THE SOCIETAL COMPANY

Many attempts have been made to reduce the harms caused by business and to make companies become socially responsible. This book approaches the subject from a new perspective arguing that reflexive law offers the best means to align the interests of large companies with those of society and that recent developments in European company law fit a reflexive model.

A reflexive company law, rather than trying to directly regulate companies, aims to affect internal decision-making processes to make companies responsive to outside interests and prevent them from operating as closed systems singularly focused on shareholder value. In this vein, the EU has recently imposed new obligations on companies to develop corporate sustainability reporting and due diligence processes as part of its objective to create a climate-neutral and sustainable economy.

This book presents an argument for how the 'societal company' – a company that has an internal culture of transnational responsibility to do no harm but that retains the autonomy necessary to be economically productive – can be established through reflexive law. The book will appeal to researchers, policy makers and lawyers interested in corporate sustainability, regulatory theory, company law and EU law.

CONTEMPORARY STUDIES IN CORPORATE LAW

Series editors: Marc Moore, Christopher Bruner

Corporate law scholarship has a relatively recent history despite the fact that corporations have existed and been subject to legal regulation for three centuries. The modern flourishing of corporate law scholarship has been matched by some broadening of the field of study to embrace insolvency, corporate finance, corporate governance and regulation of the financial markets. At the same time, new possibilities for studying the corporation emerge from corporate law's intersection with other legal fields (e.g., labour, contract, competition, intellectual property, and criminal law), inter-disciplinary application of social scientific and other methodologies (e.g., economics, finance, history, politics, sociology, and philosophy), and comparative study of prevailing corporate governance structures from significant commercial jurisdictions around the world. This series seeks to foster intellectually diverse approaches to thinking about the law and its role, scope and effectiveness in the context of corporate activity. In so doing the series aims to publish works of high intellectual content and theoretical rigour.

Titles in this series

Reconceptualising Corporate Compliance
Anna Donovan

Corporate Opportunities: A Law and Economics Analysis
Marco Claudio Corradi

The Making of the Modern Company
Susan Watson

Court-Supervised Restructuring of Large Distressed Companies in Asia: Law and Policy
Wai Yee Wan

Activist Shareholders in Corporate Governance: The Australian Experience and its Comparative Implications
Tim Bowley

Investment Management, Stewardship and Sustainability: Transformation and Challenges in Law and Regulation
Edited by Iris H–Y Chiu and Hans-Christopher Hirt

Diversity. Merit and Power in the C-Suite
Eleanore Hickman

Shareholders and Stakeholders: The Unrealised Promise of Company Law Reform in Post-War Britain
Joanne F Sonin

The Origins of Company Law: Methods and Approaches
Edited by Victoria Barnes and Jonathan Hardman

Hidden Fallacies in Corporate Law and Financial Regulation: Reframing the Mainstream Narratives
Edited by Saule T Omarova, Alexandra Andhov and Claire A Hill

The Societal Company

Sustainability, Shareholder Value, and European Company Law

John Quinn

•HART•
OXFORD • LONDON • NEW YORK • NEW DELHI • SYDNEY

HART PUBLISHING

Bloomsbury Publishing Plc

Kemp House, Chawley Park, Cumnor Hill, Oxford, OX2 9PH, UK

1385 Broadway, New York, NY 10018, USA

Bloomsbury Publishing Ireland Limited, 29 Earlsfort Terrace, Dublin 2, D02 AY28, Ireland

HART PUBLISHING, the Hart/Stag logo, BLOOMSBURY and the Diana logo are trademarks of Bloomsbury Publishing Plc

First published in Great Britain 2025

A catalogue record for this book is available from the British Library.

A catalogue record for this book is available from the Library of Congress.

Library of Congress Control Number: 2025945729

ISBN: HB: 978-1-50997-774-1
ePDF: 978-1-50997-776-5
ePub: 978-1-50997-775-8

Typeset by Compuscript Ltd, Shannon

Acknowledgements

I am grateful for all the support I have received from the Dublin City University School of Law and Government and the Faculty of Humanities and Social Sciences. I am particularly grateful to my Heads of School Gary Murphy, Iain McMenamin Ken McDonagh and Tanya Ní Mhuirthile who have all been very supportive of my work. I would also like to thank my colleague Rónán Condon who provided typically insightful feedback at various stages of the book's development.

I would like to thank the series editors Marc Moore and Christopher Bruner for their helpful feedback and the team at Hart Publishing, particularly Roberta Bassi and Verity Stuart, for their flexibility and guidance.

I am also lucky to have received help, encouragement and advice from many senior colleagues over the past few years. I would like to especially thank Deirdre Ahern, Andrew Keay, Beate Sjåfjell, Irene Lynch-Fannon, Ciara Hackett, Federico Fabbrini, Yvonne Daly, Aisling de Paor, James Gallen, Brenda Daly and Noel McGrath. Thanks also to Sacha Garben and Inge Govaere for hosting me at the College of Europe where the book was finished.

Finally, I would like to thank my amazing girlfriend Aleksandra for all her love and support.

Contents

Introduction

I. THE ARGUMENT

A PRESSING ISSUE of our time is the how to align the interests of large companies with the present and future interests of society.[1] Companies, while providing many benefits to society, also impose costs in the form of environmental damage, harms to stakeholders and human rights abuses. This is not a new observation and many initiatives have attempted to reduce the harms and negative externalities[2] of business, including through human rights principles, corporate governance frameworks, market forces and many proposals from academia. This book offers an alternative thesis that a company law with reflexive elements[3] offers the best method to orientate large companies toward the goal of promoting society's 'aggregate welfare'[4] and thereby establish the 'societal company'. In making this argument, the book analyses recent developments in European company law,[5] where the European Union (EU) has developed a company law framework around 'corporate sustainability' that aims to reduce the negative externalities of companies.[6]

II. THE PROBLEM

The theory guiding company law, at least in the Anglo-American and European traditions,[7] is that the best way for company law to promote aggregate welfare is

[1] For one example of the extensive scholarship on this point see E Ferran and P Schilling de Carvalho, 'Reconciling Shareholder Primacy and the Interests of People and Planet' (2025) *LQR* available at https://papers.ssrn.com/sol3/papers.cfm?abstract_id=5084134.

[2] Referring to the adverse impact of economic activities on the welfare of those uninvolved in these activities.

[3] Taking the term 'reflexive elements' from G Teubner, 'Substantive and Reflexive Elements in Modern Law' (1983) 17(2) *Law and Society Review* 239.

[4] As defined by *The Anatomy of Corporate Law* as all those 'who are affected by a firm's activities, including the firm's shareholders, employees, suppliers and customers, as well as third parties such as local communities and beneficiaries of the natural environment' See R Kraakman et al, *The Anatomy of Corporate Law: A Comparative and Functional Approach*, 3rd edn (Oxford, Oxford University Press, 2017) 22.

[5] Meaning the company law of the European Union as opposed to the national company law of European States.

[6] Referring to the adverse impact of economic activities on the welfare of those uninvolved in those activities.

[7] I refer here to the fact that the core legal characteristics of the company have converged across common law and continental European jurisdictions. There are, of course, differences in the traditions of common law jurisdictions, continental European jurisdictions and the company law of the EU.

to facilitate the efficient organisation and operation of business while negative externalities are best addressed through external regulation.[8] From this facilitative perspective, company law has evolved to provide the company with a set of characteristics that facilitates efficient business organisation.[9] This framework lowers the risks and costs of business[10] and in so doing enables the creation and operation of efficient companies which advance aggregate welfare by, for example, offering desirable goods and services, engaging in research and development, providing employment and creating a competitive economy.

The intellectual foundation of this facilitative model is based on a description of the company as a nexus of contracts whose efficiency is derived from its orientation toward shareholder value.[11] The nexus of contracts model reduces the company to a series of contractual rights and obligations between parties where shareholders stand out as a unique constituent given they did not expressly bargain for their position but instead claim what is left after all other contractual obligations have been satisfied, ie they claim the residual. Hence, shareholders bear the most risk and have a homogeneous interest in maximising this residual.[12] This makes them the group most suited to supervise management and limit agency costs[13] thereby maximising the company's efficiency. Under this contractual model, company stakeholders should not be the concern of company law as their interests are protected by: (1) their contracts to which they have voluntarily agreed; and (2) other areas of law,[14] while broader social issues such as environmental damage and human rights abuses are best addressed by sector specific regulation.[15]

There are two fundamental issues with the above picture. The first is that, as many authors have pointed out, the nexus of contracts model rests on faulty descriptions of the company.[16] Many alternative models highlight these shortcomings by emphasising the company's non-contractual dimensions such as the importance of stakeholders,[17] the state[18] or the company's sociological[19]

[8] As set out in F Easterbrook and D Fischel, *The Economic Structure of Corporate Law* (Harvard University Press, 1991).

[9] ibid 7–10 noting that these characteristics are what parties would, for the most part, have agreed to privately through contract but at a greater cost.

[10] See R Posner, *The Economic Analysis of Law*, 8th edn (Wolters Kluwer, 2010) 14–17.

[11] Meaning that advancing the interests of shareholders should be objective of the company.

[12] Easterbrook and Fischel, *The Economic Structure of Corporate Law* (n 8) 36–39.

[13] Agency costs referring to the potential for company directors to be negligent, opportunistic or wasteful. See M Jensen and W Meckling, 'Theory of the Firm: Managerial Behaviour, Agency Costs and Ownership Structure' (1976) 3 *Journal of Economics* 305.

[14] Eg, by contract law, employment law or insolvency law.

[15] Eg, environmental law or tort law.

[16] Eg, the characterisation of shareholders as having homogenous interests and sharing a singular focus in maximising the residual, see M Hayden and M Bodie, *Reconstructing the Corporation: From Shareholder Primacy to Shared Governance* (Cambridge, Cambridge University Press, 2020).

[17] See RE Freeman et al, *Stakeholder Theory: The State of the Art* (Cambridge, Cambridge University Press, 2010).

[18] See S Watson, 'The Corporate Legal Person' (2019) 19(1) *Journal of Corporate Law Studies* 137.

[19] See E Micheler, *Company Law: A Real Entity Theory* (Oxford, Oxford University Press, 2021).

or legal[20] characteristics. Some of these theories claim that aggregate welfare is best advanced not by prioritising shareholders but by prioritising the interests of stakeholders or the company as a distinct entity. The second issue is the harms that continue to arise from the operation of companies,[21] particularly in a transnational context where business is organised through corporate groups[22] or chains of companies.[23] Some examples include dangerous working conditions for employees,[24] child labour,[25] and environmental damage.[26] Such issues seem incapable of being addressed solely through a patchwork of regulatory law. As companies obtain increasing levels of power, operate globally and extend their reach into all aspects of society, it becomes increasingly difficult for sector specific regulation to address all contexts where a pursuit of shareholder value generates negative externalities and therefore should be constrained for the benefit of society. Even if regulatory law could address every context where economically productive business should be regulated, it is not clear that legal interventions would be able to achieve its objectives of reducing or ending negative externalities.[27] In other words, as society and companies have become more complex and globalised, sector specific regulation has become less effective.

To overcome the limitations of sector specific law, we need new modes of regulation[28] which go beyond the dichotomous approach above of a 'facilitative'

[20] See A Keay, *The Corporate Objective: Corporations, Globalisation and the Law* (Edward Elgar Publishing, 2011).

[21] For a report setting out many such examples see British Institute of International and Comparative Law, 'Study on Due Diligence Requirements Through the Supply Chain' (2020) available at https://op.europa.eu/en/publication-detail/-/publication/8ba0a8fd-4c83-11ea-b8b7-01aa75ed71a1/language-en. The report also provides examples of companies reducing their negative environmental and human rights record.

[22] Where one 'parent' company owns shares in multiple other 'subsidiary' companies. See P Underwood, *Corporate Group Legitimacy: Reconceptualising the Corporate Group* (Routledge, 2024).

[23] Which operate through contractual governance and codes of conduct. See A Beckers, *Enforcing Corporate Social Responsibility Codes on Global Self-Regulation and National Private Law* (Oxford, Hart Publishing, 2018).

[24] One notable example being the Rana Plaza disaster in building in Dhaka, Bangladesh where a building used to manufacture garments collapsed killing more than 1,100 and injuring over 2,500 persons see International Labour Organization, 'The Rana Plaza Disaster Ten Years On: What Has Changed?' (2023) available at https://webapps.ilo.org/infostories/en-GB/Stories/Country-Focus/rana-plaza#intro.

[25] For example, where children are used in the mining of cobalt. See Amnesty International, 'Human Rights Abuses in the Democratic Republic of the Congo Power the Global Trade in Cobalt' (2016) available at: https://www.amnesty.org/download/Documents/AFR6231832016ENGLISH.PDF.

[26] Eg, through pollution or contribution to climate change. See Amnesty International, 'The Cost Of Doing Business?: The Petrochemical Industry's Toxic Pollution In The USA' (2024) available at https://www.amnesty.org/en/documents/AMR51/7566/2024/en/.

[27] This argument is based on systems theory and is developed in ch 2.

[28] This is not a new claim, there is an extensive literature on alternative modes of regulation. See, for example, L Lessig, 'The Law of the Horse: What Cyber Law Might Teach' (1999) 13 *Harvard Law Review* 501 and I Ayres and J Braithwaite, *Responsive Regulation: Transcending the Deregulation Debate* (Oxford, Oxford University Press, 1992).

company law on one hand and sector specific 'regulatory law' on the other.[29] The challenge is to develop a framework that continues to enable the company's economic productivity while reducing the resulting harms. Of course, there have already been many attempts to achieve this objective. For example, the explicit aim of the United Nation's Guiding Principles on Business and Human Rights (UNGPs)[30] is to reduce harm by creating a model for responsible business practices. Sustainable finance and environmental, social and governance (ESG) investing aim to address the problem through market forces.[31] Legal initiatives, in the UK and US, have sought to make clear that company directors are permitted to have regard to interests other than shareholders, including employees and the environment.[32] Many proposals have also emerged from academia, two leading examples being to redefine the corporate purpose[33] and to reform the legal duties of the board to promote sustainable value creation.[34] This book proposes an alternative solution, where a company law with reflexive elements creates the 'societal company'.

III. THE SOCIETAL COMPANY

The starting point for the societal company is that company law should directly aim to advance aggregate welfare rather than aiming to advance it instrumentally through facilitating shareholder value or prioritising the interests of stakeholders or the company as an entity. Hence, the societal company does not follow a specific theory of the firm but rather sees the company as a social 'enterprise'[35] or 'system'[36] which exists, above all, to serve society's interests. This means that

[29] This point is made in D Hess, 'Social Reporting: A Reflexive Law Approach to Corporate Social Responsiveness' (1999) 25 The *Journal of Corporation Law* 41.

[30] UN's Guiding Principles on Business and Human Rights (2011), available at www.ohchr.org/Documents/Publications/GuidingPrinciplesBusinessHR_EN.pdf.

[31] See D Busch, G Ferrarini, and SN Grünewald (eds), *Sustainable Finance in Europe: Corporate Governance, Financial Stability and Financial Markets* (Palgrave, 2021).

[32] See A Keay, *The Enlightened Shareholder Value Principle and Corporate Governance* (Routledge, 2013); and E Orts, 'Beyond Shareholders: Interpreting Corporate Constituency Statutes' (1993) 61 *George Washington Law Review* 14.

[33] See C Mayer, *Prosperity: Better Business Makes the Greater Good* (Oxford, Oxford University Press, 2018); and C Mayer, *Capitalism and Crises: How to Fix Them* (Oxford, Oxford University Press, 2024).

[34] See B Sjåfjell, 'Beyond Climate Risk: Integrating Sustainability into The Duties of the Corporate Board' (2018) 23(2) *Deakin Law Review* 1; and A Johnston et al, 'Corporate Governance for Sustainability' available at https://papers.ssrn.com/sol3/papers.cfm?abstract_id=3502101.

[35] Relying on Parkinson's description of the company, see J Parkinson, *Corporate Power and Responsibility: Issues in the Theory of Company Law* (Clarendon Press, 1993) 23–32.

[36] Relying on Teubner's understanding of the company: see G Teubner, 'Enterprise Corporatism: New Industrial Policy and the "Essence" of the Legal Person' (1988) 36(1) *The American Journal of Comparative Law* 130. While Parkinson and Teubner rely on different theories to support their description – the theories being political theory and systems theory respectively – they arrive at a fundamental shared description of the company as something which is only legitimate through its advancement of society's interest, rather than the private interests which it is comprised of. This point is developed in ch 1.

given the inability of external regulation, and indeed voluntary frameworks and market mechanisms, to address the negative externalities of business, company law must evolve and contribute to the reduction of harm resulting from the operation of large companies. However, in order to prevent a net negative effect on aggregate welfare, this evolution must occur without disrupting the company's autonomy or core characteristics which allows for its economic efficiency and productivity. Hence, the societal company aims to find a balance between the need for companies to be economically efficient while also not harming wider society through, for example, human rights abuses and environmental harms.

To create the societal company, company law must not only be facilitative but must direct internal decision makers toward a responsibility to do no harm. This principle of doing no harm has formed the basis of several important frameworks, perhaps most notably the work of John Ruggie[37] and his work in developing UNGPs[38] and Colin Mayer[39] and his work with the British Academy[40] on the corporate purpose.[41] As these works note, this objective of companies doing no harm is only possible if a sense of responsibility exists within the company itself, rather than through external regulation that apply in specific contexts. Hence, I use the term 'societal' in the same way as Jaap Winter who expresses the need for companies to reconnect with society, the challenge being 'to ignite a sense of societal responsibility *within* corporations'.[42] This responsibility to do no harm cannot be limited to the company's immediate environment and direct stakeholders but must extend transnationally. This is because companies, whether through corporate groups or value chains connected by contract, operate beyond national boundaries and have the capacity to create negative externalities across the world.[43] Hence, the term societal encompasses that which is transnational, and is used here in the same way as

[37] J Ruggie, 'Protect, Respect and Remedy: A Framework for Business and Human Rights, Report to the UN Human Rights Council' (2008) available at https://www2.ohchr.org/english/bodies/hrcouncil/docs/8session/a-hrc-8-5.doc, 24.

[38] OHCHR, 'Guiding Principles on Business and Human Rights' (2011), available at www.ohchr.org/Documents/Publications/GuidingPrinciplesBusinessHR_EN.pdf. Guiding Principle 13 provides that the responsibility to respect human rights and requires business enterprises to avoid causing or contributing to adverse human rights impacts through their own activities and from their business relationships.

[39] C Mayer, *Capitalism and Crises: How to Fix Them* (Oxford, Oxford University Press, 2024) ch 4. C Mayer, 'Success, Law and ESG' (2024) Law Working Paper No 795/2024 *European Corporate Governance Institute* available at https://papers.ssrn.com/sol3/papers.cfm?abstract_id=4939931, 5 arguing that shareholders should be sole beneficiary of the company's residual success but that this success should be conditional on the avoidance of harm to others.

[40] British Academy, 'Principles for Purposeful Business' (2019) available at https://www.thebritishacademy.ac.uk/publications/future-of-the-corporation-principles-for-purposeful-business/.

[41] The corporate purpose is the subject of ch 7.

[42] J Winter, 'Addressing the Crisis of the Modern Corporation: The Duty of Societal Responsibility of the Board' (2020) available at https://papers.ssrn.com/sol3/papers.cfm?abstract_id=3574681 emphasis added.

[43] See L Cáta Backer, 'Theorizing Regulatory Governance Within Its Ecology: The Structure of Management in an Age of Globalization' (2018) 24(5) *Contemporary Politics* 607. The problem of negative externalities arising from transnational business operations is the subject of ch 5.

Hans Micklitz[44] who describes 'societal' justice and responsibility as existing outside the 'social responsibility' framework of the nation state.[45]

These elements of an internal responsibility to do no harm that extends transnationally are the core of the societal company. This book argues that the best way to create this sense of responsibility within companies is through reflexive law. Reflexive law[46] has its foundations in systems theory[47] which views society as being comprised of differentiated systems that are 'self-referential' in the sense that they function according to their own logic, values, norms, and language.[48] Reflexive law, rather than imposing rules from one system (the legal system) on to another (the economic system and its subsystems of companies), looks to law's ability to structure processes and procedures within systems to make them responsive to outside interests. In a company law context, new reflexive elements would aim to prevent large companies from operating as closed systems singularly focused on shareholder value[49] and instead stimulate their internal resources in a way that develops 'economic self-restraint' regarding actions which cause harm to the non-economic environment.[50] Hence, reflexive law is not directed toward goal-oriented intervention and so does not seek to directly prescribe managerial decision making nor does it aim to fundamentally alter the core characterises of the corporate form. Instead, it recognises the many different types of companies, the complexity of the challenges they face and the need for the autonomy to respond to their unique situations.[51] However, it also does not leave the regulation of companies to external rules and instead relies on mandatory processes to make the company's management responsive to its external effects.

Again, this has been the aim of the UNGPs and other voluntary frameworks,[52] as well as market-based solutions.[53] However, while these proposals have the capacity to have an impact on how companies are managed, they ultimately

[44] HW Micklitz, *The Politics of Justice in European Private Law: Social Justice, Access Justice, Societal Justice* (Cambridge, Cambridge University Press, 2018).

[45] ibid 380, describing 'societal private law' as 'imposing responsibilities on the market citizen, meaning civil society organisations and companies, to build a society beyond the nation-state.'

[46] G Teubner, 'Substantive and Reflexive Elements' (n 3).

[47] For a full exploration of systems theory see R Condon, *Network Responsibility: European Tort Law and the Society of Networks* (Cambridge, Cambridge University Press, 2022).

[48] See G Teubner, 'After Legal Instrumentalism? Strategic Models of Post-Regulatory Law' (1984) *European University Institute Working Papers* available at https://cadmus.eui.eu/handle/1814/23192.

[49] See Teubner, 'Substantive and Reflexive Elements' (n 3) 276–78.

[50] G Teubner, 'Corporate Fiduciary Duties and their Beneficiaries' in G Teubner and K Hopt (eds), *Corporate Governance and Directors' Liabilities: Legal, Economic and Sociological Analyses on Corporate Social Responsibility* (De Gruyter, 1985) 164–65.

[51] A Johnston, 'Integrating Sustainability into Corporate Governance' in C Bruner and M Moore (eds), *A Research Agenda for Corporate Law* (Edward Elgar Publishing, 2023) 57.

[52] Eg, The UN's Sustainable Development Goals available at https://sdgs.un.org/goals.

[53] See A Johnstone, 'Governing Externalities: The Potential of Reflexive Corporate Social Responsibility' *University of Cambridge Working Paper* (2012) available at https://papers.ssrn.com/sol3/papers.cfm?abstract_id=2165616 discussing Ronald Coase's argument in 'The Problem of Social Cost' (1960) 3 *Journal of Law and Economics* 1, that reduction of negative externalities

lack the coercive power of law[54] and the force necessary to reorientate many large companies toward aiming to do no harm.[55] What is needed is mandatory rules, directed toward external interests that are backed by the potential of legal enforcement, either through civil liability or by regulatory authorities, that add a coercive dimension necessary to produce a reflexion and reorientate companies toward advancing the interest of society.[56] In terms of what these reflexive procedural rules should be, this book will discuss shared governance, reporting and due diligence as mechanisms which have the capacity to change the way in which decisions are reached within companies. These three mechanisms have the capacity to: (1) increase awareness within the company of its external effects;[57] (2) provide practical guidance on how companies can mitigate or end their negative externalities; (3) harness the importance of a company's reputation to provide incentives to reduce their external harms; and (4) establish direct links and open communication channels with stakeholders and other parties that are affected by the companies activities.

IV. EUROPEAN COMPANY LAW

The EU recently introduced a series of reforms under the heading of corporate sustainability that include several reflexive elements. The early development of European company law[58] focused on facilitating freedom of establishment[59] by developing a common company law framework.[60] At the turn of the millennium, the EU focused more directly on establishing a facilitative framework for cross border business.[61] Hence, European company law has historically been primarily facilitative[62] while the EU has imposed relatively strong regulation on

should either be through direct regulation or left to private bargaining based on a cost benefit analysis.

[54] The concept of 'coerced self-regulation' is developed in I Ayres and J Braithwaite, *Responsive Regulation: Transcending the Deregulation Debate* (Oxford, Oxford University Press, 1992) 100–02.

[55] Teubner, 'Corporate Fiduciary Duties' (n 50) 160, arguing that the 'reflexion cannot be voluntary, but needs to be stimulated by powerful external forces'.

[56] See Parkinson, *Corporate Power and Responsibility* (n 35) 73 arguing that duty-based controls can only be effective if there is a realistic chance of enforcement.

[57] As Ruggie noted, for a company to reduce its harms it must first become aware of its impact: see Ruggie, 'Protect, Respect and Remedy'(n 37) [23–25].

[58] European company law does not provide a complete company code but is rather a 'two-level system' in which EU law prevails over the national company law of Member States but covers a relatively small number of matters.

[59] Meaning that companies of one EU Member State can freely pursue economic activity in another Member State.

[60] This meant establishing a base level of harmonisation between Member States but also removing national restrictions on freedom of establishment. This will be discussed in ch 3.

[61] Eg, by creating a European company as well as directives on takeovers and cross-border mergers.

[62] See L Enriques, 'EC Company Law Directives and Regulations: How Trivial Are They?' (2006) 27 *University of Pennsylvania Journal of International Economic Law* 1 describing European company law as trivial.

companies through other areas of law.[63] However, more recently, the EU introduced new company law rules which have a different aim of ensuring a 'green transition to a climate-neutral' and 'sustainable' economy[64] in line with the European Green Deal.[65]

The two main European company law developments have been in relation to corporate sustainability disclosures and due diligence. In 2014, the EU introduced the Non-Financial Reporting Directive (NFRD)[66] which was a non-mandatory framework for large companies to develop policies and disclose information relating to the environment, employees and human rights. In 2019, the Sustainable Finance Disclosure Regulation (SFDR)[67] imposed mandatory disclosure requirements on 'financial market participants'[68] while the 2023 Corporate Sustainability Reporting Directive (CSRD)[69] amended the NFRD broadening the range of information to be disclosed, extending the scope of application, standardising what was be reported and made reporting mandatory with the potential for fines by regulatory authorities.[70] The CSRD was followed by the 2024 Corporate Sustainability Due Diligence Directive (CSDDD) which requires large companies to identify actual and potential adverse human rights and environmental impacts arising from their own operations or those of their subsidiaries or from established business relationships in their supply chains.[71] Once identified, companies are required to take appropriate measures to bring an end to, or if that is not possible, to minimise those adverse impacts[72] and failing to do so can result in fines or civil liability.[73] Both the CSRD and the CSDDD will impact many companies outside the EU's territory and so will have a significant transnational effect.[74]

[63] Eg, through EU labour law, environmental law, consumer law and competition law.

[64] See Directive (EU) 2024/1760 of the European Parliament and of the Council of 13 June 2024 on corporate sustainability due diligence and amending Directive (EU) 2019/1937 and Regulation (EU) 2023/2859 [2019] OJ L, 2024/1760, recital 11.

[65] Communication from the Commission to the European Parliament, the European Council, the Council, the European Economic and Social Committee and the Committee of the Regions – The European Green Deal [2019] COM/2019/640 final, available at https://eur-lex.europa.eu/legal-content/EN/TXT/?uri=celex:52019DC0640.

[66] Directive 2014/95/EU of the European Parliament and of the Council of 22 October 2014 amending Directive 2013/34/EU as regards disclosure of non-financial and diversity information by certain large undertakings and groups [2014] OJ L 330/1.

[67] Regulation (EU) 2019/2088 of the European Parliament and of the Council of 27 November 2019 on sustainability-related disclosures in the financial services sector [2019] OJ L 317/1.

[68] Which includes credit institutions, investment firms providing portfolio management and financial advisers. ibid art 1.

[69] Directive (EU) 2022/2464 of the European Parliament and of the Council of 14 December 2022 amending Regulation (EU) No 537/2014, Directive 2004/109/EC, Directive 2006/43/EC and Directive 2013/34/EU, as regards corporate sustainability reporting [2022] OJ L 322/15.

[70] These points will be expanded in ch 4.

[71] Directive (EU) 2024/1760 (n 64).

[72] ibid art 8.

[73] ibid art 22.

[74] This is the subject of ch 6.

However, more recently again, the European Commission has reverted to a policy position based around the importance of enhancing efficient and competitive business. The Commission's Omnibus I Proposal[75] aims to reduce the regulatory burden on companies by reducing the scope of the CSRD by approximately 80 per cent and limiting the application of the CSDDD to direct contractual partners, thus limiting its transnational effects and removing the EU model for civil liability.[76] Regardless of whether these proposals are enacted, the European company law framework on corporate sustainability is the first attempt to impose mandatory company law rules directly focused on reducing external social harms caused by companies. As such it has created a roadmap and language for what such interventions could look like and offers lessons for the creation of a company law with reflexive elements.

V. CHAPTER OUTLINES

Chapter one examines the claim that the best way for company law to promote the aggregate welfare of society is by facilitating efficient business and a pursuit of shareholder value. It starts by setting out the classical conception of company law as a body of law that has 'evolved' to enable the efficient organisation of business. It discusses the nexus of contracts description of the company and its claim that the company's efficiency is derived from its orientation toward shareholder value. The chapter then sets out alternative models of the company which challenge the descriptions of the company made by the nexus of contracts model and which emphasise other aspects of the company, such as the importance of stakeholders, the role of the state in its formation or how it can be viewed as a distinct entity. These models challenge the validity of the description of the company as a nexus of contracts and in so doing undermine the argument that a facilitative company law and shareholder value are the best methods to advance aggregate welfare. The chapter then aims to go beyond these theories of the firm to more directly frame the company in terms of societal benefits, ultimately developing the concept of the societal company.

Chapter two examines the claim that the negative externalities of business are best dealt with by areas of law other than company law. It starts with a discussion of negative externalities, particularly in the context of environmental harms and human rights abuses. It then analyses the capacity of a patchwork of regulatory law and voluntary framework to reduce and end these negative

[75] European Commission, Omnibus I (2025) available at https://commission.europa.eu/publications/omnibus-i_en. It is important to note that these are proposals only and are subject to the EU legislative process, however, it is now clear that the new European Commission, whose term began in December 2024, intends to deregulate existing corporate sustainability rules in the name of facilitating business. The Omnibus is discussed in ch 3.

[76] These changes will be discussed in chs 4 and 5. For a summary of the changes see https://www.arthurcox.com/insights/omnibus-package-proposed-amendments-to-csrd-and-csddd/.

externalities. The chapter then sets out an argument that a company law with reflexive elements is the best method to advance society's aggregate welfare. Finally, it provides some examples of such elements that could provoke a reflexive response within companies including shared governance, corporate reporting and due diligence.

Chapter three examines the development of European company law and describes how European company law has evolved to facilitate the freedom of establishment and cross border business. It begins by discussing the processes of positive harmonisation and negative integration designed to uphold the freedom of establishment and give effect to the single market. It then discusses a shift in European company law toward facilitating cross border business through default legal frameworks. The chapter then discusses the policy basis on which future legislative initiatives on corporate sustainability are based and the more recent reversal of this policy which returns to a focus on economic competitiveness.

Chapter four focuses on corporate reporting, beginning by outlining the importance of financial disclosures in fostering economic reliability. It then analyses the relationship between reflexivity and corporate sustainability reporting and argues that existing rules have lacked the strength necessary to produce a reflexive response by not being mandatory, detailed, standardised and independently verified. Finally, it discusses recent EU legislative developments on corporate sustainability reporting, including the requirements of the CSRD and argues that, while unnecessarily complex, the CSRD is sufficiently detailed to provide reliability and provoke a reflexive response within companies.

Chapter five addresses due diligence, starting by describing the disparity between company law's individualistic framework of responsibility, where every company is assumed to be a distinct person, and complex transnational business organisations that operate through corporate groups and contractual governance. This disparity has allowed such complex business organisations to operate outside traditional legal frameworks of responsibility thereby encouraging the externalisation of costs leading to extensive human rights abuses and environmental harms. The chapter then discusses the concept of due diligence, both in company law and as it has been developed through the UNGPs. Finally, it analyses the CSDDD, including the scope of application, the liability regime, the methods of ensuring compliance and the process that is required, followed by some analysis of its capacity to produce a reflexive effect.

Chapter six assesses the international effects of the CSRD and CSDDD. It starts by examining how EU law can have effects beyond the EU's borders through 'jurisdictional triggers' which are used to apply EU law to persons outside the EU that have effects within its territory. Both the CSRD and the CSDDD use a jurisdictional trigger of 'business conducted within the EU' to bring non-EU based companies within their scope. Another means through which EU law can have effects beyond its borders is through 'territorial extension' which describes contexts in which EU law uses a territorial connection with the EU to influence conduct that takes place outside of its territory. The CSDDD uses territorial extension by requiring companies within its scope to conduct due diligence across all their subsidiaries and business partners regardless of their size or geographical location. The chapter also examines the potential for the CSRD and CSDDD to have a 'Brussels effect', a phenomenon whereby EU law shapes the global regulatory environment through market forces rather than the direct application of law.

Chapter seven locates the book's research question of how company law can best align the interests of large companies with the interests of society within the debate on the corporate purpose. It begins by highlighting how directors, as the people who manage companies, are responsible for carrying out the company's purpose. It then analyses the different interpretations of the duty to act in the interests of the company and demonstrates how the law of directors' duties provides directors with a broad discretion to manage the company. It then discusses the EU's attempt to reform the duties of directors and the issues revealed by their attempts to do so. Finally, it engages with the debate on the corporate purpose, arguing that while defining the corporate purpose is important, a supplementary framework of procedural rules plus enforcement are more fundamental to aligning the company with the interests of society and reducing the negative externalities of business.

1

Models of the Company

I. INTRODUCTION

THE AUTHORS OF the *Anatomy of Corporate Law* describe the appropriate goal of company law as being to serve the interests of society by advancing the 'aggregate welfare of all who are affected by a firm's activities, including the firm's shareholders, employees, suppliers and customers, as well as third parties such as local communities and beneficiaries of the natural environment'.[1] There is a general agreement regarding this 'aggregate welfare' objective of company law,[2] the debate lies in how to best achieve it. The traditional view, at least in the Anglo-American and European traditions,[3] is that company law most effectively promotes aggregate welfare by providing a set of rules that facilitates the economically efficient organisation of business. This facilitative model describes company law as having evolved to provide the company with a set of characteristics that facilitates efficiency.[4] By providing a framework that lowers the risk and cost of business,[5] company law facilitates the efficient creation and operation of companies which advance aggregate welfare by, for example, offering desirable goods and services, engaging in research and development, providing employment and forming the basis of a competitive economy.

The intellectual foundation of this facilitative model is based on a description of the company as a nexus of contracts whose efficiency is derived from its

[1] R Kraakman et al, *The Anatomy of Corporate Law: A Comparative and Functional Approach*, 3rd edn (Oxford, Oxford University Press, 2017) 22 describing aggregate welfare as a 'loose metaphor' and general aim rather than as a precise economic yardstick. A similar approach is taken by Parkinson who bases his book on a view that company law should serve the 'public interest' acknowledging that the public interest is not objectively determinable but is a shorthand description for the appropriate balancing of the interests of groups affected by the company's operations be they employees, customers, suppliers, the local community or the wider environment: J Parkinson, *Corporate Power and Responsibility: Issues in the Theory of Company Law* (Clarendon Press, 1993) 22.

[2] At least if one assumes 'beneficiaries of the natural environment' includes future generations.

[3] I refer here to the fact that the core legal characteristics of the company have converged across common law and continental European jurisdictions. There are, of course, differences in the traditions of common law jurisdictions, continental European jurisdictions and the company law of the EU. This point will be developed in Section II.

[4] F Easterbrook and D Fischel, *The Economic Structure of Corporate Law* (Harvard University Press, 1991) 7–10 noting that these characteristics are what parties would, for the most part, have agreed to privately through contract but at a greater cost.

[5] See R Posner, *The Economic Analysis of Law*, 8th edn (Wolters Kluwer, 2010) 14–17.

orientation toward shareholder value.[6] The nexus of contracts model reduces the company into a series of contractual rights and obligations between parties. From this perspective, shareholders are a unique constituent as they do not expressly bargain for their position but instead claim what is left after all other contractual obligations have been satisfied ie they claim the residual. Hence, shareholders bear the most risk and have a homogeneous interest in maximising this residual which makes them suited to supervise management and limit agency costs[7] which ultimately maximises the company's efficiency. This chain of reasoning leads to a conclusion that the best way for company law to advance aggregate welfare is by continuing to facilitate efficient business and that companies should pursue shareholder value while the social harms and negative externalities[8] of business are to be addressed by other areas of law.[9]

However, as many authors have pointed out, the nexus of contracts model rests on an inaccurate and incomplete description of the company.[10] Many alternative models highlight other aspects of the company, such as the importance of stakeholders, the role of the state in its formation or how it can function as a distinct entity. There is also increasing evidence that the negative externalities of business cannot be controlled through a patchwork of regulatory law.[11] Such challenges to the nexus of contracts model undermines the argument that a facilitative company law and a pursuit of shareholder value are the best methods to advance aggregate welfare. However, alternative models of the company also suffer from limitations, often approaching the company from a single perspective and failing to capture its multi-dimensional nature. Another difficulty is that, in moving beyond the straightforward objective of maximising the residual, these models provide for greater managerial discretion that can result in a lack of direction, increased agency costs or the continued externalisation of costs. What is required is a model that goes beyond shareholder value, that is sufficiently broad that acknowledges the multi-dimensional nature of the company, but which also directs internal decision makers toward directly advancing aggregate welfare without disrupting the evolved core characteristics of the company that facilitates its efficiency.

[6] Meaning that advancing the interests of shareholders should be objective of the company.

[7] Meaning the potential for company management to be negligent, opportunistic or wasteful with the company's resources.

[8] Referring to the adverse impact of economic activities on the welfare of those uninvolved in those activities.

[9] Or in Friedman's terms, the social responsibility of business is to make profit within the rules of the game: M Friedman, 'The Social Responsibility of Business is to Increase Its Profits' *New York Times* (13 September 1970) available at https://www.nytimes.com/1970/09/13/archives/a-friedman-doctrine-the-social-responsibility-of-business-is-to.html. Hayek expressed similar in F Hayek, 'The Corporation in a Democratic Society: In Whose Interest Ought It and Will it be Run?' in H Ansoff (ed) *Business Strategy* (Penguin, 1969) 265–267.

[10] For example, see M Moore, *Corporate Governance in the Shadow of the State* (Oxford, Hart Publishing, 2013) and G Hayden and M Bodie, *Reconstructing the Corporation: From Shareholder Primacy to Shared Governance* (Cambridge, Cambridge University Press, 2020).

[11] This point is developed in ch 2.

This chapter puts forward a new conceptualisation of the company – the societal company –under which company law directly aims to advance aggregate welfare rather than aiming to promote it instrumentally through advancing the interests of shareholders, stakeholders or the company as an entity. It argues that the optimal method through which this can be achieved is a company law with reflexive elements[12] that direct internal decision makers toward societal responsibility which is a responsibility to do no harm that extends transnationally. These reflexive elements are mandatory processes that address external issues, such as human rights abuse and environmental harms, but do not directly regulate corporate decision making nor alter the company's evolved core characteristics. Instead, the aim is to make companies responsive to outside interests and prevent them from operating as closed systems singularly focused on economic success and shareholder value.

Section II describes how modern company law has evolved to facilitate efficient business organisation. Section III sets out the link between the nexus of contracts description of the company and shareholder value. Section IV discusses alternative models of the company which challenge the premises of the nexus of contracts model. Part 4 develops the concept of the 'societal company'.

II. EVOLUTIONARY COMPANY LAW

One mechanism through which law is established is the state's recognition and enforcement of rules that have emerged from custom or practice.[13] One such example is English commercial law as articulated by Roy Goode. Goode began his Hamyln lectures with the statement that English commercial law 'has evolved from the needs and practices of the mercantile community'.[14] He goes on to describe a close connection between commercial practice and commercial law[15] where law enables and gives effect to structures and tools that satisfy the legitimate needs of the market.[16] The classic example is *Lex Mercatoria*[17] of medieval Europe, where a set of rules emerged from commercial mercantile practice which eventually became incorporated into the legal frameworks

[12] Taking the term from G Teubner, 'Substantive and Reflexive Elements in Modern Law' (1983) 17(2) *Law and Society Review* 239.

[13] See JB Murphy, *The Philosophy of Customary Law* (Oxford, Oxford University Press, 2014).

[14] R Goode, *Commercial Law in the Next Millennium: The Hamyln Lectures* (Sweet and Maxwell, 1998).

[15] For a development of this point see Lord Devlin, 'The Relation Between Commercial Law and Commercial Practice' (1951) 14(3) *Modern Law Review* 249.

[16] Goode, *Commercial Law in the Next Millennium* (n 14) 4. Goode uses a range of specific security instruments such as fixed and floating charge and retention of title clauses as examples of tools that have emerged from practice that have now been provided for by law.

[17] O Toth, *The Lex Mercatoria in Theory and Practice* (Oxford, Oxford University Press, 2017) and R Michales, 'The True Lex Mercatoria: Law Beyond the State' (2007) 14 *Indiana Journal of Global Legal Studies* 447.

of European states.[18] In Goode's vision, the purpose of commercial law is to legitimise and enforce practices and instruments that have proven to be effective in the market by facilitating trade.[19]

Similarities can be drawn between this description of commercial law and modern company law. Susan Watson, in her book on the origins of the modern company, sets out how the large global corporation emerged in the mid-seventeenth century with quasi state companies like the Bank of England and the East India Company.[20] However, alongside state-chartered companies existed joint-stock companies which were constituted by private ordering through contract, entirely outside of the state's infrastructure.[21] Such companies had many similar characteristics to modern companies in the sense that they were regarded as 'separate accounting entities'.[22] When the English Bubble Act 1720 prohibited the formation of joint-stock companies and reduced the number of state-chartered companies, the deed of settlement company emerged. The deed of settlement company used a combination of contracts and trusts to acquire many of the advantages of the modern company such as the formation of a collective fund and the limiting the liability of investors. However, this limited liability was established through contract and was restricted by the privity rule which meant that English courts held investors liable for the company's debts.[23] On Watson's historical account, the litigation arising out of deed of settlement companies formed the basis for much of what we now know as modern company law in common law jurisdictions.[24] The damaging economic effects of the Bubble Act alongside the deed of settlement case law provided the foundation for the UK's General Incorporation Acts of 1856 and 1862.[25] These Acts provided a legal framework which made incorporation widely available and represented the state's legitimisation of what had developed through joint-stock and deed of settlement companies, namely the corporate form which facilitated business, investment and ultimately economic growth which in turn provided extensive benefits to society.

[18] See B Benson, 'The Spontaneous Evolution of Commercial Law' (1989) 55(3) *Southern Economic Journal* 644.

[19] Goode, *Commercial Law in the Next Millennium* (n 14) 14. It is worth noting Goode sees a value in legal regulation in contexts where there are market imperfections and information asymmetries, at 45.

[20] S Watson, *The Making of the Modern Company* (Oxford, Hart Publishing, 2022) ch 3.

[21] ibid ch 2. This alternate track mimics companies in Roman Law where the *universitas* derived its legal status from the state while the *societas* referred to a general category of contractual relationships between members. See S Williston, 'History of the Law of Business Corporations before 1800' (1888) 2(3) *Harvard Law Review* 105.

[22] Watson, *The Making of the Modern Company* (n 20) 22–27.

[23] ibid 115–116.

[24] ibid 118 stating that English company law was 'driven by the contractual deed of settlement form'.

[25] ibid 131–133. While the Acts provided for certain mandatory rules, they still afforded private parties extensive scope to tailor their business operations.

German company law also has a long evolutionary history, with its system of shared governance between employees and shareholders representing an alternative to the Anglo-American model where, in general, only shareholders may elect directors.[26] This system of 'codetermination' involves a company's management being divided between a management and supervisory board, with employees being represented on the supervisory board. The division dates to 1861 when the German Commercial Code introduced a supervisory board for public companies that was intended to replace direct state oversight.[27] This early form of codetermination was repealed in 1934 but was reintroduced after the Second World War. Ewan McGaughey[28] describes the reemergence of codetermination as having its roots in private agreements, starting as early as 1918, which provided for legally binding employee representation through works councils[29] and representation in management.[30] This collective bargaining was possible in Germany due to two distinctive factors: (1) the period following both world wars produced an economic landscape where bargaining power between employers and employees was relatively equal;[31] and (2) the German labour movement became unified around the idea of collective representation.[32] On this account, rules on codetermination also evolved through private agreement which sought to prevent social division between labour and capital, the unity of which contributed to future German economic productivity and efficiency.[33] This is not to say that codetermination per se enhances efficiency, but rather that the distinctive conditions in Germany allowed for an efficient model of shared governance to emerge.[34]

[26] This system will be outlined in more detail in ch 2. For the differences between the two approaches see I Lynch-Fannon, *Working Within Two Kinds of Capitalism: Corporate Governance and Employee Stakeholding – US and EC Perspectives* (Oxford, Hart Publishing, 2003).

[27] See P Muchlinski, 'The Development of German Corporate Law Until 1990: An Historical Reappraisal' (2013) 14(2) *German Law Journal* 339.

[28] E McGaughey, 'The Codetermination Bargains: The History of German Corporate and Labor Law' (2016) 23(1) *Columbia Journal of European Law* 135, 154–64.

[29] Work Councils serve as a mechanism to resolve employee issues. They negotiate specific terms of union collective bargaining agreements and must be consulted with regards to lay-offs, relocation or any fundamental change in business operations. See J Rogers and W Streeck (eds), *Works Councils: Consultation, Representation, and Cooperation in Industrial Relations* (University of Chicago Press, 2009).

[30] McGaughey, 'The Codetermination Bargains' (n 28) 136.

[31] Hayden and Bodie argue that such equal bargaining power between capital and labour never existed in many countries preventing the rise of codetermination internationally. See G Hayden and M Bodie, 'The Corporation Reborn: From Shareholder Primacy to Shared Governance' (2020) 61 *Boston College Law Review* 2419.

[32] McGaughey (n 28) 136.

[33] J Addison, *The Economics of Codetermination* (Springer, 2009) 2–8.

[34] This is a path dependency point, simply because codetermination led to efficient business in Germany does not mean it should be transported to countries with different histories and evolved structures of corporate governance. See A Licht, 'The Mother of all Path Dependencies: Towards a Cross-Cultural Theory of Corporate Governance Systems' (2001) 26 *Delaware Journal of Corporate Law* 147 and L Bebchuck and M Roe, 'A Theory of Path Dependence in Corporate Ownership and Governance' (2000) 52 *Stanford Law Review* 127.

The assumed outcome of the legal instantiation of emergent contractual practices is that they are efficient by making it easier to establish, manage and invest in business, often by lowering the risks and costs involved. Over time, company law has continued to evolve becoming more detailed and refined and converging internationally, often driven by what is efficient for business. Roe describes such legal evolution as follows: '[w]hat survives is presumptively efficient: if it were inefficient, the practice, the law, or the custom would be challenged by its more efficient competitors. The success of the more efficient practice or law allows it to prosper, while its less efficient competitors wither and die'.[35] The global convergence on the fundamental rules of company law adds weight to the argument that company law, at least in relation to these core rules, is the product of an evolutionary process that has led to the most efficient way of ordering business activity. The authors of the *Anatomy of Corporate Law* describe the company has having five fundamental characteristics that exist across almost all jurisdictions: (1) legal personality; (2) limited liability of shareholders; (3) transferable shares; (4) delegated management to a board of directors; (5) shareholders having ultimate control and access to net earnings.[36] These characteristics are again emphasised by a different set of high-profile scholars in 'The Modern Corporation Statement on Company Law: Fundamental Rules of Corporate Law'.[37] It is, of course, important to note that significant differences within company law exist across different nations.[38] However, in relation to these core characteristics, company law has converged internationally indicating that they combine to offer the most efficient way of organising business. Altering these core characteristics from top-down state regulation – an extreme example being the Bubble Act – is likely to harm economic efficiency.

The principal way in which the company provides for efficiency was the subject of highly influential economics scholarship in the twentieth century that focused on bargaining and transaction costs. The seminal work is Coase's 'The Nature of the Firm' which explained that firms exist because it is frequently more efficient to engage in intra-firm transactions organised by direct authority rather than through market transactions.[39] Alchian and Demsetz disagreed with the authoritarian conception of the company and instead explained the company as a system of team production of voluntary exchange through

[35] M Roe, 'Chaos and Evolution in Law and Economics' (1996) 109(3) *Harvard Law Review* 641.

[36] Kraakman et al, *The Anatomy of Corporate Law* (n 1) 5–15.

[37] Stout et al, 'The Modern Corporation Statement on Company Law Summary: Fundamental Rules of Corporate Law' available at papers.ssrn.com/sol3/papers.cfm?abstract_id=2848833.

[38] See M Pargendler, 'The Grip of Nationalism on Corporate Law' (2020) 95 *Indiana Law Journal* 533.

[39] R Coase, 'The Nature of the Firm' (1937) 4 *Economica* 387. Coase argued that it is cheaper to direct production to occur than to contract for it separately each time and that the hierarchy within a firm allows it to be achieved through authority rather than by price, negotiation and contract at 390–92.

contract.[40] Williamson developed Coase's transaction costs thesis and explained the existence and size of firms as being the result of the costs connected with bargaining and the impossibility of achieving complete contracts in the context of complex relations.[41] Jensen and Meckling further added to this literature by focusing on the reduction of agency costs.[42]

While seminal contributions, the above articles provided an economic analysis of the firm's efficiency, not a legal one. It was Easterbrook and Fischel's *The Economic Structure of Corporate Law*[43] which drew on these insights to describe how company law facilitated efficient business. Easterbrook and Fischel describe company law in the US as being the product of an evolutionary process, whereby US states have competed against each other to attract business by offering the most beneficial governance structures and rules.[44] This 'regulatory competition'[45] between US states resulted in a set of 'enabling statutes'[46] that mimicked the preferences of the market and reduced bargaining costs.[47] On Easterbrook and Fischel's account, most of the resulting company law rules were 'default' and could be avoided through private contract. For example, shareholders gained limited liability by default if they conducted their business through a company but could contract out of it by offering a personal guarantee for a company debt if beneficial in a specific context.[48] While Easterbrook and Fischel accepted that company law in the US had some mandatory rules, they argued that those rules were not in important areas and contracting parties were required to yield to such rules in very few instances.[49]

III. THE COMPANY AS A NEXUS OF CONTRACTS AND SHAREHOLDER VALUE

Easterbrook and Fischel built on this evolutionary description of company law to develop a descriptive theory of the company as a nexus of contracts whose

[40] A Alchian and H Demsetz, 'Production, Information Costs, and Economic Organization' (1972) 62 *American Economic Review* 777 focusing on the coordination of production rather than the hierarchical nature of the firm.

[41] O Williamson, 'Transaction Cost Economics: The Governance of Contractual Relations' (1979) *Journal of Law and Economics* 22.

[42] M Jensen and W Meckling, 'Theory of the Firm: Managerial Behaviour, Agency Costs and Ownership Structure' (1976) 3 *Journal of Economics* 305.

[43] Easterbrook and Fischel, *The Economic Structure of Corporate Law* (n 4).

[44] ibid 6.

[45] See L Bebchuck, 'Federalism and the Corporation: The Desirable Limits on State Competition in Corporate Law' (1992) 105(7) *Harvard Law Review* 1435.

[46] Easterbrook and Fischel (n 4) 2.

[47] ibid 11.

[48] They may do so in order to help the company obtain credit or lower the cost of credit. The point being that limited liability is not a mandatory feature of the company but can be contracted around.

[49] Easterbrook and Fischel (n 4) 15.

efficiency was dependent on company directors maximising shareholder value.[50] Historically, shareholder value was justified by reference to private property, where shareholders were characterised as owners that are entitled to have the company operated for their private benefit. This was the view put forward by Berle and Means in *The Modern Corporation and Private Property* who argued that 'owner-shareholders ought to receive the profits of the corporation because they acquired ownership of the corporate venture and are the rightful benefactors of all corporate economic surplus to the exclusion of non-owners'.[51] Friedman also characterised shareholders as owners and company directors as their employees who had a direct responsibility to increase the profits of the business.[52] However, the idea that shareholders 'own' the company was undermined on legal grounds given share ownership conferred a different set of rights to the ownership of private property.[53] Rather than owning the company or its assets, shareholders own a corporate security which gives them certain rights, but not legal control over the company's property or earnings, only its net earnings contractual liabilities have been satisfied and a dividend is declared.[54]

The nexus of contracts model provided an alternative justification for shareholder value, under which the company is reduced to the contractual rights of its participants. Amongst this web of contracts between parties such as employees, suppliers, customers, creditors and so on, shareholders stand out as the constituent that did not expressly bargain for their rights but instead claim what is left after the company's contractual obligations have been satisfied ie they are residual claimants. Easterbrook and Fischel argued that because shareholders have no fixed contractual protection and are paid last, they have the greatest stake in the company's success. Hence, shareholders bear the most risk[55] and have a homogenous interest in maximising the residual. This makes them best placed to control directors and limit agency costs while directors focus on maximising the residual drives efficiency within the company.

The problem of agency costs[56] is central to this nexus of contracts-based justification of shareholder value. An agency relationship exists where one party (the agent) has the authority to materially affect the position of another party

[50] For a modern analysis of shareholder value see S Bainbridge, *The Profit Motive: Defending Shareholder Value Maximization* (Cambridge, Cambridge University Press, 2023).

[51] A Berle and G Means, *The Modern Corporation and Private Property* (Transaction, 1932) 6–7.

[52] M Friedman, *Capitalism and Freedom* (The University of Chicago Press, 1962) 133–35.

[53] One of the leading proponents of shareholder value agrees that shareholders have none of the rights normally associated with ownership. See S Bainbridge, 'In Defence of the Shareholder Wealth Maximisation Norm: A Reply to Professor Green' (1993) 50 *Washington and Lee Law Review* 1423, 1427–29.

[54] For a full development of this point see P Ireland, 'Company Law and the Myth of Shareholder Ownership' (1999) 62 *Modern Law Review* 32 and C O' Kelly, 'History Begins: Shareholder Value, Accountability and the Virtuous State' (2009) 60(1) *Northern Ireland law Quarterly* 35, 37–39.

[55] Easterbrook and Fischel (n 4) 38–39.

[56] See E Fama, 'Agency Problems and the Theory of the Firm' (1980) 88 *Journal of Political Economy* 228 and M Jensen and W Meckling, 'Theory of the Firm: Managerial Behaviour, Agency Costs and Ownership Structure' (1976) 3 *Journal of Economics* 305.

(the principal).[57] In company law, the management of the company is automatically delegated to a director or board of directors which reduces management costs. However, such delegation grants significant discretionary power in the directors creating the 'agency problem' – the difficulty of ensuring this discretionary power is properly exercised. The agency problem became one of the foremost issues in company law in the wake of the growth of the modern public company which had widely dispersed share structures[58] and a complete separation between ownership of shares and managerial control.[59] In such companies, there is no obvious means to prevent directors from being negligent, opportunistic[60] or wasteful.[61] Eisenberg characterises the problem in terms of shirking believing 'all agents have a potential interest in working at a slack pace, and in avoiding the effort and discomfort involved in adapting to changed circumstance … This is the problem known as shirking. All agents have a potential interest in diverting the principals' assets to their own use'.[62]

In Easterbrook and Fischel's account, the best way to limit agency costs was to make directors accountable to shareholders as the group who are directly dependent upon the company's economic success given their position as residual claimants.[63] This view was originally put forward by Berle who argued that directors should exercise their powers for the benefit of shareholders because it would curb corporate managers from serving their own interests and thereby reduce agency costs.[64] The result would be that directors are answerable to shareholders, should run the company for their benefit by maximising the residual, thereby reducing agency costs and optimising efficiency which will ultimately increase aggregate welfare. In the absence of such a clear objective of maximising the residual, so the argument goes, directors would be left unaccountable without a clear objective which could lead to confusion, a lack of direction and ultimately an increase of agency costs at the expense of aggregate welfare. In Easterbrook and Fischel's words, a 'manager who is told to serve two masters … has been freed of both and is answerable to neither … agency costs rise and *social wealth falls*'.[65]

[57] See P Watts, *Bowstead and Reynolds on Agency*, 22nd edn (Sweet and Maxwell, 2020) and S Worthington, 'Corporate Attribution and Agency: Back to Basics' (2017) 133 *LQR* 118.

[58] As first discussed in Berle and Means, *The Modern Corporation and Private Property* (n 51).

[59] See M Blair, *Ownership and Control; Rethinking the Corporate Governance for the Twenty First Century* (Brookings Institute, 1996) and B Clarke, 'Corporate Responsibility in Light of the Separation of Ownership and Control' (1997) 19 *Dublin University law Journal* 50.

[60] For example, by increasing their own salary or long-term job security.

[61] As discussed in O Williamson, *The Economics of Discretionary Behaviour: Managerial Objectives in a Theory of the Firm* (Prentice-Hall, 1964).

[62] M Eisenberg, 'The Structure of Corporation Law' (1989) 89 *Columbia Law Review* 1461, 1471.

[63] Easterbrook and Fischel (n 4) 36–39.

[64] See A Berle, 'Corporate Powers as Powers in Trust' (1930) 44 *Harvard Law Review* 1049, 1049 arguing that the powers granted to management 'are necessarily and at all times exercisable only for the ratable benefit of all the shareholders'.

[65] Easterbrook and Fischel (n 4) 38. Emphasis added.

Under the nexus of contracts description of the company and the facilitative model of company law, provision for other company constituents or stakeholders should not be part of company law as they are protected by: (1) their contracts which they have voluntarily agreed; and (2) external areas of law.[66] For example, employees agree to certain conditions and payment in their employment contract, are free to renegotiate this contract and this agreement takes place within the broader regulatory framework set by employment or labour law. Likewise, creditors may advance finance to a company in pursuit of a return through interest as defined in the contract and will frequently bargain for additional protection in the form of security.[67] These agreements exist within a broader insolvency law framework which provides that creditors are to be paid in advance of shareholders should the company be liquidated and frequently that directors owe a fiduciary duty to creditors when the company is in, or nearing insolvency.[68] These contractual and external legal protections mean that further protections from within company law for non-shareholder constituents are unnecessary and undeserved. Further, because such stakeholders are not dependent upon the residual, they would not value a share in the company's governance as much as shareholders. As an extension of this reasoning, broader social issues such as environmental damage and human rights abuses arising from the operation of companies should be addressed by sector specific regulation, not by company law.[69]

This facilitative model has been widely endorsed in the scholarship, culminating in two leading company law scholars declaring the 'End of History for Corporate Law' in 2001 as there was 'no longer any serious competitor to the view that corporate law should principally strive to increase long term shareholder value'.[70] It has also influenced company law reform in many common law jurisdictions. For example, the UK's Company Law Review Steering Group[71] stated that the role of company law is 'to *facilitate* the exercise of effective business choices so as to maximise wealth and welfare … *without public policy intervention*'.[72] Similarly, Ireland's Company Law Review Group[73] sought to transcend a 'command and control' mindset to instead 'ensure that economic

[66] ibid 36–39.

[67] See J Quinn, 'The Crystallisation of Floating Charges: Rethinking the Conceptual Framework' (2020) 20(1) *Journal of Corporate Law Studies* 179.

[68] J Quinn and P Gavin, 'The Creditor Duty Post *Sequana*: Lessons for Legislative Reform' (2023) 23(1) *Journal of Corporate Law Studies* 271.

[69] This point about the ability of external law to address negative externalities will be taken up in chapter two.

[70] H Hansmann and R Kraakman, 'The End of History for Corporate Law' (2001) 89 *Georgetown Law Review* 440, 440.

[71] The body that led the reform culminating in the UK Companies Act 2006.

[72] Company Law Review Steering Group, 'Modern Company Law for a Competitive Economy: Developing the Framework' (2000) [2.4]. Emphasis added.

[73] Whose work led to the Irish Companies Act 2014.

activity is enhanced by both the efficiency and effectiveness of the company law regime'.[74] It also, for a time, influenced the development of European company law. In 2001, the High Level Group of Company Law Experts[75] believed that European company law 'should provide a *flexible* framework'[76] that facilitated 'the running of *efficient* and competitive business enterprises'[77] and that regulation though company law should, in general, be avoided.[78] Following their report, the European Commission[79] took a 'minimalist'[80] approach to European company law while the EU imposed extensive regulation on companies through other areas of law.[81]

IV. ALTERNATIVE MODELS OF THE COMPANY

While company law has clearly evolved to provide rules that facilitate economically efficient business, the factual descriptions which underpin the nexus of contracts model, which in turn underpin the argument for shareholder value, are widely contested.[82] For example, Hayden and Bodie reject the characterisation of shareholders as having homogenous interests and sharing a singular focus in maximising the residual.[83] Another counter point is that company law is not

[74] Company Law Review Group, First Report (2001), 5 available at www.clrg.org/media/ycilc5dz/1-clrg-first-report.pdf, 9. The legislation which founded Ireland's Company Law Review Group provided that the Group 'shall seek to promote enterprise, facilitate commerce, simplify the operation of the Companies Acts, enhance corporate governance and encourage commercial probity' (Company Law Enforcement Act 2001, s 68(2)).

[75] The group charged by the European Commission to define new priorities for European company law. See 'Report of the High Level Group of Company Law Experts, A Modern Regulatory Framework for Company Law in Europe' (2002) available at www.ecgi.global/sites/default/files/report_en.pdf.

[76] ibid 5. Emphasis added.

[77] ibid 4.

[78] ibid 36. The Group instead advocated for 'specific law enforcement instruments outside company law' at 6.

[79] See Communication from the Commission to the Council and the European Parliament – Modernising Company Law and Enhancing Corporate Governance in the European Union – A Plan to Move Forward (2003) COM/2003/0284 final, available at https://eur-lex.europa.eu/legal-content/EN/ALL/?uri=celex%3A52003DC0284.

[80] As described by J Armour and WG Ringe, 'European Company Law 1999–2010: Renaissance and Crisis' (2011) 48 *Common Market Law Review* 125, 150.

[81] For example, employment law, tort law, consumer law, competition law and more recently in a digital context through privacy law and the regulation of digital markets, digital services and AI.

[82] See K Greenfield, *The Failure of Corporate Law: Fundamental Flaws and Progressive Possibilities* (Oxford, Oxford University Press, 2006), 14–19 and J Hardman, 'Tensions in Corporate Contractarianism: Rhetoric Rather than Logic' (2025) *International Journal for the Semiotics of Law* 1.

[83] See Hayden and Bodie, *Reconstructing the Corporation* (n 10) chs 5, 6 and 7. In particular, they point out that shareholders, far from having a singular interest in maximising the residual, have significantly different preferences depending on whether they are pension funds, sovereign wealth funds, minority shareholders or employee and management shareholders.

only default but includes mandatory rules[84] and provides benefits that cannot be obtained through contract.[85] Such contradictions to the descriptions made by the nexus of contracts model damage its normative argument that a facilitative company law and the prioritisation of shareholders is the best method to advance aggregate welfare. As Marc Moore notes, if a particular characterisation of a phenomenon lacks adequate description – in the sense of failing to represent materially significant features – it undermines the normative conclusions based on those descriptions.[86] Many alternative models of the company exist which highlight the inaccuracies of the assumptions made by the nexus of contracts model, emphasising the importance of the company's non-contractual dimensions.

A. Stakeholder Theory

Stakeholder theory[87] is based on the idea that providing benefits to all stakeholders should be an end in itself rather than an instrumental outcome of economic profit.[88] The theory wholly rejects the description of shareholders as being primary risk bearers or as providing a unique or superior investment, pointing out the fact that other stakeholders can be more affected by corporate decision making.[89] For example, an employee may train to develop highly specific skills with little relevance outside that company, a supplier may invest in equipment for the use of a single customer and a creditor may not receive satisfaction of their debt if the company enters insolvency.[90] The normative claim of the theory is that the best way to promote aggregate welfare is for directors to manage the company for the benefit of all stakeholders.[91]

[84] See Moore, *Corporate Governance in the Shadow of the State* (n 10) and C Bruner, 'The Enduring Ambivalence of Corporate Law' (2007) 59 *Alabama Law Review* 1385.

[85] For example, by providing for limited liability to shareholders for corporate torts. See H Hansmann and R Kraakman, 'Toward Unlimited Shareholder Liability for Corporate Torts' (1991) 100(7) *The Yale Law Journal* 1879.

[86] Moore (n 10) 4.

[87] The term 'stakeholder' is an infamously vague concept but can be generally defined as 'those groups and individuals who can affect or be affected by [corporate] actions'. RE Freeman et al, *Stakeholder Theory: The State of the Art* (Cambridge, Cambridge University Press, 2010) 9.

[88] E Freeman, *Strategic Management: A Stakeholder Approach* (Pitman, 1984) 97. See also C Stoney and D Winstanley, 'Stakeholding: Confusion or Utopia? Mapping the Conceptual Terrain' (2001) 38(5) *Journal of Management Studies* 603.

[89] L Zingales, 'In Search of New Foundations' (2000) 55 *Journal of Finance* 1623, 1632.

[90] See J Macey, 'Fiduciary Duties as Residual Claims: Obligations to Nonshareholder Constituencies from a Theory of the Firm Perspective' (1999) 84 *Cornell Law Review* 1266, 1274.

[91] See S Reynolds, F Schultz and D Hekman, 'Stakeholder Theory and Managerial Decision Making: Constraints and Implications of Balancing Stakeholder Interests' (2006) 64 *Journal of Business Ethics* 285 and A Keay, 'Stakeholder Theory in Corporate Law: Has it Got What it Takes?' (2010) 9 *Richmond Journal of Global Law and Business* 249, 254–260.

The well-known difficulty of the theory is the problem of unlimited managerial discretion, namely, how can company directors and managers effectively balance between a wide range of stakeholders which could include employees, suppliers, creditors, local communities and even the State. Inevitably, the interests of these diverse groups will not always align and stakeholder theory offers little guidance on how to resolve disputes between competing interests. The result, in Jensen's language, is that failing to prioritise any group effectively 'leaves the manager with no objective. The result will be confusion and a lack of purpose that will fundamentally handicap the firm in its competition for survival'.[92] Teubner, rejects stakeholder theory on this basis, arguing that while it frees directors from a one-sided focus on shareholders it creates new problems of orientation arising from their increased discretion.[93] A follow on argument is that this lack of clear priorities will result in a lack of accountability and an increase in agency costs which will harm economic productivity and by extension aggregate welfare.[94]

What could be described as a form of stakeholder theory has been introduced in certain jurisdictions through laws which require directors to consider or have regard to stakeholder interests. The most well-known examples of such provisions is 'enlightened shareholder value' in the UK[95] and the constituency statutes of certain US states.[96] However, rather than placing stakeholders on an equal footing, these provisions are best described as providing directors with permission to consider stakeholder interests and protect them from litigation for doing so.[97] For example, the UK's enlightened shareholder value is quite clear that stakeholders may only be had regard to within the overall context of promoting 'the success of the company for the benefit of its members as a whole'.[98] These legal developments, while certainly stakeholder orientated, do not attempt to mandate the equal consideration of stakeholders as envisioned by stakeholder theory.

[92] M Jensen, 'Value Maximisation, Stakeholder Theory and the Corporate Objective Function' (2001) 7(3) *European Financial Management* 297, 301.

[93] G Teubner, 'Corporate Fiduciary Duties and their Beneficiaries' in G Teubner and K Hopt (eds), *Corporate Governance and Directors' Liabilities: Legal, Economic and Sociological Analyses on Corporate Social Responsibility* (De Gruyter, 1985) 158.

[94] See M Roe, 'The Shareholder Wealth Maximisation Norm and Industrial Organisation' (2001) 149 *University of Pennsylvania Law Review* 2063, 2065 arguing 'a stakeholder measure of managerial accountability could leave managers so much discretion that managers could easily pursue their own agenda, one that might maximise neither shareholder, employee, consumer, nor national wealth but only their own'.

[95] See A Keay, *The Enlightened Shareholder Value Principle and Corporate Governance* (Routledge, 2013).

[96] See S Bainbridge, 'Interpreting Nonshareholder Constituency Statutes' (1991) 19 *Pepperdine Law Review* 971 and E Orts, 'Beyond Shareholders: Interpreting Corporate Constituency Statutes' (1993) 61 *George Washington Law Review* 14.

[97] P Davies, *Gower and Davies Principles of Modern Company Law*, 8th edn (Sweet and Maxwell, 2008), 519.

[98] UK Companies Act 2006, s 172(1).

B. Team Production

Another theory of the company which emphasises the role of the company's individual participants is Blair and Stout's model of 'team production'.[99] They define team production as a 'complex productive activity' that requires multiple parties to make contributions while relinquishing control to a decision-making process in the hope of shared benefits.[100] Like stakeholder theory, the model rejects the idea that shareholders are primary risk takers and sole residual claimants pointing out that stakeholders can bear equal or greater risk and that the company depends on their essential contributions to corporate production.[101] Blair and Stout attempt to conquer the problem of excessive managerial discretion by narrowing the focus of directors to those who make firm specific investments. They argue that the core strategy of a company should be to protect the enterprise-specific investments of all the members of the corporate team including shareholders, managers, rank and file employees, and possibly other groups, such as creditors. Blair and Stout describe the power of directors in public companies as 'virtually absolute'[102] and argue that their job, rather than prioritising shareholders, should be to act as a 'mediating hierarch' that prevents parties from opportunistically exploiting one another.[103] Their ultimate argument is that directors should, rather than prioritising shareholders, serve as 'trustees for the corporation itself' whose job is to 'balance team members' competing interests in a fashion that keeps everyone happy enough that the productive coalition stays together'.[104]

The difficulty with the team production model is similar to that of stakeholder theory in that directors have complete control which creates a lack of accountability and little direction for how to actually balance competing interests. Millon, while praising the model from a normative perspective,[105] criticises it on the basis that the outcome of team production, by its very nature, is non-separable and so it is impossible for directors to fairly allocate the outcomes of team production between the contributors. Given this impossibility, the team production model offers no rules or principles for how to structure board decision making leaving directors with 'unconstrained authority'.[106] This may not only lead to increased agency costs, but essentially grants directors freedom to act in any way they choose, which could allow them to pursue any direction,

[99] M Blair and L Stout, 'A Team Production Theory of Corporate Law' (1999) 85 *Virginia Law Review* 247.
[100] ibid 285.
[101] ibid 323.
[102] ibid 251.
[103] ibid 271–80.
[104] ibid 281.
[105] D Millon, 'New Game Plan or Business as Usual? A Critique of the Team Production Model of Corporate Law' (2000) 86 *Virginia Law Review* 1001, 1002–05.
[106] ibid 1026.

including shareholder value. Another objection is that the model is solely focused on those who make investments to the firm and provides no framework to address the negative externalities of business.

C. Concession Theory

The nexus of contracts, stakeholder theory and team production models of the company all take a disaggregated view by focusing on the company's separate participant groups. The concession theory approaches the company from the opposite perspective and views the company as a top-down creation of the state.[107] The theory focuses on the fact that the company is dependent upon the state for its creation through the process of registration or incorporation. The theory also emphasises that the company is dependent on the state's continuing recognition of its legal personality, which forms the basis for legal advantages such as corporate tax rates and limited liability for tort claims that cannot be obtained through private contracting. In addition, the existence of mandatory rules within company law[108] further demonstrates that the company is still subject to the externally imposed rules of the regulatory state.[109] The normative significance of the theory is that by characterising the company as being dependent upon the state, it is logical that the state retains authority to regulate it in a way that may otherwise be unjustified in private business relationships.[110]

It is incontestable that companies must be registered in accordance with rules set by the state, as Watson points out, registration is a mandatory process and it is only after its completion that a company exists.[111] It is also true that the companies depend on the state's legislation for their continued recognition as a legal person[112] and ongoing business dealings. The theory has been somewhat undermined by general incorporation legislation that has reduced registration to largely a formality with little state oversight. Registration was more relevant historically where the state was actively involved in granting recognition to companies.[113] Nevertheless, the state does provide many advantages to the company and the theory puts forward a strong justification for state regulation of companies.

[107] S Watson, 'The Corporate Legal Person' (2019) 19(1) *Journal of Corporate Law Studies* 137, 137 arguing that 'the modern company is a creature of the state with corporate legal personality derived from the state through the process of incorporation.' See also J Hardman, 'Fixing the Misalignment of the Concession of Corporate Legal Personality' (2023) 43(3) *Legal Studies* 443.

[108] For example, in relation to financial disclosures. See J Gordon, 'The Mandatory Structure of Corporation Law' (1989) 89 *Columbia Law Review* 1549.

[109] Moore (n 10) 63.

[110] L Ribstein, 'Why Corporations?' (2004) 1 *Berkeley Business Law Journal* 183, 208.

[111] Watson, 'The Corporate Legal Person' (n 107) 140.

[112] Companies can be struck from the register of companies for failing to file annual accounts or for failing to comply with other requirements of national company law.

[113] The state rarely plays an active role in companies outside of cases where it is a shareholder. See M Pargendler, 'State Ownership and Corporate Governance' (2011) 80 *Fordham Law Review* 2917.

D. Real Entity Theory

One of the earliest theoretical understandings of the company was put forward by Otto Van Gierke who viewed the company as a 'real entity'[114] rather than simply being a set of stakeholders or a creation of the state.[115] Instead, Van Gierke believed the company to have a 'life' beyond any individual or group involved in its operations.[116] A more modern version of the theory has been developed by Eva Micheler who relies on sociology as the foundation of real entity theory,[117] viewing the company as 'more than its changing parts'[118] and as having an emergent autonomy arising from the social action of its human parts.[119] This autonomy is based on the 'social fact'[120] that interactions within organisations create distinctive habits, routines, processes, and procedures and a distinctive organisational culture.[121]

A similar, albeit distinct, perspective is put forward by Keay[122] who argues that the interests of company as a distinct entity should take priority over all other company participants, including shareholders.[123] Under Keay's 'Entity Maximisation and Sustainabilty Model', the corporate objective is not 'the attainment of the public good' but rather to maximise the wealth of the entity and to sustain the entity as a going concern.[124] His model allows for the multidimensional character of the company and, like the other models, it frees directors from the pursuit of shareholder value. Again, the difficulty with this model is that aiming to advance the interests of the company as a distinct entity remains

[114] O Gierke (Frederic Maitland Trans), *Political Theories of the Middle Age* (Oxford, Oxford University Press, 1900).

[115] For an expansion of these ideas see F Maitland, 'The Corporation Sole (1900) 16(4) *LQR* 335 and A Machen, 'Corporate Personality' (1911) 24 *Harvard Law Review* 253.

[116] See M Horwitz, *The Transformation of American Law 1870–1960* (Oxford, Oxford University Press, 1992) 73 claiming Van Gierke insisted that corporate personality was as real as the individuality of a physical person.

[117] See E Micheler, *Company Law: A Real Entity Theory* (Oxford, Oxford University Press, 2021).

[118] ibid 178.

[119] ibid 179.

[120] See E Durkheim (S Lukes (ed)), *The Rules of Sociological Method* (Macmillan Press, 1982) 50–60.

[121] Micheler, *A Real Entity Theory* (n 117) 31 conceiving of companies as 'as autonomous actors with processes that shape and are shaped by natural actors'. See also R Adelstein, 'Firms as Social Actors' (2010) 6(3) *Journal of Institutional Economics* 329.

[122] A Keay, 'Ascertaining the Corporate Objective: An Entity Maximisation and Sustainability Model' (2008) 71(5) *The Modern Law Review* 663 and *The Corporate Objective: Corporations, Globalisation and the Law* (Elgar, 2011).

[123] Keay, *The Corporate Objective*, (n 122),173–230.

[124] ibid 174–76. Keay does argue that this approach will have benefits for the public good, but that this is best achieved through a focus on the entity's interests. Micheler does not argue that directors should act in the interests of the entity but rather notes the many controls that are on directors which advance the interests of different groups, primarily shareholders and creditors but sometimes the public interest. She argues that for non-shareholder interests to be integrated into the company as an entity requires the integration of their interests into the decision-making process of the company. See Micheler, *A Real Entity Theory* (n 117) 265 and ch 7.

an abstract concept leaving directors the discretion to decide what is in the entity's interests in every given scenario.[125] Directors faced with such discretion and complexity may, in practice, continue to pursue shareholder value simply to comply with existing corporate norms with disregard for negative externalities or pursue their own interests.

E. A New Model

What unites the above theories is their challenge to the descriptive claims of the nexus of contracts model[126] where shareholders are presented as the company's primary contributor and risk bearer, elevating their status above other stakeholders, the company itself and the state. In doing so, they undermine the nexus of contracts based justification that a facilitative company law and the pursuit of shareholder value as the best method to advance aggregate welfare. The other commonality between these models is that they provide for greater managerial discretion compared to the simple and clear objective of maximising the residual and prioritising the interests of shareholders. This presents a difficulty as excessive discretion can lead to a lack of direction, increased agency costs or directors simply continuing to prioritise shareholders or externalising costs. Describing directors as 'mediating hierarchs'[127] between stakeholders or arguing that they should prioritise the interests of the company as an entity ultimately fails to guide directors on how to prioritise competing interests[128] or on how to reduce negative externalities or advance aggregate welfare. What is required is a model that goes beyond shareholder value, that is sufficiently broad, that can capture the many aspects of the company but which also directs internal decision makers toward advancing aggregate welfare without disrupting the company's evolved characteristics that facilitate its efficiency. In an attempt to develop such a model, this book puts forward the 'societal company'.

V. THE SOCIETAL COMPANY

The starting point for the societal company is to describe the company in a way that acknowledges the company's multidimensional nature and that all the

[125] Keay does directly address the problem of managerial discretion, relying on different mechanisms such as market forces, corporate governance codes, social norms and regulation as potential sources of accountability: Keay, *The Corporate Objective* (n 122) Chapter 7.

[126] Millon refers to this type of scholarship as communitarian focused, noting that little work has been done to connect them but they remain united by their criticism of the status quo. See D Millon, 'Communitarians, Contractarians, and the Crisis in Corporate Law' (1993) 50 *Washington and Lee Law Review* 1373.

[127] Blair and Stout, 'A Team Production Theory of Corporate Law' (n 99) 271–80.

[128] This was Berle's point in the well-known Berle-Dodd debate. See A Berle, 'Corporate Powers as Powers in Trust' (1930) 44 *Harvard Law Review* 1049.

above theories capture important aspects of the company, be they contractual, stakeholder, state or sociological dimensions. This requires a description of the company as something complex,[129] that cannot be accurately described from a single viewpoint.[130] Rather, the dynamism of companies,[131] the different forms they take and the number of different sectors in which they operate means that companies can fit multiple models simultaneously – they can be dependent on the state, and can function both as a network of participants and as a separate entity depending on from what perspective it is viewed.[132]

Orts' response to this complexity is to describe the company as an 'institution',[133] aiming to find a 'broad middle ground'[134] between bottom-up theories that disaggregate the company into its constituent parts[135] and top-down, state focused theories.[136] Orts, relying on institutional theory,[137] describes companies as socially established entities that are both authorised by the state and controlled by individual participants.[138] He argues that once companies are registered and recognised by the state they become institutions which, from a legal perspective, means they become distinct entities that allow participants to self-govern through contract, the company's constitution and delegation of management to directors.[139] He also sees the company as a social institution that owes its survival to self-activating social processes.[140] Orts believes this description is sufficiently broad to encompass all main theories of the company,[141]

[129] See E Orts, 'The Complexity and Legitimacy of Corporate Law' (1993) 50(4) *Washington and Lee Law Review* 1565.

[130] Much like Lynam Johnson who noted the 'limitations (and risks) of adhering to a single all-purpose outlook'. See, L Johnson, 'Individual and Collective Sovereignty in the Corporate Enterprise' (1992) *Columbia Law Review* 2215, 2217.

[131] For a discussion of the modern company's dynamism see C Bruner, *The Corporation as Technology: Re-calibrating Corporate Governance for a Sustainable Future* (Oxford, Oxford University Press, 2022). Bruner rejects a single outlook of the company in favour of recognising the legal, cultural, economic and historical contexts that have contributed to the development of the modern company and company law ultimately describing the company as a dynamic legal technology that can be calibrated and re-calibrated in varying contexts, 13–16.

[132] M Eisenberg analogised the company with a photon which, depending on the way it is observed, can be both a particle and a wave. He argued that from the internal perspective, a company is a set of individuals contracting but from the external perspective of the market and the legal system, the company acts as a unified entity. See M Eisenberg, 'The Conception that the Corporation is a Nexus of Contracts and the Dual Nature of the Firm' (1998) 24 *Journal of Corporation Law* 819.

[133] E Orts, *Business Persons: A Legal Theory of the Firm* (Oxford, Oxford University Press, 2013). This 'legal theory of the firm' focuses on the consequences that flow from the legal rules but does not attempt to reduce the company to its legal dimension.

[134] ibid 19.

[135] Like the nexus of contracts, stakeholder and team production models.

[136] Like the concession theory.

[137] Citing E Hughs, 'The Ecological Aspect of Institution' (1936) 1 *American Sociological Review* 180; J Knight, *Institutions and Social Conflict* (Cambridge, Cambridge University Press, 1992); and JP Murmann, *Knowledge and Competitive Advantage: The Coevolution of Firms, Technology and National Institutions* (Cambridge, Cambridge University Press, 2003).

[138] Orts, *Business Persons* (n 133) 14.

[139] ibid 15.

[140] ibid 2.

[141] ibid 15.

however, due do its breadth it has few normative implications for the role of company law in advancing aggregate welfare, in Orts' words, it does not imply a 'positive legal theory'.[142] Rather than relying on theory for his normative argument,[143] Orts argues for a pragmatic institutionalism[144] where company law should be adapted by reference to 'particular contexts and situations rather than in general'.[145]

A different approach, that still allows for the company's complexity but which has greater normative implications is defining the company directly in terms of its role in promoting aggregate welfare or society's interests. This moves beyond instrumental theories which argue that aggregate welfare is best advanced through the prioritisation of shareholders, stakeholders or the company as an entity. Parkinson followed such an approach, declining to select between theories of the firm,[146] instead describing the company as a 'social enterprise'.[147] Parkinson rooted this description in a political theory of private power which regards corporate power as legitimate only if used in the public interest.[148] Parkinson's argument was that company law should only advance private interests to the extent they benefit society and analysed company law from this perspective proposing multiple potential reforms that could orientate corporate power toward the public interest.[149] A similar approach is taken by Teubner who relies not on political theory but on systems theory and autopoiesis[150] to go beyond individualist and collectivist theories of the

[142] ibid 18.

[143] A caution against this approach is made by HLA Hart who argued against the growth of theory on the back of definition, especially definitions of complex and ambiguous words such as state, possession or corporation. See HLA Hart, 'Definition and Theory in Jurisprudence' in *Essays in Jurisprudence and Philosophy* (Clarendon Press, 1983) 21–25.

[144] Orts (n 133) 17 relying on the work of HLA Hart and J Dewey whose approach to company law was pragmatic in the sense that they reject a theory first approach in favour of looking to specific contexts and the consequences that arise from the application of law. For example, Hart, after outlining a hypothetical contract law issue involving a company, concluded that the problem could not be solved by theory but only by reference to 'a detailed description of the conditions' and the 'specific rules in a particular case': Hart, 'Definition and Theory in Jurisprudence' (n 143) 41. Dewey was the first to make this kind of argument, urging for the disengagement of theories of the company from specific issues and disputes: see J Dewey, 'The Historic Background of Corporate Legal Personality' (1926) 35(6) *Yale Law Journal* 655, 669. For a broader view of Dewey's pragmatism see R Sleeper, *The Necessity of Pragmatism: John Dewey's Conception of Philosophy* (University of Illinois Press, 2001).

[145] ibid 19.

[146] Parkinson, *Corporate Power and Responsibility* (n 1) 31 describing the debate between theories as a distraction.

[147] ibid 23 relying on R Dahl, 'A Prelude to Corporate Reform' (1972) *Business and Society Review* 17.

[148] ibid 31.

[149] ibid ch 11.

[150] A concept from biology regarding the self-reproducing, self-organising, self-maintaining character of cellular organisms which has been extended to sociology. See, G Teubner, *Law as an Autopoietic System* (Blackwell, 1993) and G Teubner, *Critical Theory and Legal Autopoiesis: The Case for Societal Constitutionalism* (Manchester, Manchester University Press, 2019).

firm[151] – emphasising the company's 'ambivalence' and how it fluctuates between theories[152] – to describe the company as a self-referential social system.[153] Like Parkinson, Teubner uses this 'systems' understanding as a basis to redefine the company in terms of social benefits, arguing that company law must become orientated toward broader social expectations, emphasising the public interest in economic organisation.[154] In Teubner's view, 'a corporate enterprise does not exist simply as a self-serving and self-realizing institution for the unique benefits of its shareholders and workers, but rather exists, above all, to fulfil a broader role in society'.[155]

The societal company follows Parkinson and Teubner to avoid following a specific theory of the firm to focus instead on how company law can best promote aggregate welfare. Of course, as Parkinson points out, even after highlighting the limitations of the nexus of contracts model, it is quite possible that a facilitative company law and a pursuit of shareholder value best achieves this goal.[156] The fundamental problem with this argument, a point which will be fully developed in chapter two, is the inability of a patchwork of regulatory law, and indeed voluntary frameworks and market mechanisms, to effectively limit or end the negative externalities of companies.[157] Hence, company law, to optimally advance aggregate welfare, must allow for economically efficient business but also must include elements which are focused on limiting the negative externalities of business. This is necessary to correct for the imbalance created by the facilitative model where companies are free to focus on their economic success without regard for their external consequences.[158] Hence, the basic objective of the societal company is for companies to do no harm. This principle of do no

[151] G Teubner, 'Enterprise Corporatism: New Industrial Policy and the "Essence" of the Legal Person' (1988) 36(1) *The American Journal of Comparative Law* 130, 132.

[152] ibid 138.

[153] ibid 133–137 Relying on N Luhmann, *Social Systems* (Stanford University Press, 1995) to emphasise how the company as an organised action system has a cyclical linkage of identity and action, meaning it is constantly reproducing itself through new communications and actions.

[154] See G Teubner, 'Company Interest the Public Interest of the Enterprise in Itself' (1986) 94 *Journal of Political Economy* 691.

[155] Teubner, 'Corporate Fiduciary Duties' (n 93) 157. He makes the same point in G Teubner, 'Corporate Responsibility as a Problem of Company Constitution' (1983) *European University Institute Working Paper* available at https://cadmus.eui.eu/atmire/bitstream/1814/23191/1/1983_EUIWP_051.pdf, 3.

[156] Parkinson (n 1) 24.

[157] In making this argument, I again rely on Teubner's argument on functional differentiation and the limits of regulatory law. See Teubner, 'Substantive and Reflexive Elements' (n 12). The basic point is that as companies obtain increasing levels of power, operate globally and extend their reach into all aspects of society, it becomes increasingly difficult for sector specific regulation to address all contexts where a pursuit of shareholder value generates negative externalities and therefore should be constrained for the benefit of society.

[158] Once within the boundaries of the regulatory framework set by other areas of law – the external rules of the game in Friedman's terms (n 9) – but as will be argued in chapter two, a patchwork of regulatory law is insufficient to address the negative externalities of business.

harm has formed the basis of several important frameworks, perhaps most notably the work of John Ruggie[159] and his work in developing UNGPs[160] and Colin Mayer[161] and his work with the British Academy[162] on the corporate purpose.[163]

Given the limitations of external regulatory controls, for companies to do no harm a sense of societal responsibility must exist within the company itself and so, as Winter states, the challenge becomes how to 'ignite a sense of societal responsibility within corporations'.[164] This, of course, is the aim of many human rights principles, corporate governance frameworks, and proposals from academia. What distinguishes the societal company, is the argument that this internal sense of responsibility to do no harm is best achieved through a company law with reflexive elements[165] which serve to make companies responsive to outside interests and stop them from operating as closed systems singularly focused on economic success and shareholder value. These elements are procedural only and so do not seek to directly control corporate decision making nor change the company's evolved structure.[166] Rather, they require directors and managers to follow processes that are focused on societal issues such as environmental harms and human rights abuses. The aim is to 'externally stimulate' the company's internal processes to create a 'regulated autonomy'[167] which allows the company to retain the autonomy necessary to be economically productive[168] but which directs managerial discretion toward the public interest creating an internal sense of responsibility.[169] Through this company law with reflexive elements, the societal company model aims to strike the precarious balance

[159] J Ruggie, 'Protect, Respect and Remedy: A Framework for Business and Human Rights, Report to the UN Human Rights Council' (2008) available at www2.ohchr.org/english/bodies/hrcouncil/docs/8session/a-hrc-8-5.doc, 24.

[160] OHCHR, 'Guiding Principles on Business and Human Rights' (2011), available at www.ohchr.org/Documents/Publications/GuidingPrinciplesBusinessHR_EN.pdf. Guiding Principle 13 provides that the responsibility to respect human rights requires business enterprises to avoid causing or contributing to adverse human rights impacts through their own activities and from their business relationships.

[161] C Mayer, *Capitalism and Crises: How to Fix Them* (Oxford, Oxford University Press, 2024), ch 4. C Mayer, 'Success, Law and ESG' (2024) *European Corporate Governance Institute Working Paper* available at https://papers.ssrn.com/sol3/papers.cfm?abstract_id=4939931, 5 arguing that shareholders should be sole beneficiary of the company's residual success but that this success should be conditional on the avoidance of harm to others.

[162] British Academy, 'Principles for Purposeful Business' (2019) available at www.thebritishacademy.ac.uk/publications/future-of-the-corporation-principles-for-purposeful-business/.

[163] The Corporate Purpose is the subject of ch 7.

[164] J Winter, 'Addressing the Crisis of the Modern Corporation: The Duty of Societal Responsibility of the Board' (2020) available at https://papers.ssrn.com/sol3/papers.cfm?abstract_id=3574681, 1.

[165] Teubner (n 12).

[166] I am not saying that reflexive elements are part of company law's evolutionary development but rather that reflexive company law is not a 'regulatory' company law that aims to directly mandate how companies take decisions or change the 'core' characteristics of the company mentioned in ch 1.

[167] Teubner (n 93) 162.

[168] Ultimately, only directors in a given company can decide what is in the company's interests in a given context or whether to take a decision which favours employees, creditors, shareholders etc.

[169] This mirrors Parkinson's view that corporate decision making will only adequately serve the public interest if it explicitly takes it into account: see, Parkinson (n 1) 2.

between the need for companies to have an internal sense of societal responsibility while remaining economically productive. The justification for these reflexive elements and a description of their content is set out in chapter two.

VI. CONCLUSION

Debates on the correct description of the company have been ongoing for well over a century and will continue long into the future. Over the past quarter of a century the nexus of contracts model has emerged as dominant, influencing the development of company law to be primarily facilitative and providing the intellectual foundation for the idea that shareholder value within external regulation is the optimal method to advance aggregate welfare. This chapter has argued for an alternative approach, where company is defined directly in terms of its role in promoting aggregate welfare or society's interests.

2

A Reflexive Company Law

I. INTRODUCTION

THE LAST CHAPTER developed the claim that the inclusion of reflexive elements into company law would better promote 'aggregate welfare'.[1] This claim runs contrary to the traditional view that company law should facilitate business[2] and that broader social concerns and negative externalities are best dealt with by sector specific regulation through other areas of law.[3] The difficulty for this approach, which is followed by most nations and, until recently, by the EU, is that despite numerous external regulations aiming to reduce the negative externalities of business, such harms continue to arise.[4] The inability of patchworks of regulatory law to reduce the negative externalities of business has led to an increasingly widely held view that company law has a role to play in limiting the negative externalities of business.[5]

Given the power of modern companies and the number of different areas in which they operate, it is increasingly difficult for sector specific rules to cover

[1] Using the same definition as ch 1 taken from R Kraakman et al, *The Anatomy of Corporate Law: A Comparative and Functional Approach* 3rd edn (Oxford, Oxford University Press, 2017) 22 as being the 'aggregate welfare of all who are affected by a firm's activities including the firm's shareholders, employees, suppliers and customers, as well as third parties such as local communities and beneficiaries of the natural environment'.

[2] As discussed in ch 1. This facilitation of business does not mean that company law has no regulatory rules but rather that its regulatory rules are also directed toward efficient business, for example, through prohibitions on fraud.

[3] See F Easterbrook and D Fischel, *The Economic Structure of Corporate Law* (Harvard University Press, 1991) 36–39.

[4] Particularly in relation to environmental harms and human rights abuses. For a detailed report outlining many examples of such issues see British Institute of International and Comparative Law et al, 'Study on Due Diligence Requirements Through the Supply Chain' (2020) available at https://op.europa.eu/en/publication-detail/-/publication/8ba0a8fd-4c83-11ea-b8b7-01aa75ed71a1/language-en.

[5] See, eg B Sjåfjell and C Bruner (eds), *The Cambridge Handbook of Corporate Law, Corporate Governance and Sustainability* (Cambridge, Cambridge University Press, 2019) 6 stating that the 'idea that law and policy can be compartmentalised, with environmental issues left to environmental law, labour issues left to labour law, and so on, while imagining that the result will somehow become a consistent whole, is outdated and has proven unworkable in practice'. See also K Greenfield, 'Saving the World with Company Law?' (2007) *Boston College Law School Legal Studies Research Paper Series* available at https://papers.ssrn.com/sol3/papers.cfm?abstract_id=978242, 15 highlighting the peculiarity of recognising a need for the legal regulation of companies yet at the same time arguing that company law should not be part of this regulatory framework.

all the contexts in which shareholder value or economic productivity should be constrained for the benefit of aggregate welfare.[6] In other words, as society becomes increasingly complex and fragmented, regulatory law loses its capacity to achieve its stated objectives. Reflexive law acknowledges the shortcomings of both facilitative and regulatory law and takes an intermediate position where law aims to 'externally stimulate' the internal 'procedures' and 'mechanisms' within systems.[7] By taking this intermediate position, a company law with reflexive elements aims to prevent the company operating as a closed system singularly focused on its own economic success; the ultimate aim being to externally stimulate internal reflexion in a way that develops 'economic self-restraint' regarding actions which have detrimental effects on the non-economic environment.[8]

One example of a reflexive element is shared governance, where the law provides for stakeholders other than shareholders to be represented in the company's management structure. Shared governance is a feature of many European jurisdictions,[9] where employees are represented on the boards of large companies and could be extended to include 'general public directors'[10] selected by the state or other regulatory authorities.[11] Another example is duties to conduct due diligence and reporting which require companies to develop information gathering and reporting procedures regarding their direct impact and the impact of their subsidiaries and value chains.[12] However, such rules are, in and of themselves, insufficient to provoke a reflexive response and must be backed by the potential for legal enforcement, either privately through civil liability or public through supervision and fines from regulatory authorities. Without the threat of enforcement, law loses its coercive dimension and legal frameworks become simply another optional framework dependent upon voluntary compliance that lacks the force necessary to produce the reflexion.

This chapter discusses the potential for a company law with reflexive elements to address the negative externalities of business. Section II examines the claim that the negative externalities of business are best dealt with through sector specific regulation rather than by company law. Section III

[6] See E Elhauge, 'Sacrificing Corporate Profits in the Public Interest' (2005) 80(3) *New York University Law Review* 733, 802 and J Parkinson, *Corporate Power and Responsibility: Issues in the Theory of Company Law* (Clarendon Press, 1993) 347.

[7] See G Teubner, 'Substantive and Reflexive Elements in Modern Law' (1983) 17(2) *Law and Society Review* 239.

[8] G Teubner, 'Corporate Fiduciary Duties and their Beneficiaries' in G Teubner and K Hopt (eds), *Corporate Governance and Directors' Liabilities: Legal, Economic and Sociological Analyses on Corporate Social Responsibility* (De Gruyter, 1985) 164–65.

[9] See NV Munkholm, 'Board Level Employee Representation in Europe: An Overview' (2018) *European Centre of Expertise Working Paper* available at https://eu.eventscloud.com/file_uploads/e0bd9a01e363e66c18f92cf50aa88485_Munkholm_Final_EN.pdf.

[10] Borrowing the term from C Stone, *Where the Law Ends: The Social Control of Corporate Behaviour* (Harper & Row, 1975).

[11] See Parkinson, *Corporate Power and Responsibility* (n 6) 387.

[12] The leading examples being the EU's Corporate Sustainability Reporting and Due Diligence Directives.

develops a theory of reflexive law. Section IV focuses on shared governance and the potential for public interest directors to produce a reflexive effect. Section V briefly discusses due diligence, reporting, directors' duties and the importance of enforcement for an argument that reflexive law can create the societal company.

II. NEGATIVE EXTERNALITIES

While economic growth and the creation of wealth are high social priorities, there are clearly certain matters that rank above economic productivity which ought not be sacrificed in its pursuit.[13] One such area is the environment, now broadly discussed under the term 'sustainability'.[14] The term first came to prominence in a 1987 United Nations report which defined sustainability as meeting 'the needs of the present without compromising the ability of future generations to meet their own needs'.[15] Sustainability has since become closely associated with environmental concerns where it can be understood as aiming to safeguard the Earth's 'life-support system, on which the welfare of current and future generations depends'.[16] There is increasing evidence from environmental science that 'business as usual' is unsustainable because it is leading to global warming and environmental degradation.[17] For example, the International Panel on Climate Change (IPCC) estimates that global temperatures will have risen by 1.5°C above pre-industrial levels by 2040[18] and have concluded that it is now 'unequivocal that human influence has warmed the atmosphere, ocean and land'.[19] Environmental scientists have sought to define Earth's 'planetary boundaries' as the ecological limits within which humanity can continue to develop in the long term[20] with some concluding that four of the nine planetary boundaries have already been exceeded.[21]

[13] See Parkinson (n 6) 21–25.

[14] See Sjåfjell and Bruner (eds), *The Cambridge Handbook of Corporate Law* (n 5).

[15] The United Nations Brundtland Commission Report available at www.un-documents.net/our-common-future.pdf.

[16] See D Griggs et al, 'Sustainable Development Goals for People and Planet' (2013) 495 *Nature* 305, 307.

[17] See J Bélanger and D Pilling, *The State of the World's Biodiversity for Food and Agriculture* (FAO Commission on Genetic Resources for Food and Agriculture Assessments, 2019).

[18] V Masson-Delmotte et al (eds), 'Global Warming of 1.5C: An IPCC Special Report' (2018) available at www.ipcc.ch/site/assets/uploads/sites/2/2019/06/SR15_Full_Report_Low_Res.pdf.

[19] V Masson-Delmotte et al, 'Summary for Policymakers' in *Climate Change 2021: The Physical Science Basis* (2021) 4 available at www.ipcc.ch/report/ar6/wg1/downloads/report/IPCC_AR6_WGI_SPM.pdf.

[20] First developed by J Rockström et al, 'Planetary Boundaries: Exploring the Safe Operating Space for Humanity' (2009) 14(2) *Ecology and Society* 1 and subsequently built upon by W Steffen et al, 'Planetary Boundaries: Guiding Human Development on a Changing Planet' (2015) 347(6223) *Science* 736.

[21] See M Leach et al, 'Between Social and Planetary Boundaries: Navigating Pathways in the Safe and Just Space for Humanity' (2013) *World Social Science Report* 84.

Companies, as the dominant organisation in many of the world's economic sectors, lie at the heart of facing these environmental challenges. The argument is that their current activity, despite the economic value generated, is contributing to climate change and environmental degradation which could threaten the Earth's capacity to support life in the long term.[22] If the actions of companies, through, for example, the extraction of fossil fuels,[23] use of carbon and pollution contributes to potentially detrimental environmental degradation, arguments that such companies are economically efficient and contribute to a competitive economy lose significance. Considering these environmental challenges, there is a need for more sustainable business practices and a better balance between economically productive activity and protection of the environment.[24] Similarly, economic productivity cannot justify human rights abuses, for example, in contexts where corporate production leads to harmful working conditions,[25] child labour or pollution that damages an ecosystem on which locals depend.[26]

Increasingly, it is not individual companies that are the main drivers of these negative externalities but rather multiple connected companies where a parent or 'lead firm' facilitates, ignores or fails to detect instances of environmental damage or human rights abuses arising from the operation of its subsidiaries or contractual partners. Such corporate groups[27] and supply and value chains[28] have become highly efficient systems which frequently control the entire production process from the extraction of raw materials to the delivery of finished products and have 'globalised' in the sense that they have broken free of territorial boundaries and national law and instead operate through their own regimes of private governance.[29] In doing so, they largely escape traditional modes of legal regulation and pose a particularly difficult problem in attempting to address human rights and environmental harms arising from the operation of companies.

The environmental and human rights issues mentioned above have been the subject of numerous frameworks and agreements designed to mitigate climate

[22] See C Bruner, 'Corporate Governance Reform and the Sustainability Imperative' (2024) 131 *Yale Law Journal* 1217.

[23] See C Hackett, 'The Challenge of MNCs and Development: Oil Extraction, CSR, Nigeria and corruption' (2016) 2(2) *Journal of Human Rights in the Commonwealth* 1.

[24] For an EU funded project, led by Beate Sjåfjell, addressing these issues see Sustainable Market Actors for Responsible Trade (SMART) www.smart.uio.no/.

[25] See L Catá Backer, 'Are Supply Chains Transnational Legal Orders: What we can learn from the Rana Plaza Factory Building Collapse' (2016) 1 *UC Irvine Journal of International, Transnational and Comparative Law* 11.

[26] For the broader debate on this point see R Dworkin, 'Why Efficiency – A Response to Professors Calabresi and Posner' (1979) 8 *Hofstra Law Review* 563; R Dworkin, 'Is Wealth a Value?' (1980) 9(2) *The Journal of Legal Studies* 191; R Posner, 'The Value of Wealth: A Comment on Dworkin and Kronman' (1980) 9(2) *The Journal of Legal Studies* 243.

[27] Referring to the common ownership of shares between companies, where typically, one parent company owns shares in multiple subsidiaries. See J Dine, *The Governance of Corporate* Groups (Oxford, Oxford University Press, 2000), 40.

[28] See A Beckers, 'Global Value Chains in EU Law' (2023) 42 *Yearbook of European Law* 322.

[29] See L Cáta Backer, 'Theorizing Regulatory Governance within its Ecology: The Structure of Management in an Age of Globalization' (2018) 24(5) *Contemporary Politics* 607.

change and improve human rights standards. In the climate change context, the 2015 Paris Agreement brought nations together to 'strengthen the global response to the threat of climate change' by establishing a goal of limiting global warming to below '2°C above pre-industrial levels and pursuing efforts to limit the temperature increase to 1.5°C'.[30] The United Nations has also been at the forefront of confronting these challenges through their Sustainable Development Goals (SDGs)[31] and the Guiding Principles on Business and Human Rights (UNGPs).[32] These developments have had a significant impact and established new strategies and frameworks on how to meet these challenges. Nevertheless, they remain non-binding frameworks that lack the force of legal rules.[33] Adherence to them depends on the importance given to moral or social issues by individuals within companies and while they influence certain individuals, they are frequently an impotent means of regulation in the face of economic incentives to externalise costs.[34] The continuing examples of both environmental and human rights harms[35] also undermine arguments that such issues can be addressed through private bargaining.[36]

A. The Role of Company Law

If we agree that there is a place for law in addressing environmental and human rights challenges, the question, for present purposes, becomes what role, if any, is there for company law. The traditional argument from proponents of shareholder value is to accept that certain interests or values rank ahead of economic

[30] United Nations, Paris Agreement (2015) Art 2(1). See also the Communication from the Commission to the European Parliament, the European Council, the Council, the European Economic and Social Committee and the Committee of the Regions – The European Green Deal [2019] COM/2019/640 available at https://commission.europa.eu/publications/communication-european-green-deal_en.

[31] United Nations, 'Sustainable Development Goals' available at www.un.org/sustainable development/.

[32] OHCHR, 'Guiding Principles on Business and Human Rights: Implementing the United Nations "Protect, Respect and Remedy" Framework' (2011) available at www.ohchr.org/sites/default/files/documents/publications/guidingprinciplesbusinesshr_en.pdf.

[33] See J Quinn and R Condon, 'Beyond the Individual-Company: From Corporate Social Responsibilities to Corporate Social Liability' (2025) *Transnational Legal Theory* available at www.tandfonline.com/doi/full/10.1080/20414005.2025.2479318?src=exp-la#abstract.

[34] See Teubner, 'Corporate Fiduciary Duties' (n 8) 158 citing M Weber, *Gesammelte Aufsätze zur Religionssoziologie*, 6th edn (JCB Mohr, 1972) Vol 1, 544 and J Habermas, *Theorie des kommunikativen Handelns* (Suhrkamp, 1981) 312.

[35] See British Institute of International and Comparative Law, 'Study on Due Diligence Requirements Through the Supply Chain' (n 4) and Lebaron et al, 'Governing Global Supply Chain Sustainability through the Ethical Audit Regime' (2017) 14(6) *Globalizations* 958.

[36] See A Johnstone, 'Governing Externalities: The Potential of Reflexive Corporate Social Responsibility' *University of Cambridge Working Paper* (2012) available at https://papers.ssrn.com/sol3/papers.cfm?abstract_id=2165616 discussing R Coase's argument in 'The Problem of Social Cost' (1960) 3 *Journal of Law and Economics* 1, that reduction of negative externalities should either be through direct regulation or left to private bargaining based on a cost benefit analysis.

efficiency but that such matters are best addressed by other areas of law directly focused on regulation.[37] The argument is that, as examples, environmental law should provide safeguards against pollution through conditions imposed for the granting of licences, compliance frameworks or fines and other penalties[38] and employment law should protect employees from unfair dismissal, harassment and an unsafe work environment.[39] If new challenges emerge, new rules or new areas of law should be developed to regulate and prevent negative externalities while company law continues to facilitate economically efficient business.[40] Such regulatory interventions are 'inefficient' in the sense that they limit the alternatives available to companies but are necessary to protect aggregate welfare. The crucial point is that these external regulations maintain the broadly facilitative rules of company law and directors remain free to promote the interests of shareholders and maximise the residual within the external 'rules of the game'.[41] This has been, until recently, the exact approach of the EU where European company law has remained relatively underdeveloped, from a regulatory perspective, compared to EU employment law,[42] tort law,[43] environmental law,[44] competition law,[45] privacy law,[46] and most recently, digital services[47] and AI.[48]

[37] Easterbrook and Fischel, *The Economic Structure of Corporate Law* (n 3) 37.

[38] For a full discussion of the limits of such an approach to environmental law see E Orts, 'Reflexive Environmental Law' (1994) 89(4) *Northwestern University Law Review* 1227.

[39] The general argument can be traced as far back as 1920 where Pigou proposed a tax on corporate activities that generate externalities in order to create incentives to either reduce the harmful activities or to take precautions in relations to the harm they created: A Pigou, *The Economics of Welfare* (1920, Macmillan) 170.

[40] This argument was made by Hayek who argued that negative externalities are best remedied by the 'gradual improvement of law': F Hayek, 'The Corporation in a Democratic Society: In Whose Interest Ought It and Will It Be Run?' in HI Ansoff (ed), *Business Strategy* (Penguin, 1969) 266.

[41] M Friedman, *Capitalism and Freedom* (The University of Chicago Press, 1962) 133–35. Friedman argued that it was the responsibility of society to create a legal framework that allowed the invisible hand of the market to promote the interests of society, citing Adam Smith, *The Wealth of Nations* (1776), 421.

[42] See https://eur-lex.europa.eu/summary/chapter/17.html.

[43] Eg, Directive 85/374/EEC of 25 July 1985 (Defective Products Directive).

[44] See www.europarl.europa.eu/factsheets/en/sheet/71/environment-policy-general-principles-and-basic-framework.

[45] Articles 101–106 of the Treaty on the Functioning of the European Union (TFEU) prohibiting practices that have the objective or effect of preventing, restricting or distorting competition within the internal market.

[46] See Regulation (EU) 2016/679 of the European Parliament and of the Council of 27 April 2016 on the protection of natural persons with regard to the processing of personal data and on the free movement of such data, and repealing Directive 95/46/EC (General Data Protection Regulation) [2016] OJ L 119/1.

[47] See Regulation (EU) 2022/2065 of the European Parliament and of the Council of 19 October 2022 on a Single Market for Digital Services and amending Directive 2000/31/EC (Digital Services Act) [2022] OJ L 277/1.

[48] See Regulation (EU) 2024/1689 of the European Parliament and of the Council of 13 June 2024 laying down harmonised rules on artificial intelligence and amending Regulations (EC) No 300/2008, (EU) No 167/2013, (EU) No 168/2013, (EU) 2018/858, (EU) 2018/1139 and (EU) 2019/2144 and Directives 2014/90/EU, (EU) 2016/797 and (EU) 2020/1828 (Artificial Intelligence Act) [2024] OJ L, 2024/1689.

The difficulty is that there is increasing evidence that patchworks of regulatory law are unable to address environmental and human rights issues leading to the belief that company law has at least some role to play in limiting the negative externalities of business. This is based on the view that external controls can never address all the contexts in which shareholder value or economic productivity should be constrained for the benefit of aggregate welfare.[49] This is because of the power companies have, the number of different areas in which they operate,[50] the unavoidable time lag of law[51] and the practical difficulties faced by litigants in enforcing the law.[52] Lipton summarises it as follows: 'we cannot rely solely on legal prohibitions to curb all antisocial corporate activity, because it is impossible to specify in advance – let alone enforce laws against – every potential form of corporate misbehavior'.[53] There is also a more general point, developed below, that regulatory law is frequently unable to achieve its stated objectives as society becomes increasingly complex.

These shortcomings support an argument that company law should form part of the legal framework which seeks to limit the negative externalities of companies. However, the argument against such reform is that company law has a unique ability to alter the company's internal decision-making processes through changes to corporate governance structures or directors' duties. As such, company law reform has the potential to disrupt the structure that has evolved to maximise efficiency. Advocates of shareholder value argue that such regulatory intervention would decrease economic efficiency with a net negative impact on aggregate welfare.[54]

III. REFLEXIVE LAW

Gunther Teubner's work on corporate responsibility[55] emphasises the shortcomings of both facilitative and regulatory law and instead argues for a 'reflexive'

[49] See E Elhauge, 'Sacrificing Corporate Profits in the Public Interest' (n 6) 802.

[50] See Parkinson (n 6) 347–49.

[51] See G Teubner, 'Corporate Responsibility as a Problem of Company Constitution' (1983) *European University Institute Working Papers* available at https://cadmus.eui.eu/handle/1814/23191, 19–21.

[52] See A Lafarre, 'Mandatory Corporate Sustainability Due Diligence in Europe' (2022) *European Corporate Governance Institute Blog* available at https://www.ecgi.global/publications/blog/mandatory-corporate-sustainability-due-diligence-in-europe-the-way-forward noting the barriers facing tort claimants such as high costs and asymmetric power relations.

[53] A Lipton, 'Not Everything is About Investors: The Case for Mandatory Stakeholder Disclosure' (2020) 37 *Yale Journal on Regulation* 499, 505.

[54] Net negative impact meaning that any benefit to aggregate welfare from changes to company law would be outweighed by the harms resulting from a decrease in economic productivity. See M Roe et al, 'The European Commission's Sustainable Corporate Governance Report: A Critique' (2020) Law Working Paper No 553/2020 *European Corporate Governance Institute* available at https://papers.ssrn.com/sol3/papers.cfm?abstract_id=3711652.

[55] See Teubner and Hopt (eds), *Corporate Governance and Directors' Liabilities* (n 8) and G Teubner, 'Corporate Responsibility as a Problem of Company Constitution' (1983) *European University Institute Working Papers* available at https://cadmus.eui.eu/handle/1814/23191.

approach.[56] As referenced in the last chapter, for Teubner, the challenge of corporate responsibility lies in how law can restrict the company's internal profit maximising rationality and redefine the interests of the company in terms of broader social benefits.[57] However, Teubner also recognises the importance of the company as a vehicle for economic productivity believing that a contradiction lies at the heart of the company between its needs for economic performance and social responsibility.[58] He argues that reflexive law can help achieve a balance between these contradicting obligations through the external 'stimulation' or 'mobilisation' of internal 'self-control resources' causing a shift away from a singular focus on economic success.[59]

Reflexive law lies between the 'formal' and 'substantive' branches of law described by Weber.[60] Formal law refers to foundational rules through which private parties orient their affairs,[61] for example, property rights or the enabling framework of company law.[62] Over time, the growing complexity of modern society overwhelms formal law, in the sense that growing complexity increases the potential for harmful effects resulting from private bargaining. As Pigou argued, governments need to intervene, through regulation or taxation, to correct for externalities because the 'divergence between private and social net product' arises out of a 'disservice rendered to persons other than the contracting parties' and so cannot be 'mitigated by a modification of the contractual relation between any two contracting parties'.[63] This leads to the rise of the regulatory state and its 'substantive law' which is used for 'purposive, goal-oriented intervention'[64] like, for example, the environmental law or employment law rules mentioned above.

However, as society becomes increasingly complex, it begins to 'functionally differentiate' and substantive law loses its ability to achieve its purposes through direct intervention.[65] In making this argument, Teubner relies on Luhman[66] and

[56] See Teubner, 'Substantive and Reflexive Elements in Modern Law' (n 7).

[57] See G Teubner, 'Company Interest the Public Interest of the Enterprise in Itself' (1986) 94 *Journal of Political Economy* 691.

[58] Teubner, 'Corporate Fiduciary Duties' (n 8) 162.

[59] ibid 160.

[60] See M Rheinsstein, *Max Weber on Law in Economy and Society* (Harvard University Press, 1954) 60–65. See also P Zumbanssen, 'Law After the Welfare State: Formalism, Functionalism and the Ironic Turn of Reflexive Law' (2008) 56(3) *American Journal of Comparative* Law 769.

[61] See Teubner (n 7) 240.

[62] I refer here to the fundamental characteristics of the company that exist across almost all jurisdictions as described in R Kraakman et al, *The Anatomy of Corporate Law* (n 1) 5–15 as being: (i) legal personality; (ii) limited liability of shareholders; (iii) transferable shares; (iv) delegated management to a board of directors; (v) shareholders having ultimate control and access to net earnings.

[63] Pigou, *The Economics of Welfare* (n 39) 192.

[64] Teubner (n 7) 240.

[65] See M Dorf, 'The Domain of Reflexive Law' (2023) 103 *Columbia Law Review* 384, 395.

[66] N Luhmann, 'Evolution Des Rechts' in Karl Engisch et al (eds) *Rechtstheorie: Zeitschrift Für Logik, Methodenlehre Kybernetik Und Soziologie Des Rechts 3* (Frankfurt, Suhrkamp, 1970).

Habermas[67] and their work on systems theory[68] which views society as being comprised of differentiated systems that are 'self-referential' in the sense that they function according to their own logic, values, norms, and language.[69] This differentiation between systems makes it difficult for any single system (for example, the legal system) to influence other systems in the way intended.[70] Hence, conventional reform strategies where law directly intervenes to address social issues often fail due to society's complexity and differentiation.[71] The limitations of substantive law in the face of this functional differentiation provides the basis for Teubner to argue for a third form of law – reflexive law – which recognises the limits of law's ability to direct change in a specified or detailed manner.[72] Rather than trying to impose rules from one system on to another, reflexive law focuses on how law can structure processes and procedures within different systems to establish 'regulated autonomy'.[73] The core argument is that functionally differentiated systems cannot be regulated through substantive rule making, rather restrictions must be built into the 'structure of every functional subsystem'.[74]

Teubner regards the economic system, like many other systems, as being unable to re-translate its external consequences 'into its own language'.[75] The same can be said of economic sub-systems such as companies or enterprises[76] which are inclined toward self-interested profit-maximisation.[77] Applying reflexive law to companies means looking to the internal decision making processes and imposing legal rules the aim of which is to make companies reflect on and be responsive to outside interests, in effect, to prevent them from operating as closed

[67] J Habermas, *Communication and the Evolution of Society* (Thomas McCarthy Trans, 1979).

[68] For a full exploration of systems theory see R Condon, *Network Responsibility: European Tort Law and the Society of Networks* (Cambridge, Cambridge University Press, 2022) and L LoPucki, 'Systems Approach to Law' (1997) 80 *Cornell Law Review* 479. Systems theory has been discussed in a company law context but as a means of better understanding the company itself rather than in the context of corporate social responsibility. See T Belinfanti and L Stout, 'Contested Visions: The Value of Systems Theory for Corporate Law' (2017) 166 *University of Pennsylvania Law Review* 579 and C Witting, 'The Place of Managers in the Corporate Governance Architecture' (2024) 24(1) *Journal of Corporate Law Studies* 267.

[69] For a broader discussion of this point see G Teubner, *Law as an Autopoietic System* (Blackwell, 1993) and G Teubner, 'After Legal Instrumentalism? Strategic Models of Post-Regulatory Law' (1984) *European University Institute Working Papers* available at https://cadmus.eui.eu/handle/1814/23192.

[70] See D Hirsch, 'Green Business and the Importance of Reflexive Law: What Michael Porter Didn't Say' (2010) 62(4) *Administrative law Review* 1063, 1107.

[71] Orts, 'Reflexive Environmental Law' (n 38) 1261 criticising R Dworkin's, *Law's Empire* (Harvard University Press, 1986) on the basis that once a society grows significantly complex, a strategy of legal imperialism law is no longer effective.

[72] Teubner (n 7) 253–55.

[73] ibid 254.

[74] Teubner (n 8) 162.

[75] Teubner, 'After Legal Instrumentalism?' (n 69) 40.

[76] See G Teubner, 'Enterprise Corporatism: New Industrial Policy and the "Essence" of the Legal Person' (1988) 36(1) *The American Journal of Comparative Law* 130.

[77] G Teubner, 'Company Interest: The Public Interest of the Enterprise in Itself (1986) 94 *Journal of Political Economy* 691, 695.

systems.[78] The law's role is therefore to externally stimulate internal reflexion[79] in a way that develops 'economic self-restraint' regarding actions which have detrimental effects on the non-economic environment.[80] This, of course, is the aim of voluntary frameworks like the SDGs and UNGPs but Teubner regards such voluntary frameworks as insufficiently powerful to provoke the necessary reflexion.[81] Teubner's ultimate argument is that law should 'design' the structural preconditions for an 'organizational conscience' that reflects the balance needed between the company's social functions and its economic performance.[82]

In considering what legal rules could achieve the necessary reflexion, Teubner looks to 'mechanisms' that will ensure the company takes 'into account the non-economic interests of workers, consumers, and the general public'.[83] However, he rejects a 'stakeholder' approach where company directors owe duties to different interest groups because such groups lack the capacity to select and appropriately weigh broader social concerns.[84] He regards stakeholder theory as freeing company law from a one-sided focus on shareholders but creating new problems of orientation,[85] ie the problem of directors having excessive discretion discussed in chapter one. He argues that sufficiently strong 'procedural standards and organizational devices' can overcome the problem of managerial absolutism.[86]

Teubner's recommendations are for a duty of cooperation and consultation implemented through the representation of stakeholder and public representatives on company boards, ie shared governance.[87] He also argues for a duty of audited disclosures[88] and for a duty to 'organise' in large scale, complex organisations whereby 'top management' should be made responsible for creating a system of coordination, supervision, monitoring and control, ie due diligence.[89] Such changes, by focusing on internal processes and decision making, allow for complexity in a way that regulatory law cannot and provide flexibility for businesses to adapt to specific circumstances.[90] Hence, reflexive law is not directed

[78] See Teubner (n 7) 276–78.

[79] Teubner (n 8) 164.

[80] ibid 165.

[81] ibid arguing that the 'reflexion cannot be voluntary but needs to be stimulated by powerful external forces'.

[82] ibid 166. Teubner emphasises the importance of this balance and that the societal function of the company should not be 'stressed one sidedly at the expense of economic performance' at 162.

[83] ibid 165.

[84] ibid 151.

[85] ibid 158.

[86] ibid 167.

[87] ibid 171, specifically referencing representation for 'employee welfare, consumers, environment and community, law-enforcement, planning and research etc'.

[88] ibid 168–69 noting that disclosures can be expanded 'to cover problem areas other than the protection of shareholders' interests.' and the potential for a 'social audit'.

[89] ibid.

[90] See G Teubner, 'Social Order from Legislative Noise? Autopoietic Closure as a Problem for Legal Regulation' in G Teubner and A Fabbrajo (eds), *State, Law, and Economy as Autopoietic Systems: Regulation and Autonomy in a New Perspective* (Giuffrè, 1992).

toward goal-oriented intervention and does not seek to directly prescribe managerial decision making, nor does it aim to fundamentally alter the core characterises of the corporate form. Instead, it recognises the many different types of companies, the complexity of the challenges they face and the need for autonomy to respond to their unique situation.[91] However, it also does not leave the regulation of companies to external rules or private bargaining, instead relying on mandatory processes to make the company's internal decision makers responsive to its external effects.

IV. SHARED GOVERNANCE

One of the core characteristics of the company is that its executive (day-to-day) management is delegated to directors but shareholders retain control over certain fundamental decisions, such as altering the company's constitution or voluntarily liquidating the company.[92] Another decision under the exclusive control of shareholders, at least in common law jurisdictions, is the power to elect and remove directors.[93] The overarching justification for this exclusive power is that it is efficient as an outcome of private ordering[94] and because shareholders, as non-contractual claimants, depend upon maximising the residual and so are best placed to select and monitor directors. According to Easterbrook and Fischel, extending voting rights to other stakeholders with heterogenous preferences would produce intransigent election results, or voting cycles[95] which would ultimately lead to the company's 'self destruction'.[96]

Hayden and Bodie, in their argument for shared governance between shareholders and employees,[97] present a series of persuasive criticisms of these justifications.[98] They highlight that shareholders, far from having a unified and singular interest in maximising the residual, have significantly different

[91] A Johnston, 'Integrating Sustainability into Corporate Governance' in C Bruner and M Moore (eds), *A Research Agenda for Corporate Law* (Edward Elgar Publishing, 2023), 57.

[92] This control is exercised through shareholder voting. It should be acknowledged that the significance of these voting rights varies depending on the type of company. For example, voting rights are likely to be less significant in companies with a widely dispersed share ownership as compared to companies with controlling shareholders. See Kraakman et al, *The Anatomy of Corporate Law* (n 1) 72–74.

[93] Kraakman et al (n 1) 57.

[94] Without rehashing arguments from ch 1, the argument is that if the company's internal governance structures have 'evolved' then this is likely to be the most efficient form of governance.

[95] As based on Kenneth Arrow's impossibility theorem. See G Hayden and M Bodie, *Arrow's Theorem and the Exclusive Shareholder Franchise* (2009) 62 *Vanderbilt Law Review* 1219.

[96] Easterbrook and Fischel, *The Economic Structure of Corporate Law* (n 3) 69–70.

[97] For a detailed discussion of the role employees within US and EU corporate governance see I Lynch-Fannon, *Working Within Two Kinds of Capitalism: Corporate Governance and Employee Stakeholding: US and EC Perspectives* (Bloomsbury, 2003).

[98] G Hayden and M Bodie, *Reconstructing the Corporation: From Shareholder Primacy to Shared Governance Reconstructing the Corporation* (Cambridge, Cambridge University Press, 2021).

preferences depending on whether they are pension funds, sovereign wealth funds, minority shareholders or employee and management shareholders.[99] This point is further evidenced by the rise of environmental, social, and governance (ESG) investing which proves that many shareholders have broader preferences than simply maximising the residual.[100] According to Hayden and Bodie, the heterogeneous interests of shareholders proves that the corporate governance system already allows for divergent preferences and that one of the principal functions of a governance system is to accommodate such divergences.[101] Hence, shared governance does not necessarily lead to intransigence.

Hayden and Bodie base their argument for shared governance on social choice theory and their analysis of preference aggregation[102] – the mechanism through which governance systems facilitate the move from individual preferences to group choices through voting. The fundamental issue in preference aggregation is who is granted the right to vote. According to social choice theory, the most important factor in being granted the right to vote is the degree to which a person is affected by the outcome of an election. Often, there is no direct way to establish this, and so markers of interest are used with modern democracies relying on residency as the primary marker of interest. In companies, however, despite several constituents having a significant interest, many jurisdictions allow only shareholders to vote. The authors use their analysis of social choice theory to argue that both shareholders and employees have sufficient markers of interest to justify voting rights as special constituents within the firm as opposed to other corporate constituents who lie outside it.[103] The case for employees is that they directly contribute to the company's production and create value through their labour as well as being dependent upon the company's ongoing success for their employment.[104] Hayden and Bodie rely on a firm-market distinction as the justification for excluding other stakeholders from participation in the company's governance.[105] They argue that stakeholders beyond shareholders and employees have insufficient markers of interest to justify voting rights and believe they are best protected by contract and regulation external to company law. They highlight the example of customers and suppliers, who, while clearly having a 'stake' in the company, generally have only a tenuous interest in the company's long-term success. The authors then rely on German codetermination as evidence that shared governance between employees and shareholders can work in practice.

[99] ibid 17.
[100] See J Macey, 'ESG Investing: Why Here? Why Now?' (2022) 19 *Berkeley Business Law Journal* 258.
[101] Hayden and Bodie, *Reconstructing the Corporation* (n 98) ch 5.
[102] ibid ch 2.
[103] ibid ch 10.
[104] ibid 169–71.
[105] ibid 171.

A. German Codetermination

The boards of German companies that have over 500 employees are divided into a management board (*Vorstand*) and a supervisory board (*Aufsichtsrat*) which includes employee representatives. The supervisory board has the power to appoint directors to the management board, may inspect the company's books and records at any time,[106] and the management board must inform the supervisory board of its policies.[107] The supervisory board can also call shareholders meetings and certain transactions may need supervisory board approval depending on the company's constitutional documents.[108] This separation of management and supervisory boards in Germany dates back to 1861 when the German Commercial Code introduced a supervisory board for public companies that was intended to replace oversight by the then socialist Government.[109] However, despite an intention that the supervisory board would reflect the interests of the state, employees and investors,[110] the supervisory board was comprised only of shareholder representatives.[111] Subsequently, Germany introduced a series of reforms clarifying the role of each board[112] leading to the first implementation of codetermination in 1922 when employees were given the power to elect representatives to the supervisory board.[113] This first form of codetermination was repealed by the Nazi Government in 1934 but codetermination was reintroduced in 1951 by an Act which required any company with over 1,000 employees in the iron, coal or steel industries to have a two-tier board.[114] The supervisory board was to consist of five shareholder representatives and five employee representatives with an eleventh neutral member from outside the company.[115] In 1952, Germany expanded codetermination to every public company (AG) and private company (GmbH) with over 500 employees.[116] The supervisory board was to be made of a number divisible by three, with employee representation making up

[106] C Rasnic, 'Germany's Statutory Works Councils and Employee Codetermination: A Model for The United States?' (1992) 14 *Loyola of Los Angeles International & Comparative Law Journal* 275, 283.

[107] K Hopt, *The German Two-Tiered Board (Aufsichtsrat): A German View on Corporate Governance* in *Comparitive Corporate Governance* (De Gruyter 1997) 6.

[108] ibid 5.

[109] For a comprehensive history see P Muchlinski, 'The Development of German Corporate Law Until 1990: An Historical Reappraisal' (2013) 14(2) *German Law Journal* 339.

[110] C Jungman, 'The Effectiveness of Corporate Governance in One-Tier and Two-Tiered Board Systems' (2006) 4 *European Company and Financial Law Review* 426, 449.

[111] R Weitholter, 'Interessen und Organisation der Aktiengesellschaft im Amerkenischen und Deutschen Recht' (Verlag CF Muller, Karlsrue, 1961), 280 as referenced in J du Plessis and O Sandrock, 'The Rise and Fall of Supervisory Codetermination in Germany?' (2005) *International Company and Commercial Law Review* 69, 71.

[112] Hopt, *The German Two-Tiered Board* (n 107) 6.

[113] See J du Plessis, 'Reflections on Some Recent Corporate Governance Reforms in Germany: A Transformation of the German Aktienrecht?' (2003) *Deakin Law Review* 389.

[114] Montan-mitbestimmunggsgesetz (Coal, Steel and Mining Codetermination Law) 1951 [1].

[115] Montan-mitbestimmunggsgesetz (Coal, Steel and Mining Codetermination Law) 1951 [45].

[116] Betriebsverfassungsgesetz, [77].

one third.[117] The Codetermination Act 1976[118] expanded codetermination to all companies with over 2,000 employees, the supervisory board being made up of one half shareholders and one half employees, the deciding vote being held by a shareholder elected chair.[119]

Hayden and Bodie's arguments above provide a theoretical justification for extending representation on company boards beyond shareholders while German codetermination proves that shared governance between shareholders and employees can work in practice and form the basis of a successful and efficient economy. Yet, it is not clear how shared governance between employees and shareholders could address the negative externalities of companies such as environmental harms and human rights abuses. Employee representatives will necessarily focus on the interests of employees who are likely to be concerned with working conditions, benefits and job security rather than broader societal challenges.[120] An obvious demonstration of this point is the Volkswagen emissions scandal where the auto manufacturer used software in its diesel vehicles to lower emissions during tests artificially improving results.[121] Volkswagen has a unique codetermination arrangement arising from its privatisation in 1960 where several board seats were reserved for local government representatives. Traditionally, the local government representatives sided with employees on contentious matters effectively creating a de facto employee majority on the company's supervisory board.[122] The arrangement meant that Volkswagen has the most employee dominated governance structure of all multinational companies yet, as Bodie points out, the emissions scandal 'demonstrates that high levels of worker participation in corporate governance do not guarantee good behaviour or sustainable practices'.[123] Ultimately, employee representatives may be just as self-interested as shareholder representatives and consent to the externalisation of costs if it is in their interests.

While Hayden and Bodie persuasively argue that stakeholders beyond employees do not have sufficient markers of interest to be included in a company's management structure, they do not consider 'public interest' directors selected by the state or a regulatory body.[124] Given the potential impact

[117] J Shearman, 'Corporate Governance – an Overview of the German Aufsichtsrat' (1995) *Journal of Business Law* 517, 519.

[118] Mitbestimmungsgesetz, 1976.

[119] See S Donnelly, 'The Public Interest and the Company in Germany' in J Parkinson, A Gamble and G Kelly (eds), *The Political Economy of the Company* (Oxford, Bloomsbury, 2000) 85.

[120] See Bruner, 'Corporate Governance Reform and the Sustainability Imperative' (n 22) 1265–66.

[121] N Sharpe, 'Volkswagen's Bad Decisions & Harmful Emissions: How Poor Process Corrupted Codetermination in Germany's Dual Board Structure' (2017) 7 *Michigan Business and Entrepreneurial Law Review* 49, 62.

[122] ibid 66.

[123] M Bodie, 'Worker Participation, Sustainability and the Puzzle of the Volkswagen Emissions Scandal' in Sjafjell and Bruner (eds) *The Cambridge Handbook of Corporate Law* (n 5).

[124] As discussed in B Tomlinson et al, 'Environment-Selected Directors: An Interactive Simulation Experiment of Environmental Representation on Corporate Boards' (2020) *Ecological Economics* 178 and Ralph Nader et al, *Taming the Giant Corporation* (Norton, 1976).

of companies, directors representing environmental or human rights matters would have a sufficient marker of interest necessary to justify a position on large companies or companies operating in high-risk sectors. Stone, much like Teubner, believed that companies will only become responsible through 'intrusion' into the boardroom because companies do not respond to external legal or other stimuli.[125] One of Stone's arguments was that companies should have a minority of 'general public directors' appointed by the state.[126]

The effect of such minority directors would be to improve the inward flow of information highlighting the potential impact of a company's action on external parties rather than focusing on mere compliance, or economic success within the external rules of the game.[127] This could provoke a reflexion within the boardroom whereby other directors are directly confronted by the social consequences of their decisions.[128] Such directors could also serve an important role in allowing for consultation with stakeholders and the outflow of information to the public or to regulatory authorities.[129] While the introduction of public interest directors would change the structural characteristics of the company, it is not an argument for the dilution of ultimate shareholder control[130] but rather for societal interests to be represented, given a seat at the table so to speak, which would provide an opportunity to advocate and provide a different perspective to the board.

V. PROCEDURAL DUTIES AND ENFORCEMENT

Beyond shared governance, reflexive elements could be introduced into company law through procedural duties. One such example is a duty on the company to gather and disclose information related to its environmental and human rights impact. If sufficiently strong, such rules could create a reflexive effect through: (1) creating a new internal awareness of the company's external effects;[131]

[125] See C Stone, *Where the Law Ends: The Social Control of Corporate Behaviour* (Harper & Row, 1975).

[126] ibid ch 15.

[127] ibid 168. See also, Lord Wedderburn, 'The Legal Development of Corporate Responsibility for Whom Will Corporate Managers Be Trustees?' in Teubner and Hopt (eds), *Corporate Governance and Directors' Liabilities* (n 8).

[128] Elhauge has argued that the company's structure has removed many of the social and moral sanctions that operate at an individual level which encourage people to consider the effects of their conduct on others. He argues that under the correct conditions, directors, as executive decision makers, can still be influenced by such social and moral considerations. Elhauge, 'Sacrificing Corporate Profits in the Public Interest' (n 6) 800.

[129] See Parkinson (n 6) 387.

[130] Shareholders would still have a majority of representatives.

[131] As Ruggie noted, for a company to reduce its harms it must first become aware of its impact: J Ruggie, 'Protect, Respect and Remedy: A Framework for Business and Human Rights, Report to the UN Human Rights Council' (2008) available at www2.ohchr.org/english/bodies/hrcouncil/docs/8session/a-hrc-8-5.doc, [23–25].

(2) limiting the company's ability to engage in greenwashing,[132] cherry picking[133] or boiler plate reporting;[134] (3) making companies reflect on the importance of their reputation and consequentially take steps to reduce their negative externalities in order to have positive information to report.[135] However, such effects are dependent upon reporting rules that are mandatory, detailed, standardised and independently verified so that the reports are accurate and reliable. The EU's Corporate Sustainability Reporting Directive (CSRD)[136] has all four of these elements and is the most developed framework of corporate reporting on environmental and human rights matters. The subject of corporate reporting will be taken up in chapter four.

Another example of a procedural duty is the application of due diligence rules which require a company to investigate its negative external impacts and take steps to mitigate and end those impacts. Corporate due diligence is a key component of the UNGPs[137] and several jurisdictions, including France[138] and Germany[139] and the EU[140] have recently enacted due diligence requirements into law. The EU's Corporate Sustainability Due Diligence Directive (CSDDD)[141] is again the most far reaching of these laws,[142] given its detailed procedural requirements. For example, the CSDDD requires companies within its scope to develop a due diligence policy, a code of conduct, a corrective action plan where an adverse external impact cannot be immediately ended, to engage with stakeholders in the development of these policies, plans and codes and requires a further process to monitor the adequacy and effectiveness of the company's due diligence practices. Crucially, given the transnational fragmentation of modern business structures, the CSDDD requires a company's due diligence practices to extend

[132] Meaning making public favourable information while not reporting unfavourable information.

[133] Meaning making public false or misleading information.

[134] Meaning making public generalised reports with irrelevant information.

[135] See D Hess, 'Social Reporting: A Reflexive Law Approach to Corporate Social Responsiveness' (1999) 25 *The Journal of Corporation Law* 41.

[136] Directive (EU) 2022/2464 of the European Parliament and of the Council of 14 December 2022 amending Regulation (EU) No 537/2014, Directive 2004/109/EC, Directive 2006/43/EC and Directive 2013/34/EU, as regards corporate sustainability reporting [2022] OJ L 322/15.

[137] UNGPs (n 32) Guiding principle 17. Principles 19–24 introduce supplementary concepts on how due diligence should be operationalised which include concepts such as 'leverage' (the ability to affect change) and 'tracking' (monitoring the effectiveness of responses to human rights impact).

[138] The French Duty of Vigilance (French Law No 2017-399 *Loi de Vigilance*).

[139] The German Supply Chain Due Diligence Act (*LkSG – Lieferkettensorgfaltspflichtengesetz* 2021).

[140] Directive (EU) 2024/1760 of the European Parliament and of the Council of 13 June 2024 on corporate sustainability due diligence and amending Directive (EU) 2019/1937 and Regulation (EU) 2023/2859 [2024] OJ L, 2024/1760.

[141] ibid.

[142] See M Bodie, 'Shareholders All the Way Down: EU Corporate Sustainability Reforms and the Structure of Corporate Governance' (2024) 52 *Georgia Journal of International and Comparative Law* 559, 566 describing the CSDDD as the most dramatic regulatory reform to date. See also L Enriques, M Gatti and R Shapira, 'How the EU's Sustainability Due Diligence Directive Could Reshape Corporate America' (2025) *European Corporate Governance Institute Working Paper* available at www.ecgi.global/publications/working-papers/how-the-eus-sustainability-due-diligence-directive-could-reshape.

to its subsidiaries and contractual partners both inside and outside the EU. The subject of due diligence will be taken up in chapter five while the subject of the international effects of the CSRD and CSDDD is the subject of chapter six.

A. Enforcement

The distinction between a reflexive law approach and many other proposals which also aim to realign the activities of large companies with the interests of society is its claim that law is necessary for companies to develop an internal sense of responsibility.[143] Voluntary frameworks, changes to the company's constitution, contractual and market based solutions, while all capable of having effects, ultimately lack the coercive power of law[144] and the force necessary to reorientate many large companies toward reducing their negative externalities. However, this argument for the role of law depends upon supervision, the existence of legal penalties and a realistic possibility of enforcement, otherwise law loses its coercive dimension and legal frameworks become simply another optional framework dependent upon voluntary compliance or market forces. As Parkinson argued, the effectiveness of duty-based controls is dependent upon a realistic chance of enforcement.[145] Hence, the societal company is dependent not only on company law having reflexive elements, but also on these elements being accompanied by legal enforcement to ensure compliance[146] and therefore the force necessary to produce the reflexion.

New procedural duties could be enforced privately through a civil liability framework where a company can be held liable for a failure to follow the relevant process which results in harm. A threat of civil liability can provide an important incentive for companies to internalise their negative externalities. This is one of the rationales for tort law,[147] with recent empirical finding

[143] For example, both Mayer and Ruggie see law as unnecessary to achieve such a goal, respectively believing in principles and the company's constitution as superior methods. See J Ruggie, 'The Concept of "Due Diligence" in the UN Guiding Principles on Business and Human Rights: A Reply to Jonathan Bonnitcha and Robert McCorquodale' (2017) 28(3) *The European Journal of International Law* 921, 924 and C Mayer, *Prosperity: Better Business Makes the Greater Good* (Oxford, Oxford University Press, 2018).

[144] The concept of 'coerced self-regulation' is developed in I Ayres and J Braithwaite, *Responsive Regulation: Transcending the Deregulation Debate* (Oxford, Oxford University Press, 1992) 100–02.

[145] Parkinson (n 6) 73.

[146] In the context of reporting, the potential harm to the company's reputation is a key dimension in provoking the company to reduce its external harms rather than the threat of fines or legal action, nevertheless, in order for a company's reputation to be affected the company must comply with reporting rules and publish detailed and accurate information in compliance with the legal standard. Hence, corporate reporting must have an external verification system (auditing) that is supervised by a regulatory authority that can impose legal penalties for compliance failures.

[147] See A Pacces, 'Civil Liability in the EU Corporate Sustainability Due Diligence Directive Proposal: A Law & Economics Analysis' (2023) Law Working Paper No 691/2023 *European Corporate Governance Institute* available at https://papers.ssrn.com/sol3/papers.cfm?abstract_id=4391121.

in the US providing evidence that increased exposure to civil liability for environmental damage had a material effect in reducing the pollution emitted by companies.[148] This incentive is particularly important in the transnational context, where multiple company organisational structures present difficult legal barriers to victims seeking to transfer liability up and across corporate groups and value chains.[149] New civil liability frameworks have the capacity to transcend some of these traditional barriers, reduce the effectiveness of judgment proofing[150] and provide a remedy for injured parties.[151] However, the broader effect of such a framework is an incentive for companies to invest in and comply with their procedural responsibilities, which increases the potential for a reflexive response and a rebalancing of the company's economic productivity and its societal responsibility. The CSDDD developed two models for civil liability, one at the proposal stage and one in the final Directive.[152] These models and civil liability more generally will be discussed in chapter five.

Private enforcement through civil liability has well known limitations,[153] such as high costs, delays[154] and, in the transnational context, difficulties arising from *forum non conveniens*,[155] conflict of laws[156] and choice of laws.[157] Given these limitations, and because the purpose of reflexive reforms is to serve the public interest, it is necessary for public enforcement to play a part in the supervision

[148] P Akey and I Appel, 'The Limits of Limited Liability: Evidence from Industrial Pollution (2021) 76 *Journal of Finance* 5.

[149] These barriers are discussed in detail in ch 5.

[150] Described by LoPucki as a relationship between two or more entities in which one entity generates disproportionately high risks of liability and another owns a disproportionately high level of assets. L LoPucki, 'The Essential Structure of Judgment Proofing' (1998) 51 *The Stanford Law Review* 147, 149.

[151] There seems to be an increasing willingness for private parties to engage in environmental litigation. See J Setzer and C Higham, 'Global Trends in Climate Change Litigation: 2024 Snapshot' (Grantham Research Institute 2024) available at www.lse.ac.uk/granthaminstitute/publication/global-trends-in-climate-change-litigation-2024-snapshot/.

[152] The European Commission's Omnibus I proposes to remove the EU civil liability model entirely.

[153] See A Keay, 'An Assessment of Private Enforcement Actions for Directors' Breaches of Duty' (2014) 33(1) *Civil Justice Quarterly* 76. J Armour et al, 'Private Enforcement of Corporate Law: An Empirical Comparison of the United Kingdom and the United States' (2009) 6 *Journal of Empirical Legal Studies* 687.

[154] A Lafarre, 'Mandatory Corporate Sustainability Due Diligence in Europe: The Way Forward' (2022) *European Corporate Governance Institute Blog* available at www.ecgi.global/publications/blog/mandatory-corporate-sustainability-due-diligence-in-europe-the-way-forward.

[155] Referring to the problem of finding the appropriate jurisdiction to hear the case. See N Brannigan, 'Resolving Conflicts: Establishing *Forum Non Conveniens* in A New Hague Jurisdiction Convention' (2022) 18(1) *Journal of Private International Law* 83.

[156] Referring to the problem of determining which jurisdiction's laws will apply to a dispute involving different parties located in different jurisdictions. See A Briggs, *The Conflict of Laws* (Oxford, Oxford University Press, 2019).

[157] Referring to the problem of how the jurisdictional location of a company is to be determined. See J Dammann, 'A New Approach to Corporate Choice of Law' (2005) 38 *Vanderbilt Journal of Transnational Law* 51.

and enforcement of a company law with reflexive elements.[158] Public enforcement authorities can monitor and enforce standards in contexts where there is no incentive or framework which facilitates private claims.[159] In Parkinson's words, 'deterrence, and the creation and refinement of standards of conduct and performance, have the quality of "public goods" which private enforcers, pursuing only private gain are liable to under-produce'.[160] Public enforcement of company law is already common across national jurisdictions[161] and in different contexts in EU law[162] and is an essential component of the argument that the societal company can be established through reflexive law.

VI. CONCLUSION

Company law is a crucial component to the facilitation of economic efficiency and productivity which remain key components of promoting aggregate welfare. However, company law also has a unique ability to affect internal corporate decision-making processes and create an internal sense of responsibility within companies to reduce their negative externalities. Reflexive law offers a means through which a balance can be struck between the two competing functions of the company to be both economically productive and socially responsible. A company law with reflexive elements, through public interest directors' procedural duties, allows the company to retain its autonomy and leaves the company's fundamental characteristics intact while also imposing mandatory processes to prevent it from functioning as a closed system singularly focused on economic productivity. In this way, reflexive law offers a superior method to facilitative law, regulatory law, voluntary frameworks and market mechanisms to establish the societal company.

[158] For a discussion of private and public enforcement see E Ferran and PS de Carvalho, 'Reconciling Shareholder Primacy and the Interests of People and Planet' (2025) *LQR* available at https://papers.ssrn.com/sol3/papers.cfm?abstract_id=5084134.

[159] A Keay, 'The Public Enforcement of Directors' Duties: A Normative Inquiry' (2014) 43 *Common Law World Review* 89, 111.

[160] Parkinson (n 6) 238.

[161] See Kraakman et al (n 1) 41.

[162] See O Cherednychenko, 'Public and Private Enforcement of European Private Law: Perspectives and Challenges' (2015) 23 *European Review of Private Law* 481.

3

The Development of European Company Law

I. INTRODUCTION

THE COMPANY LAW of the European Economic Community (EEC) and the European Union (EU) broadly developed in line with the facilitative model described in chapter one. Accordingly, European company law has traditionally aimed to facilitate efficient business and economic development leaving the negative externalities of business to be addressed by other areas of European law.[1] Given that European company law operates alongside the national company law of Member States,[2] its primary role in facilitating business has been to aid the formation of a common market and enable cross border business between the Member States.

Since the formation of the European Economic Community (EEC) in 1957,[3] the creation of a common market based on free movement of goods, people, services and capital has been central to the European integration project.[4] To give effect to these four freedoms it was necessary to ensure freedom of establishment – the freedom for nationals and companies of one Member State to pursue economic activity in another Member State.[5] The early development of European company law facilitated freedom of establishment through processes of 'positive integration' which ensured a basic level of harmonisation across Member States and 'negative integration'[6] where the European Court of Justice (ECJ) invalidated Member States rules limiting freedom of establishment.[7]

[1] Eg, European employment law, tort law, privacy law and environmental law.

[2] And so, the EEC and the EU did not have to develop a complete companies Act or Code. Rather, European company law operates as a second layer of company law that prevails over the national company law of Member States but covers a relatively small number of areas.

[3] Formed by the Treaty of Rome https://eur-lex.europa.eu/legal-content/EN/TXT/?uri=LEGISSUM:xy0023.

[4] See C Barnard, *The Substantive Law of the EU: The Four Freedoms* (Oxford, Oxford University Press, 2022).

[5] Freedom of establishment was provided for by Arts 43 and 48 of the Treaty of Rome.

[6] See art 26(2) of the Treaty on the Functioning of the European Union (TFEU) describing a common market 'characterized by the abolition, as between Member States, of obstacles to the free movement of goods, persons, services and capital'.

[7] See Case C-212/97 *Centros Ltd v Erhvervs-og Selskabsstyrelsen* ECLI:EU:C:1999:126, [1999] ECR I-1459.

At the turn of the millennium, the positive harmonisation process slowed and European company law focused primarily on issues of cross-border business. At this time, the EU explicitly adopted a shareholder value oriented approach to company law. A Report by High Level Group of Company Law Experts ('the Expert Group')[8] described shareholders as primary risk bearers, repeatedly emphasised the importance of limiting agency costs and believed that regulation through company law should be, for the most part, avoided.[9] The Expert Group ultimately described the purpose of company law as being to provide a legal framework to 'facilitate the running of efficient and competitive business enterprises'.[10] The European Commission broadly endorsed the Report[11] and what followed were Directives on takeovers, cross-border mergers and shareholder rights that aimed to provide a facilitative legal framework for cross-border business.

In 2006 and again in 2017, Luca Enriques described European company law as 'trivial'[12] from a regulatory perspective as its rules either mimicked what was already in place under national law,[13] were default and could be avoided or were simply unimportant as they did not impact how companies were 'directed, managed and controlled'.[14] Recently however, a shift has taken place in the EU's policy approach to company law, with several legislative initiatives focusing directly on reducing the negative externalities of business under the heading of 'corporate sustainability'. This shift was part of the EU's policy focus on mitigating the effects of climate change in line with the European Green Deal,[15] meeting its obligations under the Paris Agreement[16] and limiting human rights abuses from the operation of value chains. The result was proposals to introduce new rules on directors' duties, sustainable finance, expand sustainability reporting and impose a duty to conduct due diligence that extended to subsidiaries

[8] Report of the High Level Group of Company Law Experts, 'A Modern Regulatory Framework for Company Law in Europe' (2002) available at www.ecgi.global/sites/default/files/report_en.pdf.

[9] ibid 36.

[10] ibid 29.

[11] Communication from the Commission to the Council and the European Parliament – Modernising Company Law and Enhancing Corporate Governance in the European Union – A Plan to Move Forward (2003) COM/2003/0284 final, available at https://eur-lex.europa.eu/legal-content/EN/ALL/?uri=celex%3A52003DC0284.

[12] L Enriques, 'EC Company Law Directives and Regulations: How Trivial Are They?' (2006) 27 *University of Pennsylvania Journal of International Economic Law* 1. He reiterated the point again in 2017, see L Enriques, 'A Harmonized European Company Law: Are We There Already?' (2017) 66(3) *International and Comparative Law Quarterly* 763.

[13] For example, Brian Cheffins argued that the 'EU has typically done little more than superimpose a series of measures on domestic regulations already in place': B Cheffins, *Company Law: Theory, Structure and Operation* (Clarendon Press, 1997) 448.

[14] Enriques, 'EC Company Law Directives and Regulations: How Trivial Are They?' (n 12) 7. Enriques did admit certain exceptions to his triviality thesis, mainly in relation to certain accounting rules.

[15] European Commission Communication on the European Green Deal (2019) see https://commission.europa.eu/strategy-and-policy/priorities-2019-2024/european-green-deal_en.

[16] See https://unfccc.int/sites/default/files/english_paris_agreement.pdf.

and contractual partners. These proposals ultimately led to the enactment of the Sustainable Finance Disclosure Regulation (SFDR),[17] the Corporate Sustainability Reporting Directive (CSRD)[18] and the Corporate Sustainability Due Diligence Directive (CSDDD).[19] These Directives represent not only a shift in focus but also a shift in methods as they include mandatory rules and provide for civil liability and supervision by regulatory authorities. However, the Directives, while clearly representing a change in the focus of European company law, remained procedural in nature by requiring companies to conduct internal processes rather than directing corporate decision making or changing the core structures of the company set out under national law. Thus, as will be discussed in chapters four and five, they broadly fit a reflexive approach, although the EU never explicitly endorsed such a theory.

Yet more recently again, in early 2025, the European Commission reverted to a policy position based around the importance of enhancing efficient and competitive business. The Commission's Omnibus I Proposal[20] aims to reduce the regulatory burden on companies by reducing the scope of the CSRD by approximately 80 per cent and limiting the application of the CSDDD to direct contractual partners, thus limiting its broader impact on EU and international supply chains.[21] Given that the CSDDD was already diluted immediately prior to its introduction, European company law is oscillating between the competing objectives discussed in the last chapter, namely the importance of fostering economic efficiency, business autonomy and competitiveness with need for sustainable development and a reduction of environmental harms and human rights abuses. The stated reason for the policy reversal is the need to simplify the EU's corporate sustainability framework. While the EU's development of corporate sustainability rules followed a clear policy of reducing environmental harms and human rights abuses, it lacked a theoretical clarity and the coherence in legislative development to achieve a single integrated approach across sustainable finance, reporting and due diligence.[22] While this may sound critical, the EU is the first jurisdiction to attempt to develop a mandatory company law

[17] Regulation (EU) 2019/2088 of the European Parliament and of the Council of 27 November 2019 on sustainability-related disclosures in the financial services sector [2019] OJ L 317/1.

[18] Directive (EU) 2022/2464 of the European Parliament and of the Council of 14 December 2022 amending Regulation (EU) No 537/2014, Directive 2004/109/EC, Directive 2006/43/EC and Directive 2013/34/EU, as regards corporate sustainability reporting [2022] OJ L 322/15.

[19] Directive (EU) 2024/1760 of the European Parliament and of the Council of 13 June 2024 on corporate sustainability due diligence and amending Directive (EU) 2019/1937 and Regulation (EU) 2023/2859 [2024] OJ L, 2024/1760.

[20] European Commission, 'Omnibus I' (2025) available at https://commission.europa.eu/publications/omnibus-i_en. It is important to note that at the time of writing these are proposals only and are subject to the EU legislative process.

[21] The proposal also proposes to remove the CSDDD's EU wide model of civil liability. The proposed changes will be discussed in chs 4 (CSRD) and 5 (CSDDD).

[22] As Mayer and Shift have noted, the weakness of the EU's Corporate Sustainability Framework is its complexity. See C Mayer, 'Success, Law and ESG' (2024) Law Working Paper No 795/2024 *European Corporate Governance Institute* available at https://papers.ssrn.com/sol3/papers.

framework that is focused on reducing the negative externalities of companies that apply transnationally – it is understandable that the end result was not a streamlined, integrated model. Nevertheless, it has created a roadmap for what such interventions could look like and provides many lessons for the creation of a company law with reflexive elements.

This chapter discusses the development of European company law and the shift from a facilitative approach to one orientated toward limiting negative externalities. Section II describes freedom of establishment under EU law and how European company law has given effect to that freedom through harmonisation and negative integration. Section III focuses on European company law's embrace of shareholder value and the ensuing framework to facilitate cross-border business. Section IV discusses the policy shift toward corporate sustainability and the more recent policy reversal toward enhancing economic competitiveness.

II. FREEDOM OF ESTABLISHMENT

The formation of the EU lies in political efforts to achieve cooperation and integration among European States in the wake of World War II.[23] A key point in this process was French Foreign Minister Robert Schuman's plan for the coordination between European States on coal and steel production.[24] The premise of Schuman's declaration, heavily influenced by Jean Monnet,[25] was that common trade and economic integration was a prerequisite for peace in Europe.[26] The culmination of these political efforts was the formation of the European Coal and Steel Community in 1951 made up of Belgium, Germany, France, Italy, Luxembourg and the Netherlands.[27] These founding members agreed to broaden their economic cooperation in 1957 through the Treaty of Rome and the formation of the EEC. The Treaty of Rome was amended in 1993 by the Maastricht Treaty which formed the EU and again in 2009 by the Lisbon

cfm?abstract_id=4939931, 14. See also analysis from Shift available at https://shiftproject.org/the-european-commissions-omnibus-simplification-proposal-shifts-preliminary-reflections/.

[23] See P Craig and G de Búrca, *EU Law: Text, Cases, and Materials* (Oxford, Oxford University Press, 2020) ch 1.

[24] See *The Schuman Declaration* available at https://european-union.europa.eu/principles-countries-history/history-eu/1945-59/schuman-declaration-may-1950_en.

[25] Schuman's declaration was influenced by Jean Monnet's belief that common trade and common economic integration was a prerequisite for peace in Europe. See DR Troitino, 'Jean Monnet: Neofunctionalism at Work in the European Integration', in DR Troitino, RMa de la Guardia and G Sanchez (eds), *The European Union and its Political Leaders: Understanding the Integration Process* (Springer, 2022) 121–40.

[26] *The Schuman Declaration* (n 24) states: 'The pooling of coal and steel production … will change the destinies of those regions which have long been devoted to the manufacture of munitions of war, of which they have been the most constant victims'.

[27] See https://eur-lex.europa.eu/EN/legal-content/summary/treaty-establishing-the-european-coal-and-steel-community-ecsc-treaty.html.

Treaty which renamed the Treaty of Rome the Treaty on the Functioning of the European Union (TFEU).

The aim of the EEC was to form a common market[28] between its Member States based on the free movement of goods, people, services, and capital.[29] To give effect to these four freedoms, it was necessary to ensure that both the nationals and companies of one Member State could freely pursue economic activity in another Member State. This is known as the freedom of establishment as defined by the ECJ[30] as 'the actual pursuit of economic activity through a fixed establishment in another Member State for indefinite periods'.[31] The TFEU prohibits 'restrictions on the freedom of establishment of nationals of a Member State in the territory of another Member State'.[32] The TFEU also provides that, for the purposes of freedom of establishment, 'companies or firms' shall be treated in the same way as nationals of Member States.[33] These provisions allow for primary establishment, where a national or a company of one Member State seeks to establish economic activities in a different Member State. The TFEU also guarantees secondary establishment by applying these restrictions to the 'setting-up of agencies, branches or subsidiaries'.[34]

These treaty provisions form the basis for early European company law which applies through Regulations that are directly binding on Member States, Directives that are binding on Member States in relation to the result to be achieved but which leave the methods to be decided by Member States,[35] and decisions from the ECJ which makes determinations on the validity of Member State law in respect of the Treaties.[36] Hence, European company law does not provide a complete company code or Companies Act with rules covering company formation to governance to liquidation, nor can it be compared to federal law in the US as state law and federal law address wholly separate areas.[37] Instead, European company law is a 'two-level system'[38] in which EU

[28] This European 'common market' is referred to as the 'single market' in the Single European Act and is now referred to as the 'internal market' by the TFEU. For simplicity, I use the term 'common market' throughout.

[29] See the TFEU, art 26(2).

[30] Previously the Court of Justice of the European Communities renamed by the 2009 Lisbon Treaty.

[31] *R v Secretary of State for Transport, ex p Factortame* [1991] ECR 1-3905 at [20]. See also Case C-55/94 *Gebhard v Colsiglio dell'Ordine degli Avvocati e Procuratori di Milano* ECLI:EU:C:1995:411 [1995] ECR I-4165 which defined freedom of establishment as the participation 'on a stable and continuous basis, in the economic life of a Member State other than his State of origin', [25].

[32] TFEU, art 49.

[33] ibid art 54.

[34] ibid art 49.

[35] ibid art 288.

[36] Article 258 of the TFEU allows for the Commission to a bring a matter to the ECJ where it considers that a Member State has failed to fulfil an obligation under the Treaties while art 267 allows the ECJ to deliver preliminary rulings regarding the interpretation of the Treaties where such a question is raised before the court of a Member State.

[37] N De Luca, *European Company Law*, 2nd edn (Cambridge, Cambridge University Press, 2021) 6.

[38] S Grundmann, *European Company Law* (Intersentia, 2007) 15.

law prevails over the national company law of Member States and is directly binding on companies within the EU but covers a relatively small number of matters and, in certain instances, sits alongside national provisions covering the same areas.

A. Positive Harmonisation

An initial concern of the EEC was that differences between the company law of Member States could limit the development of the common market[39] and a consensus emerged that a certain degree of harmonisation of company law was necessary to allow companies to freely and easily establish themselves in different Member States.[40] The other driving force behind harmonisation was the potential effects of 'regulatory competition' whereby national legislatures would reform their company law to attract business to their jurisdiction.[41] Such regulatory competition had already taken place in the US which resulted in Delaware becoming the state of choice for most US companies.[42] The formation of the EEC meant that regulatory competition could be much more effective and in early EEC meetings, France expressed particular concern that the Netherlands could become the 'Delaware of Europe' given its relatively permissive company law.[43] As well as the potential to imbalance the common market, there was also a concern that regulatory competition could lead to a 'race to the bottom' and the erosion of shareholder and creditor rights.[44] While it was not clear that the conditions for US style regulatory competition existed in Europe[45] or whether

[39] See J Armour and WG Ringe, 'European Company Law 1999–2010: Renaissance and Crisis' (2011) 48 *Common Market Law Review* 125, 129–31 highlighting that different rules may require companies to change or develop new business frameworks thereby increasing the cost of cross-border business.

[40] De Luca, *European Company Law* (n 37) 17.

[41] See D Murphy, *The Structure of Regulatory Competition* (Oxford, Oxford University Press, 2004).

[42] L Bebchuk, 'Federalism and the Corporation: The Desirable Limits on State Competition in Corporate Law' (1992) 105 *Harvard Law Review* 1435.

[43] See M Gelter, 'EU Company Law Harmonization between Convergence and Varieties of Capitalism' (2019) Law Working Paper 355/2017 *European Corporate Governance Institute* available at www.ecgi.global/sites/default/files/working_papers/documents/finalgelter_3.pdf, 7.

[44] See L Enriques, 'EC Company Law and the Fears of a European Delaware' (2004) 15 *European Business Law Review* 1259 and M Gelter, 'The Structure of Regulatory Competition in European Corporate Law' (2005) 5 *Journal of Corporate Law Studies* 247.

[45] For example, Armour has argued regulatory competition requires companies actively engaging in regulatory arbitrage between jurisdictions and for national jurisdictions to be willing to change their laws to attract companies and that there was limited evidence to suggest these two factors existed. See J Armour, 'Who Should Make Corporate Law? EC Legislation versus Regulatory Competition' (2005) Law Working Paper No 54/2005 *European Corporate Governance Institute* available at www.ecgi.global/sites/default/files/working_papers/documents/ssrn-id860444.pdf, 8–11.

such competition would have resulted in a race to the bottom,[46] the EEC decided that legislative harmonisation was necessary.[47]

Article 50 of the TFEU provides the legal basis for the harmonisation of European company law by stating that the European Parliament and Council will approve Directives to achieve freedom of establishment 'by coordinating to the necessary extent the safeguards which, for the protection of the interests *of members and others*, are required by Member States of companies or firms ... with a view to making such safeguards *equivalent* throughout the Union'. The EEC sought to reach this 'equivalence' at a basic level only rather than attempting to introduce a European company law code.[48] The positive harmonisation process started in 1961 with the Council of the EEC's programme for the abolition of restrictions on freedom of establishment.[49] In delivering this programme, the EEC Commission sought to establish equivalent guarantees to protect the interests of shareholders and creditors across the Member States which led to the enactment of the First Company Law Directive in 1968.[50]

The First Company Law Directive applied to all private and public limited companies and covered the disclosure of company documents[51] and the validity of obligations entered into by a company.[52] The First Directive also required Member States to open a central register which, as Grundmann notes, was a crucial development and continues to be the core tool of information disclosure in the EU.[53] The Second Company Law Directive,[54] introduced 11 years later,

[46] As discussed in ch 1, many scholars believe that regulatory competition leads to better outcomes for those involved in business through an evolutionary 'race to the top'. See F Easterbrook and D Fischel, *The Economic Structure of Company Law* (Harvard University Press, 1991) ch 1.

[47] See V Edwards, *EC Company Law* (Oxford, Oxford University Press, 1999) 2–4.

[48] See Enriques, 'A Harmonized European Company Law' (n 12).

[49] See https://op.europa.eu/en/publication-detail/-/publication/76a1267a-3190-401c-a4c5-3ae825c9e7d1.

[50] Council Directive 68/151/EEC of 9 March 1968 on co-ordination of safeguards which, for the protection of the interests of members and others, are required by Member States of companies within the meaning of the second paragraph of Article 58 of the Treaty, with a view to making such safeguards equivalent throughout the Community [1968] OJ L 65. It has been repealed and replaced by Directive 2009/101/EC which was subsumed into consolidating Directive (EU) 2017/1132 of the European Parliament and of the Council of 14 June 2017 relating to certain aspects of company law (codification) [2017] OJ L 169/46.

[51] ibid Art 2 which mandated the disclosure of the company's constitution, any amendments to the constitution, the appointment, termination and particulars of the persons authorised to represent the company as well as for the winding up of the company. The Directive also provided that once a year the company should disclose the company's capital, the balance sheet and the profit and loss account.

[52] The Directive provided that contracts could not be repudiated on grounds of being ultra vires. See S Nashenveng, 'Companies Liabilities under the First EC Directive" (2001) 12 *European Business Law Review* 89.

[53] S Grundmann, 'European Company Law in Transformation – Striving for Participation and Sustainability' (2023) 42 *Yearbook of European Law* 210, 213.

[54] Second Council Directive 77/91/EEC of 13 December 1976 on coordination of safeguards which, for the protection of the interests of members and others, are required by Member States of companies within the meaning of the second paragraph of Article 58 of the Treaty, in respect of the formation of public limited liability companies and the maintenance and alteration of their capital,

addressed the formation of public companies, pre-emption rights and capital maintenance rules which included a €25,000 minimum capital requirement for public companies and prohibitions on financial assistance.[55] Its aim was to achieve 'minimum equivalent protections for both shareholders and creditors of public limited companies'.[56] The Third[57] and Sixth[58] Company Law Directives established common rules for the merger and division of companies within Member States.[59] The Fourth Directive provided details on how annual accounts should be maintained and disclosed,[60] the Seventh Directive provided rules for consolidated accounts for corporate groups[61] and the Eighth Directive[62] related to the approval of persons responsible for carrying out the statutory audits of accounting documents.[63]

This first set of European Company Law Directives, introduced between 1968 and 1989, provided a basic level of harmonisation on fundamental matters of company law. Many of the rules contained in the Directives already existed in many Member States and so placed few additional regulatory burdens on companies. The main effect of the harmonising Directives was to prevent deregulation and the erosion of shareholder and creditor rights which may have occurred had regulatory competition taken place. In Grundmann's terms, this period of European company law was focused on 'outside reliability', principally

with a view to making such safeguards equivalent [1977] OJ L 26/1. It has been amended several times, including by Directive 92/101/EEC which extended its application to the subsidiaries of public limited companies. The Directive, as amended, has been subsumed into the consolidating Directive (EU) 2017/1132 of the European Parliament and of the Council of 14 June 2017 relating to certain aspects of company law (codification) [2017] OJ L 169/46.

[55] Financial assistance referring to a company using its funds to assist in the purchase of its own shares.

[56] See Directive (EU) 2017/1132 (n 54) recital 3.

[57] Third Council Directive 78/855/EEC of 9 October 1978 based on Article 54 (3) (g) of the Treaty concerning mergers of public limited liability companies [1978] OJ L 295/36. It has been amended by Directives 2007/63/EC and 2009/109/EC and is now codified as part of Directive (EU) 2017/1132.

[58] Directive 82/891/EEC as amended by Directive 2007/63/EC and now codified in Directive (EU) 2017/1132.

[59] These Directives are now part of the 2017 consolidating Directive (EU) 2017/1132 (n 54).

[60] Fourth Council Directive 78/660/EEC of 25 July 1978 based on Article 54 (3) (g) of the Treaty on the annual accounts of certain types of companies [1978] OJ L 222/11. It was amended by Directives 83/349/EEC and 89/666/EEC as disclosure requirements were broadened by European law.

[61] Seventh Council Directive 83/349/EEC of 13 June 1983 based on the Article 54(3)(g) of the Treaty on consolidated accounts [1983] OJ L 193/1.

[62] Eighth Council Directive 84/253/EEC of 10 April 1984 based on Article 54 (3) (g) of the Treaty on the approval of persons responsible for carrying out the statutory audits of accounting documents [1984] OJ L 126/20.

[63] The Fourth, Seventh and Eighth Directives have been consolidated into Directive 2013/34/EU of the European Parliament and of the Council of 26 June 2013 on the annual financial statements, consolidated financial statements and related reports of certain types of undertakings, amending Directive 2006/43/EC of the European Parliament and of the Council and repealing Council Directives 78/660/EEC and 83/349/EEC (the Accounting Directive) [2013] OJ L 182/19. The Eleventh Directive (Directive 89/666/EEC) extended these financial disclosure requirements to branches of companies governed by the law of another Member State.

protecting creditors and investors who depend on having a reliable basis for their creditor–debtor relationship.[64]

Attempts at harmonisation beyond these basic elements failed to be enacted into law. For example, agreement was never reached on the Fifth Company Law Directive which sought to require all public companies in the EEC to have a two-tiered board structure with employee representation.[65] The Directive was met with substantial opposition, partly from the UK as a jurisdiction with single tier boards without employee representation, but also from Italy and other Member States.[66] The opposition led to a second draft which allowed Member States to choose between a one or two tiered board and increased the threshold of application. The second draft was also subject to strong opposition, which resulted in a third draft[67] that allowed yet greater flexibility for employee representation, but an agreement could not be reached and the proposal was abandoned.[68] A separate proposal to create a legal framework for corporate groups also failed to be enacted into law.[69]

These failures highlighted issues with the positive harmonisation project. First, there was a lack of consensus for company law directives that introduced new rules on complex company law issues such as employee representation and corporate groups. This problem was exacerbated by enlargement, particularly the accession of the UK and Ireland who as common law jurisdictions widened the divergence between the company law of Member States.[70] A further factor was the principle of subsidiarity introduced in the Maastricht Treaty which provides that the EU should refrain from legislative intervention unless such intervention can be more effective than national rules.[71] Implementing rules already in existence in the national law of multiple Member States contravenes this principle and undercut the legitimacy of harmonisation to prevent deregulation.[72] Ultimately, the lack of consensus on more ambitious forms of

[64] Grundmann, 'European Company Law in Transformation (n 53) 211.

[65] Proposal for a Fifth Directive concerning the Structure of the Public Limited Companies (1972). The proposal required all public companies with over 500 employees to allow employees to elect up to one third of members to a supervisory board.

[66] See J du Plessis and J Dine, 'The Fate of the Draft Fifth Directive on Company Law: Accommodation instead of Harmonisation' (1997) *Journal of Business Law* 23, 35–37.

[67] Amended Proposal for a Fifth Directive Founded on Art 54(3)(G) of the EEC Treaty Concerning the Structure of the Public Limited Companies and the Powers and Obligations of their Organs (1983).

[68] See P Davies, 'Employee Representation and Corporate Law Reform: A Comment from the United Kingdom' (2000) 22 *Comparative Labor Law and Policy Journal* 135.

[69] See K Bohlhoff and J Budde, 'Company Groups – The EEC Proposal for a Ninth Directive in the Light of the Legal Situation in the Federal Republic of Germany' (1984) 6 *Journal of Comparative Business and Capital Market Law* 163.

[70] Armour and Ringe, 'European Company Law 1999–2010' (n 39) 128–29.

[71] See F Fabbrini, 'The Principle of Subsidiarity' in R Schütze and T Tridimas (eds), *Oxford Principles of European Union Law* (Oxford, Oxford University Press, 2018).

[72] See Grundmann, *European Company Law* (n 38) 300.

harmonisation and the introduction of subsidiarity pushed European company law toward cross-border issues that could not be effectively addressed through national law.

B. Negative Integration

While harmonisation initiatives began to stagnate in the late 1980s, European company law continued to develop through case law which invalidated Member State rules restricting freedom of establishment. A significant issue within transnational company law is how should the jurisdictional location of a company be determined.[73] Certain countries, including the UK, Ireland and the Netherlands (as well as all US states) follow an 'incorporation' approach whereby a company's location is where it is legally registered regardless of where it conducts most of its business. The alternative approach is for a company's location to be determined by its main centre of operations or 'real seat',[74] an approach followed by most Member States including Germany, France and Italy. Under the real seat approach, a company legally formed and registered in, for example, Spain that had its primary centre of business in France would be regarded as a French organisation but not as a company as it had not been registered under French law. Accordingly, the company would have no legal personality, potentially lose its ability to enforce its rights while its shareholders could become personally responsible for the company's debts. The 'real seat' doctrine was effectively a restriction on cross-border business as companies feared conducting substantial operations in a real seat jurisdiction as it may be determined that their main centre of operation was located there. Hence, the real seat approach seemed at odds with freedom of establishment as, fundamentally, it amounted to a refusal to recognise the validity of a legally formed company from one Member State attempting to establish itself in another Member State.

As briefly noted above, freedom of establishment covers both primary establishment, where a company moves from one Member State to another and secondary establishment where a company sets up a branch or subsidiary in a different Member State. Companies moving from one Member State to another is relatively rare,[75] partly because the treaty provisions on freedom of establishment, while preventing the 'new' jurisdiction from imposing restrictions on incoming companies, do not explicitly prevent the 'original' jurisdiction

[73] See J Dammann, 'A New Approach to Corporate Choice of Law (2005) 38 *Vanderbilt Journal of Transnational Law* 51 and W Ebke, 'The European Conflict-of-Corporate-Laws Revolution: *Überseering, Inspire Art* and Beyond' (2005) 16(1) *European Business Law Review* 9.

[74] See K Baelz and T Baldwin, 'The End of the Real Seat Theory (Sitztheorie)' (2002) 3(12) *German Law Journal* 8 and W Ebke, 'The Real Seat Doctrine in the Conflict of Corporate Laws' (2001) 36(3) *International Lawyer* 1015.

[75] See M Siems, 'Convergence, Competition, *Centros* and Conflicts of Law: European Company Law in the 21st Century' (2002) 27 *European Law Review* 47.

from imposing restrictions on the moving company. In *Daily Mail*[76] an English company sought to transfer its central management and control to the Netherlands to avoid paying tax on the sale of assets in the UK while still seeking to be formally registered as a UK company.[77] To relocate, the company needed permission from the UK treasury but never obtained it and instead sought a declaration that such permission was unnecessary as an invalid restriction on the freedom of establishment. The ECJ refused to grant the declaration stating that Articles 49 and 54 of the TFEU[78] 'confer no right on a company incorporated under the legislation of a Member State and having its registered office there to transfer its central management and control to another member State'.[79] The court further stated that while Directive 73/148/EEC[80] allowed natural persons to move residence freely between Member States, this applied to natural persons only and that the Directive could not 'be applied by analogy to legal persons'.[81] The Court described companies as 'creatures of national law' who must comply with restrictions imposed by the national law of the country in which they are formed.[82]

While the *Daily Mail* case seemed to directly contravene the principle of freedom of establishment, the judgment did not prevent companies moving to another Member State, but rather made clear that the Treaty provisions did not prevent a Member State imposing restrictions or obligations on a company attempting to move. The obvious workaround for companies was to set up a secondary establishment in the form of subsidiary or branch in the new Member State given this is expressly allowed for by the Treaty. Hence, the ECJ has consistently invalidated attempts to place restrictions on a company creating a secondary establishment in a new Member State. For example, the court has held that Member States cannot require a business to be conducted through a primary establishment only[83] and that Member States are prohibited from 'hindering the establishment' of entities that are explicitly mentioned in its laws[84] ie agencies, branches or subsidiaries expressly referred to in Article 49 of the TFEU. Hence, had the company in *Daily Mail* been sought to establish a branch or subsidiary in the Netherlands, the UK Treasury could not have imposed restrictions.

[76] Case 81/87 *The Queen v Treasury and Commissioners of Inland Revenue, ex p Daily Mail and General Trust plc* ECLI:EU:C:1988:456, [1988] ECR 5483.

[77] ibid [16].

[78] Formerly Arts 43 and 48 of the Treaty of Rome.

[79] *Daily Mail* (n 76) [24].

[80] Council Directive 73/148/EEC of 21 May 1973 on the abolition of restrictions on movement and residence within the Community for nationals of Member States with regard to establishment and the provision of services [1973] OJ L 172/14.

[81] *Daily Mail* (n 76) [28].

[82] ibid [19].

[83] Case C-101/94 *Commission v Italy* ECLI:EU:C:1996:221, [1996] ECR I-2691.

[84] Case C-20098 *X AB and Y AB* ECLI:EU:C:1999:566, [1999] ECR I-8261.

The leading decision on secondary establishment is *Centros*[85] which involved a company registered in the UK whose founders and sole shareholders wished to establish a branch in Denmark.[86] The company had never traded in the UK and the Danish registrar of companies refused to register the branch for two reasons: (1) they claimed that the new 'branch' was going to be the company's main place of business and therefore was not a branch; and (2) they believed the founders were attempting to avoid Danish minimum capital requirements[87] by registering in the UK which had no such requirements. The ECJ held that the Registrar's refusal was an unjustified obstacle to the freedom of establishment[88] and the fact that the company was registered in the UK purely for the purpose of establishing itself in Denmark through a branch was 'immaterial'.[89] The court rejected the Danish Government's claims that their refusal to register the branch was justified on the basis that upholding minimum capitalisation requirements served to protect creditors and reduced the risk of fraudulent bankruptcy on the basis that the ruling did not prevent Denmark adopting different measures to protect creditors or prevent fraud that would be compatible with European law.[90]

The significance of the *Centros* judgment was its potential to undermine the real seat approach. In *Centros*, it was clear that the company's primary place of business was going to be in Denmark and that the UK registered company was simply a vehicle to avoid Danish capitalisation requirements. Yet the court prohibited Denmark from preventing the secondary establishment, despite the branch being the company's main centre of operations. A series of subsequent cases further undermined the real seat approach. In *Inspire Art*,[91] the ECJ held that Dutch rules requiring companies registered abroad that were doing business only in the Netherlands to add a suffix to their name, indicating their status as a foreign company and increasing the potential for the personal liability of directors, unjustifiably impeded the freedom of establishment.[92] In *Sevic*,[93] a German company sought to register its merger with a company from Luxembourg. The German court refused on the basis that the register provided for mergers between German companies only and did not apply to cross-border mergers. The ECJ stated this was contrary to the treaty provisions on freedom of establishment which 'covers all measures which permit or even merely

[85] *Centros* (n 7).

[86] For analysis see E Micheler, 'The Impact of the Centros Case on Europe's Company Law' (2000) 21 *Company Lawyer* 179.

[87] Which were then 200,000 Dkr or approximately €15,000.

[88] *Centros* (n 7) [29–30].

[89] ibid [17].

[90] ibid [38]. Applying the test set out in *Gebhard* (n 31).

[91] Case C-167/01 *Kamer van Koophandel en Fabrieken voor Amsterdam v Inspire Art Ltd* ECLI:EU:C:2003:512, ECR I-10155.

[92] ibid [101].

[93] Case C-411/03 *Sevic Systems AG* ECLI:EU:C:2005:762, [2005] ECR I-10805.

facilitate access to another member state and the pursuit of economic activity within that state'.[94]

Another seminal freedom of establishment case is *Uberseeing*[95] where a Dutch company (Uberseeing) initiated legal proceedings against a German company (NCC) for defective work. Before these proceedings were brought, Uberseeing was acquired by two German nationals. The German regional court (*Oberlandesgerict*) held that the effect of the takeover was to transfer the company's centre of administration to Germany but since the company was incorporated under Dutch law, it did not have legal capacity in Germany as an unregistered entity without legal personality and therefore could not engage in legal proceedings.[96] Uberseeing appealed the judgment and the German High Court (*Bundesgerichtshof*) referred the relevant questions to the ECJ. The court began by distinguishing the *Daily Mail* case on the grounds that *Daily Mail* involved restrictions by a home jurisdiction on a company seeking to move[97] while *Uberseeing* related to a Member State refusing to recognise a company validly incorporated in another Member State.[98] The court held the failure to recognise Uberseeing, which effectively required it to reincorporate in Germany to enforce its rights,[99] was 'tantamount to outright negation of freedom of establishment'.[100] The Court stated that certain situations may justify restrictions on freedom of establishment in line with the *Gebhard* test[101] but outright negations of freedom of establishment could not be justified.[102] The significance of *Uberseeing* is that Member States must recognise the validity of companies from other Member States even in contexts where they would not be recognised under a 'real seat' approach. The legal effect was that a company with its registered office and central administration located in the EU cannot be denied access

[94] Case C-208/00 *Überseering BV v Nordic Construction Company Baumanagement GmbH (NCC)* ECLI:EU:C:2002:632, [2002] ECR I-9919.

[95] ibid.

[96] ibid [9].

[97] ibid [62].

[98] ibid [66].

[99] ibid [79].

[100] ibid [80–81].

[101] *Gebhard* (n 31) providing that permissible restrictions on freedom of establishment must be: (i) applied in a non-discriminatory manner; (ii) justified by imperative requirements of the public interest; (iii) effective to secure their objective; and (iv) not disproportionate in their effect. An example of justifiable restrictions on freedom of establishment were evident in Case C-196/04 *Cadbury Schweppes plc v Commissioners of Inland Revenue* ECLI:EU:C:2006:278, [2006] ECR I-4585. In that case, an English company established a subsidiary in Ireland to minimise its tax liability. The subsidiary carried on no business in Ireland and provisions in the UK tax code prohibited such tax avoidance structures. The court determined that the prohibitions were a restriction on freedom of establishment but that such restrictions were justified by the public interest of preventing tax avoidance by 'wholly artificial arrangements' at [51].

[102] *Überseering* (n 94) [92–93]. See also Case C-210/06 *Cartesio Oktató és Szolgáltató bt* ECLI:EU:C:2008:72, [2008] ECR I-9641 where the ECJ held that where a Member State allows for the integration of an immigrating company into its legal system by converting to a domestic legal form, the original Member State cannot apply disproportionate restrictions on the company.

to another Member State[103] unless such restrictions meet the high threshold of the *Gebhard* test and the case effectively marked the end of the real seat doctrine.

This early development of European company law demonstrates the EEC's and EU's commitment to establishing a common market that shared fundamental rules on company law and that had few restrictions on the freedom of establishment. In other words, the aim of company law, implemented through the processes of positive harmonisation and negative integration, was to facilitate the free establishment of companies in order to create a common market.

III. FACILITATING CROSS BORDER BUSINESS

The lack of agreement on further company law harmonisation, alongside the introduction of the principle of subsidiarity, orientated European company law toward cross-border issues. The first example of this was the creation of new forms of business organisation that could transcend national borders. Such organisations could not be grounded in the TFEU's provisions on freedom of establishment as it would not fit the criteria of a 'company or firm' attempting to conduct business in a different Member State. Instead, the Council used their special legislative powers pursuant to now Article 352 of the TFEU[104] to create the first of these organisations – the European Economic Interest Grouping (EEIG).[105] An EEIG is created by contract between at least two companies or firms from at least two different Member States.[106] The EEIG's purpose is to facilitate companies from different jurisdictions pooling their knowledge or resources in a way that produces better results than the members acting alone.[107] A second form of business organisation, the *Societas Europaea* (*SE*), was created in 2001[108] and is a legal entity that can operate freely across the EU.[109] However, the *SE* must still be grounded in national law and must have its registered office in the Member State where it has its central administration and is governed by the law of that jurisdiction for matters not covered by the Regulation.[110] Recital 1 of

[103] E Wymeersch, 'The Transfer of Company Seat in European Company Law' (2003) 40 *Common Market Law Review* 661, 680.

[104] Formerly Art 235 of the Treaty of Rome. The Article basically provides powers to the Council to adopt legislation where 'action' by the Union is 'necessary' to 'adopt the appropriate measures'.

[105] Council Regulation (EEC) 2137/85 of 25 July 1985 on the European Economic Interest Grouping (EEIG) [1985] OJ L 199/1.

[106] ibid Art 4.

[107] See https://eur-lex.europa.eu/EN/legal-content/summary/european-economic-interest-grouping.html.

[108] Council Regulation (EC) 2157/2001 of 8 October 2001 on the Statute for a European company (SE) OJ L 294/1.

[109] An *SE* is established by at least two companies from different Member States and so, like the EEIG, is a composite organisation. See E Werlauff, 'The SE Company – A New Common European Company' (2003) 14 *European Business Law Review* 85.

[110] Article 63 of the Regulation states that matters such as winding up and insolvency are governed by the applicable national law.

the Regulation provides that the completion of the common market requires not only for barriers to trade to be removed, but also that the 'structures of production' be adapted to the 'Community dimension' ie a common market requires its own organisational business structures. Recital 3 states that restructuring and cooperation between companies from different Member States gives rise to 'legal and psychological difficulties and tax problems' and while the harmonisation can overcome some of those difficulties, companies remain restricted by national law frameworks. Recital 7 states that *SE* permits the creation and management of companies 'free from the obstacles arising from the disparity and the limited territorial application of national company law'. Hence, its aim is to allow the formation of a company that is, in part at least, free from the law of a single Member State and the issues that result in attempts to conduct business across borders.

The work of the High Level Group of Company Law Experts ('the Expert Group') formed in 2001[111] laid the foundations for the further expansion of legal mechanisms to enable cross-border business. The Expert Group was charged with developing a new proposal for a Takeover Directive after a series of legislative failures[112] and to define new priorities for the development of European company law.[113] The work of the Expert Group proposed a substantial shift in the underlying objectives of European company law, their perspective clearly influenced by the nexus of contracts/shareholder value model. The Expert Group viewed shareholders as primary risk bearers, repeatedly emphasised the importance of limiting agency costs and believed that regulation through company law should be, for the most part, avoided. In their first report on takeovers[114] the Expert Group described shareholders as residual claimants and primary risk bearers who 'are best equipped to decide on the affairs of the company as the ultimate effects of their decisions will be borne by them'.[115] The Expert Group disagreed with the US approach to takeovers where many states allow a board of directors to defend against a takeover bid,[116] instead favouring a model where shareholders had complete control:[117]

[111] See www.eurofound.europa.eu/en/resources/article/2001/commission-launches-high-level-group-company-law.

[112] The Commission first announced a proposed Directive on takeover bids in its 1985 White Paper on completing the Common Market. In 1989, the Commission proposed a Thirteenth Directive on company law concerning takeovers. Following objections from the Council, the Commission presented a revised proposal which failed to secure a majority in the parliament on 4 July 2001. See R Gilson, 'The Political Ecology of Takeovers: Thoughts on Harmonising the European Corporate Governance Environment' (1992) 61 *Fordham Law Review* 161.

[113] The Expert Group, 'A Modern Regulatory Framework for Company Law' (n 8).

[114] High Level Group of Company Law Experts, *Issues Related to Takeover Bids* (2002) available at https://papers.ssrn.com/sol3/papers.cfm?abstract_id=315322.

[115] ibid 21.

[116] See B Clarke, 'Regulating Poison Pill Devices' (2004) 4(1) *Journal of Corporate Law Studies* 51.

[117] High Level Group of Company Law Experts, *Issues Related to Takeover Bids* (n 114) stating shareholders 'should always be able to decide whether to tender their shares to a bidder and for what price', 2.

> [i]t is sometimes argued that allowing the board to frustrate a takeover bid can be justified as a means to help take into consideration the interests of shareholders and other stakeholders in the company, notably the employees. The Group rejects these views … Shareholders should be able to decide for themselves and stakeholders should be protected by specific rules (eg on labour law or environmental law).[118]

The Expert Group acknowledged that the interests of other stakeholders could be negatively affected by a takeover bid, particularly employees, but believed that such effects did 'not justify defensive measures by the board which deny shareholders the opportunity to successfully tender their shares to a bidder'.[119] The Expert Group were also concerned with agency costs, describing company managers as the 'agents of shareholders'[120] and emphasising that managers subject to a takeover bid face a conflict of interest given their interests lie 'in saving their jobs and reputation instead of maximising the value of the company for shareholders'.[121] The Expert Group believed an important aspect of takeovers, alongside creating wealth by exploiting synergies,[122] was to impose market discipline on company directors[123] stating that poorly managed companies could be taken over by rivals and that such 'discipline' allows a 'reallocation of resources [which] is in the long term best interests of all stakeholders, and society at large'.[124]

The Expert Group's next report put forward recommendations on what they believed should be the key priorities for modernising European company law.[125] They began by summarising European company law as an effort to coordinate equivalent safeguards to prevent a 'race to the bottom'.[126] The Group believed that meeting the needs of companies had not been a prominent feature of this harmonisation exercise and that the EU may have lost sight of the primary purpose of company law which should be to provide a legal framework to 'facilitate the running of efficient and competitive business enterprises.'[127] The Expert Group's core vision was that European company law 'should provide a flexible framework'[128] and that the use of company law for regulatory purposes should be avoided.[129] They believed the 'objective of combating fraud and abuse

[118] ibid 2.
[119] ibid 13.
[120] ibid.
[121] ibid 21.
[122] ibid 19.
[123] ibid.
[124] ibid.
[125] The Expert Group (n 8).
[126] ibid 29.
[127] ibid.
[128] ibid 5.
[129] ibid, 36 stating 'If we consider that, in company law regulation, it is important to provide for a framework for competitive business, this calls for flexible rules and forms of rulemaking, for light regulatory regimes where possible, scope for party autonomy and for less cumbersome and burdensome procedures'. The group did however advocate for increased regulation through disclosures at 45–47.

of companies should be achieved through specific law enforcement instruments outside company law'.[130] Shareholders were again described as residual claimants that are 'ideally placed to act as a watchdog' to ensure that 'management pursues – and remains accountable to – their interests'.[131]

The Expert Group's reports, as Deakin noted,[132] were a clear endorsement of a shareholder value orientated approach, where company law does not attempt to regulate but rather aims to enable efficient business through default rules and the supervision of directors by shareholders. The Commission's response to the Expert Group did not provide such an explicit endorsement of shareholder value. In its 'Plan to Move Forward',[133] the Commission noted the importance of long-term sustainable growth and endorsed companies with strong corporate governance records that were sensitive to social and environmental matters.[134] Nevertheless, the Commission's main objective in reforming company law was 'fostering efficiency and competitiveness of business'[135] the ultimate aim being economic growth and job creation.[136] The Commission, in agreeing with the Expert Group, emphasised that 'flexibility' should be available to companies as much as possible.[137] The Commission also noted the importance of upholding the principle of subsidiarity and sought to focus primarily on cross-border issues where EU action may be the only way to achieve the pursued objectives.[138] The Commission's emphasis on flexibility was the key characteristic of future legislative developments and as Armour and Ringe describe, the Commission's plan ultimately represented a 'minimalist' approach to European company law focused on facilitating business rather than regulation.[139]

In 2007, the Commission took a step closer to the Expert Group's position and proposed a reconsideration of European company law and a repeal of the harmonising Directives in order to 'promote a simplified business environment for companies'.[140] When referring to the harmonising Directives, the Commission stated 'repealing the EU rules and increasing flexibility' by leaving company matters to Member States was a 'viable option' which would fit with the 'need to equip the EU with a streamlined company law acquis for the 21st century'.[141] The European Parliament agreed with promoting a simplified

[130] ibid 6.
[131] ibid 47.
[132] S Deakin, 'Reflexive Governance and European Company Law' (2009) 15(2) *European Law Journal* 224, 234–35.
[133] European Commission, Modernising Company Law (n 11).
[134] ibid 3.
[135] ibid 3 and 9.
[136] ibid 9.
[137] ibid.
[138] ibid.
[139] Armour and Ringe, 'European Company Law 1999–2010' (n 39) 150.
[140] European Commission, Communication on a Simplified Business Environment for Companies in the Areas of Company Law, Accounting and Auditing (2007) COM 394 available at https://eur-lex.europa.eu/LexUriServ/LexUriServ.do?uri=COM:2007:0394:FIN:EN:PDF.
[141] ibid 9.

business environment but rejected the repeal of the harmonising Directives[142] in favour of amendments in line with the recommendations of Simpler Legislation in the Internal Market (SLIM) Group.[143] The end result of this simplification process was the consolidation of the early harmonisation Directives into an accounting directive[144] and a general consolidation Directive.[145]

A. Legislative Initiatives for Facilitating Cross-Border Business

The first Directive introduced following the Expert Group's report and Commission's plan was the 2004 Takeover Directive.[146] The Directive applied to all EU listed companies and sought to create a common framework for takeover bids.[147] A main focus of the Directive was the protection of shareholder interests,[148] including minority shareholders[149] and accordingly, in line with the Expert Group's recommendations, shareholders retained control in a takeover context rather than the board of directors. Article 3(1)(c) of the Directive provides that the board of directors 'must not deny the holders of securities the opportunity to decide on the merits of the bid'. Again, in line with recommendations of the Expert Group, many of the provisions of the Directive are default rules which can be opted out of.[150] Article 9 of the Takeover Directive sets out the 'board neutrality rule' which requires boards of directors to seek approval from shareholders before taking any action, other than seeking alternative bids, which may frustrate a takeover bid. Article 11 provides a 'breakthrough rule' which allows a bidder to overcome certain voting rights and other obstacles to

[142] See European Parliament, *A Simplified Business Environment for Companies in the Areas of Company Law, Accounting and Auditing* (2009) available at https://eur-lex.europa.eu/LexUriServ/LexUriServ.do?uri=OJ:C:2009:279E:0036:0040:EN:PDF.

[143] See E Wymeersch, 'European Company Law: The "Simpler Legislation for the Internal Market" (SLIM) Initiative of the EU Commission' (2000) *Financial Law Institute Working Paper Series* available at https://financiallawinstitute.ugent.be/wp-content/uploads/2020/wps/WP2000-09.pdf. As an example, The First and Second Directives were amended by Directive 2003/58/EC. However, it was not clear that these amendments had the effect of simplifying the legislation and the EU recast the reforms with the First Directive becoming Directive 2009/101/EC34 and the Second Directive becoming Directive 2012/30/EU35.

[144] Directive 2013/34/EU of the European Parliament and of the Council of 26 June 2013 on the annual financial statements, consolidated financial statements and related reports of certain types of undertakings, amending Directive 2006/43/EC of the European Parliament and of the Council and repealing Council Directives 78/660/EEC and 83/349/EEC [2013] OJ L 182/19.

[145] Directive (EU) 2017/1132 (n 54).

[146] Directive 2004/25/EC of the European Parliament and of the Council of 21 April 2004 on takeover bids [2004] OJ L 142/12. See B Sjåfjell, *Towards a Sustainable European Company Law: A Normative Analysis of the Objectives of EU Law* (Wolters Kluwer, 2009).

[147] Directive 2004/25/EC, art 1(1).

[148] ibid recital 1.

[149] ibid art 5.

[150] See B Clarke, 'The Takeover Directive: Is a Little Regulation Better Than No Regulation?' (2009) 15(2) *European Law Journal* 174 and A Johnston, 'The European Takeover Directive: Ruined by Protectionism or Respecting Diversity' (2004) 25 *Company Lawyer* 270.

a successful takeover. However, Article 12 allows Member States to opt out of both Articles 9 and 11.

One year later, the Cross-Border Merger Directive[151] came into effect. The Directive aimed to facilitate cross-border mergers 'with a view to the completion and functioning of the common market'[152] through the introduction of a legal framework that offered a draft set of terms[153] and set out the steps required to legally complete a merger.[154] The *Sevic* case had already demonstrated that cross-border mergers were valid as a matter of EU law and the Directive's main effect was to provide a framework that provided certainty and reduced costs.[155] In 2007, the EU introduced the Shareholder Rights Directive[156] which aimed to facilitate the cross-border engagement of shareholders. It introduced minimum standards for shareholders accessing information before a general meeting,[157] encouraged electronic communication,[158] set out a framework for long distance shareholder voting[159] and set out provisions on proxy voting.[160] Another development during this period was the introduction of two non-binding recommendations: one on the remuneration of directors of listed companies;[161] and one on the role of non-executive or supervisory directors of listed companies,[162] thus demonstrating the EU's more flexible approach to company law.

These legal initiatives are different to the first wave of harmonising Directives in two ways: (1) they primarily focus on cross-border issues; and (2) they are facilitative and optional to a much greater degree.[163] Armour and Ringe writing in 2011 summarised the period as one of 'choice' with an increasing number of optional legislative instruments that provide leeway for individual

[151] Directive 2005/56/EC of the European Parliament and of the Council of 26 October 2005 on cross-border mergers of limited liability companies [2005] OJ L 310/1 which is now part of the consolidating Directive 2017/1132/EU of the European Parliament and of the Council of 14 June 2017 relating to certain aspects of company law (codification) [2017] OJ L 169/46. See T Papadopoulos, 'EU Regulatory Approaches to Cross-Border Mergers: Exercising the Right of Establishment' (2011) 1 *European Law Review* 71.

[152] Directive 2005/56/EC, recital 1.

[153] ibid art 5.

[154] ibid arts 6–9.

[155] De Luca, *European Company Law* (n 37) 514–15.

[156] Directive 2007/36/EC of the European Parliament and of the Council of 11 July 2007 on the exercise of certain rights of shareholders in listed companies [2007] OJ L 184/17. See D Zetzsche, 'Shareholder Passivity, Cross-Border Voting and the Shareholder Rights Directive' (2008) 8 *Journal of Corporate Law Studies* 289.

[157] Directive 2007/36/EC (n 156) art 5.

[158] ibid art 9.

[159] ibid arts 7 and 8.

[160] ibid, arts 10–12.

[161] Commission Recommendation 2004/913/EC of 14 December 2004 fostering an appropriate regime for the remuneration of directors of listed companies [2004] OJ L 385/55.

[162] Commission Recommendation 2005/162/EC of 15 February 2005 on the role of non-executive or supervisory directors of listed companies and on the committees of the (supervisory) board [2005] OJ L 52/51.

[163] Although it is worth noting again that the mandatory rules introduced by the early harmonising Directives were, to a large extent, already in existence at the national level.

arrangements.[164] Armour and Ringe's conclusion was that this period of European company law 'fits with an overall picture of company law that views it as enabling law, providing efficient rules for conducting business, lowering transaction costs, and bringing about intervention only insofar as it is absolutely necessary'.[165]

B. The 2012 Action Plan

In 2012, the Commission set out a new 'Action Plan' for more engaged shareholders and sustainable companies.[166] The plan retained the previous focus on agency costs by expressing concern at shareholders' lack of interest 'in holding management accountable for their decisions and actions'.[167] The Commission's plan comprised of three main elements: (1) enhancing transparency with a view to ensure companies provide better information to their investors and society at large; (2) engaging shareholders; and (3) supporting companies' growth and their competitiveness by simplifying cross-border operations of European businesses.

The primary developments under the plan came in the form of a second Shareholder Rights Directive[168] and the Non-Financial Reporting Directive (NFRD).[169] The NFRD was, in many ways, a landmark piece of legislation[170] foreshadowing future developments around corporate sustainability. The NFRD required 'public interest entities'[171] with more than 500 employees to publish information regarding their impact on the environment, employee matters and human rights. The NFRD states that the publication of such information 'is vital for managing change towards a sustainable global economy by combining

[164] Armour and Ringe, 'European Company Law 1999–2010' (n 39) 173.

[165] ibid 174.

[166] European Commission, *Action Plan: European Company Law and Corporate Governance – A Modern Legal Framework for More Engaged Shareholders and Sustainable Companies* COM (2012) 740 available at https://eur-lex.europa.eu/legal-content/EN/ALL/?uri=celex%3A52012DC0740.

[167] ibid 3.

[168] Directive (EU) 2017/828 of the European Parliament and of the Council of 17 May 2017 amending Directive 2007/36/EC as regards the encouragement of long-term shareholder engagement [2017] OJ L 132/1 which sought to further enhance shareholder engagement through better identification of shareholders (Art 3a) and oversight of remuneration (Art 9a). See D Ahern, 'The Mythical Value of Voice and Stewardship in the EU Directive on Long-term Shareholder Engagement: Rights Do Not an Engaged Shareholder Make' (2018) 20 *Cambridge Yearbook of European Legal Studies* 88.

[169] Directive 2014/95/EU of the European Parliament and of the Council of 22 October 2014 amending Directive 2013/34/EU as regards disclosure of non-financial and diversity information by certain large undertakings and groups [2014] OJ L 330/1.

[170] See J Quinn and B Connolly, 'The Non-Financial Information Directive: An Assessment of its Impact on CSR' (2017) 14(1) *European Company Law* 15.

[171] Directive 2014/95/EU, art 1. Public interest entities are defined as those with: securities traded on stock exchanges; certain credit and insurance undertakings; and other entities designated as such by Member States.

long-term profitability with social justice and environmental protection.'[172] Despite its focus on social issues, the NFRD continued the trend of flexible frameworks, operating on a comply or explain basis[173] with a non-binding disclosure standard that allowed companies to choose what information to report.[174]

IV. CORPORATE SUSTAINABILITY

Sustainability has long been a part of the European project with Article 3(3) of the TFEU stating that the EU will work toward 'sustainable development of Europe' and Article 5 providing that the EU 'shall contribute to peace, security, the sustainable development of the Earth'. While sustainability was mentioned by the Commission's 2012 Action Plan and the NFRD, sustainability remained a secondary concern to facilitating business and the common market.

This position changed with a series of policy reports, starting in 2018, that placed sustainability and climate change at the forefront of the EU agenda. The first key document was the Commission's communication on a 'clean planet for all',[175] the opening paragraph of which provided that 'immediate and decisive climate action is essential' and expressed an EU commitment to lead global climate action, meet its obligations under the Paris agreement and achieve net-zero greenhouse gas emissions by 2050.[176] The European Green Deal[177] published in 2019 reiterated these intentions stating an aim 'to transform the EU into a fair and prosperous society, with a modern, resource-efficient and competitive economy where there are no net emissions of greenhouse gases in 2050 and where economic growth is decoupled from resource use'.[178] As part of the means to achieve this objective, the European Green Deal emphasised the importance of company law and that sustainability should be 'embedded into the corporate governance framework'.[179]

A more detailed description of potential company law reform was set out in the European Commission's Action Plan for Financing Sustainable Growth.[180]

[172] ibid recital 3.

[173] ibid art 1 stating that companies that do not have a policy for the relevant non-financial matter must provide a 'reasoned explanation for not doing so.'

[174] These points are expanded upon in ch 4.

[175] Communication from the Commission to the European Parliament, the European Council, the Council, the European Economic and Social Committee, the Committee of the Regions and the European Investment Bank – 'A Clean Planet for all – A European strategic long-term vision for a prosperous, modern, competitive and climate neutral economy' (2018) COM/2018/773 final available at https://eur-lex.europa.eu/legal-content/EN/TXT/?uri=CELEX%3A52018DC0773.

[176] ibid 1.

[177] Communication from the Commission on the European Green Deal (2019) COM/2019/640 final available at https://eur-lex.europa.eu/legal-content/EN/TXT/?uri=celex:52019DC0640.

[178] ibid [2.2.1].

[179] ibid.

[180] Communication from the Commission to the European Parliament, the European Council, the Council, the European Central Bank, the European Economic and Social Committee and the

The plan emphasised the need for corporate boards to develop a sustainability strategy that would include reporting and an obligation to conduct due diligence through a company's supply chain.[181] The plan also referenced the potential need for a reform of directors' duties to have regard to the company's long-term interest. The High Level Expert Group's report on Sustainable Finance[182] further recommended that a clear commitment to sustainability be 'embedded in the duties of company directors and into the governance rules related to company management, supervision and incentive structures.'[183] The Group recommended placing explicit duties on directors to consider the likely consequences of any decision in the longer term, the interests of the company's employees as well as the impact of the company's operations on the environment and the world's cultural and natural heritage.[184] Two further reports on company law followed in 2020, one on 'Due Diligence Requirements Through the Supply Chain'[185] and one on 'Directors' Duties and Sustainable Corporate Governance'.[186] The report on due diligence was over 500 pages and described numerous examples of the ongoing environmental and human rights abuses arising from the operation of transnational companies.[187] The report on directors' duties was highly critical of shareholder value, stating that a focus on 'shareholder value maximisation' reduces the 'economic, environmental and social sustainability of European businesses[188] and that a failure to capture sustainability risks could 'amount to overwhelming environmental, social and economic consequences for companies, shareholders, investors, and society at large'.[189]

This change in policy led to a suite of legislative initiatives focused around corporate sustainability starting with the SFDR in 2019[190] followed by the

Committee of the Regions 'Action Plan: Financing Sustainable Growth' (2018) COM/2018/097 final available at https://eur-lex.europa.eu/legal-content/EN/TXT/?uri=CELEX:52018DC0097.

[181] ibid 11.

[182] EU High Level Group on Sustainable Finance, 'Sustainable Financing a European Economy" (2018) available at https://ec.europa.eu/info/sites/info/files/170713-sustainable-finance-report_en.pdf.

[183] ibid 39.

[184] ibid, 40.

[185] British Institute of International and Comparative Law, 'Study on Due Diligence Requirements Through the Supply Chain' (2020) available at https://op.europa.eu/en/publication-detail/-/publication/8ba0a8fd-4c83-11ea-b8b7-01aa75ed71a1/language-en.

[186] EY, 'Study on Directors' Duties and Sustainable Corporate Governance' (2020) available at https://op.europa.eu/en/publication-detail/-/publication/e47928a2-d20b-11ea-adf7-01aa75ed71a1/language-en.

[187] This will be discussed in more detail in ch 5.

[188] EY, 'Study on Directors' Duties and Sustainable Corporate Governance' (n 186), quotes are from the abstract.

[189] ibid vi. This report, and its extensive criticism from across academia is discussed in ch 7.

[190] Regulation (EU) 2019/2088 of the European Parliament and of the Council of 27 November 2019 on sustainability-related disclosures in the financial services sector [2019] OJ L 317/1. The Regulation aimed to harness private funding to enable the transition to a net-zero economy by increasing transparency on the sustainability of financial products allowing ESG orientated investors to select companies and projects which support sustainability related activities. For analysis see E Partiti, 'Addressing the Flaws of the Sustainable Finance Disclosure Regulation: Moving from Disclosures

Taxonomy Regulation[191] in 2020, the CSRD in 2022 and the CSDDD in 2024. The CSRD stated that the aim of introducing increased reporting obligations was to help form a 'stable, sustainable and inclusive economic system' the ultimate aim being to benefit 'individual citizens'.[192] The EU believed new reporting obligations would help create this stable and sustainable economic system by reducing the 'information gap' that caused 'significant negative consequences'.[193] These negative consequences included: that investors were unable to take sufficient account of sustainability-related risks; and that non-governmental organisations, social partners, communities and other stakeholders were less able to hold companies to account for their impacts on people and the environment.[194] The CSRD also noted the increased demand for corporate sustainability information due to the evolving nature of risk, which now included climate-related financial risks, biodiversity loss, and health and social issues, including child labour and forced labour.[195] In a similar fashion, the CSDDD noted that the behaviour of companies across all sectors of the economy is key to the EU's sustainability objectives of achieving a just transition to a sustainable economy.[196] It stated, that this was particularly important in the context of large companies that operate through value chains that have effects on human rights and the environment.[197]

This brief summary of the EU corporate sustainability initiatives demonstrate the shift in policy toward limiting the negative externalities of business, particularly in relation to environmental harms and human rights abuses. As will be discussed in chapters four and five, these legislative initiatives not only represented a change in focus but also a change in methods as they include mandatory rules and provide for civil liability and supervision by regulatory authorities, thus ending the flexible approach that was the hallmark of European company law since the early 2000s.

A. A Potential Reversal: The Omnibus

Starting in late 2024, the EU signalled a reversal of policy away from sustainability and back to facilitating efficient and competitive business. Much like

to Labelling and Sustainability Due Diligence' (2024) 25 *European Business Organization Law Review* 299.

[191] Regulation (EU) 2020/852 of the European Parliament and of the Council of 18 June 2020 on the establishment of a framework to facilitate sustainable investment, and amending Regulation (EU) 2019/2088 [2020] OJ L 198/13. The Regulation creates a classification system for 'environmentally sustainable' economic activities.

[192] CSRD (n 18) recital 9.

[193] ibid recital 14.

[194] ibid.

[195] ibid recital 11.

[196] CDDD (n 19) recitals 3 and 4.

[197] ibid recital 4. The CSDDD also states that all companies have a responsibility to respect human rights, which are universal, indivisible, interdependent and interrelated at recital 7.

in 2007, this reorientation of policy focused on providing a simplified business environment for companies.[198] The process started with a report by Mario Draghi on the 'The Future of European Competitiveness' which emphasised the need for Europe to create a regulatory landscape that facilitates competitiveness and resilience.[199] The report noted that the regulatory burden on European companies is high compared to other jurisdictions[200] and expressed concerns at the 'innovation gap' between Europe, China and the US.[201] In the Budapest Declaration on the New European Competitiveness Deal, the European Council endorsed Draghi's report describing it as a 'wake up call' and expressing an intention to 'urgently close the innovation and productivity gap'.[202] More specifically, the declaration called for 'a simplification revolution, ensuring a clear, simple and smart regulatory framework for businesses and drastically reducing administrative, regulatory and reporting burdens' and that the EU 'must adopt an enabling mindset'.[203]

This return to a policy focus on economic productivity and competitiveness led to the European Commission's 2025 Omnibus I Proposal[204] which aims to simplify the current corporate sustainability framework. The Omnibus describes the new and difficult context in which EU businesses are operating caused by higher energy costs, the rise of trade tensions and the impact of the comparatively stringent EU corporate sustainability rules. The Omnibus also notes that the ability of the EU to preserve and protect its values depends on the capacity of its economy to adapt and compete in an unstable and potentially hostile geopolitical environment. Based on these concerns, the proposal set out to simplify and streamline the regulatory framework created by the CSRD and the CSDDD, but without undermining the policy objectives of either piece of legislation or the overall ambition of the European Green Deal.

The changes proposed by Omnibus I will be outlined in more detail in chapters four and five, the main points being that it proposes for the CSRD to apply to approximately 80 per cent fewer companies and be accompanied by a less demanding reporting standard, and for the CSDDD's EU model of liability to be removed and its application limited to direct contractual partners. While the Omnibus is a proposal only and must now progress through the EU legislative process,[205] it is clear that the new European Commission, whose term began in December 2024, intends to deregulate existing corporate sustainability rules in

[198] European Commission, *Communication on a Simplified Business Environment* (n 140).

[199] M Draghi, 'The Future of European Competitiveness' (2024) available at https://commission.europa.eu/topics/eu-competitiveness/draghi-report_en#paragraph_47059.

[200] ibid 69.

[201] ibid 6.

[202] Budapest Declaration on the New European Competitiveness Deal (2024) available at https://www.consilium.europa.eu/en/press/press-releases/2024/11/08/the-budapest-declaration/.

[203] ibid [4].

[204] European Commission, 'Omnibus I' (2025) available at https://commission.europa.eu/publications/omnibus-i_en.

[205] This will involve negotiations between the European Commission, Parliament and Council.

the name of facilitating business. This has, unsurprisingly, led to criticism from sustainability advocates[206] and ESG orientated investors.[207] However, as can be seen from the above description, and as will be developed further in chapters four and five, the EU's corporate sustainability rules are the product of multiple distinct reports and legislative processes that have resulted in a complex and somewhat disjointed framework. As Colin Mayer has argued, the shortcoming of the EU corporate sustainability rules is that they are too complex.[208] This complexity increases the burden on companies and orients decision makers within companies away from the fundamental goal of becoming more aware of and reducing negative externalities and toward a 'compliance' mindset. Hence, it is perhaps unsurprising that there has been extensive lobbying from business[209] and a political re-evaluation of the corporate sustainability legislation. Shift[210] believes that the unduly complex nature of the EU rules arise from developing corporate sustainability rules in the wrong order.[211] They argue that EU corporate sustainability should have started with the development of sustainability and due diligence policies, then what companies needed to report to substantiate those efforts, and then what their investors needed to report. However, the EU worked in the reverse order, starting with requirements for investors under the SFDR, then reporting requirements under the CSRD updating the NFRD, and finally due diligence requirements under the CSDDD. Shift's analysis is that this incorrect ordering, as well as their development taking place in different branches of the Commission, has meant there is a lack of connecting logic between the instruments resulting in an unnecessarily complex framework with disconnected timelines.

Shift's core argument is that the SFDR, CSRD and CSDDD could have been much simpler if the EU had followed a single, integrated approach to corporate sustainability. The EU's development of corporate sustainability rules followed a clear policy of reducing environmental harms and human rights abuses, but lacked a theoretical clarity and the coherence in legislative development to achieve a single integrated approach across sustainable finance, reporting and due diligence. While this may sound critical, the EU is the first jurisdiction to

[206] Eg, see https://greencentralbanking.com/2025/03/07/eu-omnibus-regulation-is-a-massive-step-backwards-says-sustainability-expert/.

[207] Eg, see https://www.iigcc.org/insights/eu-omnibus-proposals-on-sustainable-finance-what-it-means-for-investors and https://www.eurosif.org/press-room/eurosif-warns-omnibus-proposals-risk-undermining-investment-and-competitiveness/.

[208] Mayer, 'Success, Law and ESG' (n 22) 14. Mayer argues for a simpler solution through redefining the corporate purpose. His arguments are set out in ch 7.

[209] See Eiris Foundation, 'Financial Sector Lobbying of the EU Corporate Sustainability Due Diligence Directive: a Social LobbyMap Analysis' available at www.thegoodlobby.eu/eu-business-lobbying-on-sustainability-exposed/.

[210] Shift are a centre of expertise focusing on the UN's Guiding Principles on Business and Human Rights. See https://shiftproject.org/.

[211] See https://shiftproject.org/the-european-commissions-omnibus-simplification-proposal-shifts-preliminary-reflections/.

attempt to develop a mandatory company law framework that is focused on reducing the negative externalities of companies that apply transnationally – it is understandable that the end result was not a streamlined, integrated model. However, the Omnibus, rather than addressing these issues, exacerbates them by proposing new rules and thresholds which increase uncertainty while making no attempt to integrate the framework. A preferable approach would have been to simplify the corporate sustainability framework through integration of sustainable finance, reporting and due diligence into a single Directive, with a single threshold of application, timeline for implementation and set out the mandatory processes that were to be followed.[212]

V. CONCLUSION

For most of the existence of the EEC and the EU, the function of European company law was to contribute to the formation of the common market. It did this through differing methods of positive harmonisation, negative integration and legal frameworks that encouraged cross-border business. From a regulatory point of view, European company law was largely trivial[213] aiming to enable efficient and productive business. However, a shift in policy focus from the EU resulted in a new approach to company law, one where the objective was the reduction of environmental harms and human rights abuses. More recently again, the European Commission has signalled a return to a policy approach of promoting efficient and competitive business. Yet despite this reversal in policy, the EU's initiatives on corporate sustainability provide an example of what a company law with reflexive elements could look like and therefore warrants detailed analysis.

[212] This would be particularly welcome in the context of reporting, where, as will be discussed in ch 4, the CSRD interrelates to multiple other Directives and a highly complex set of reporting standards.

[213] Enriques, 'EC Company Law Directives and Regulations'; and Enriques, 'A Harmonized European Company Law' (n 12).

4

Corporate Sustainability Reporting

I. INTRODUCTION

ONE OF THE core elements of company law across all jurisdictions is that companies are required to disclose certain information through a public register. European company law is no exception and disclosure requirements were introduced by the First Directive on company law in 1968[1] which has since been significantly amended and expanded.[2] European company law rules on financial disclosures are now contained in the European Accounting Directive[3] which requires companies[4] to prepare annual financial statements that present a true and fair view of 'material' information relating to the company's assets, liabilities, financial position and profit or loss.[5] These statements are to be prepared in accordance with the relevant accounting standards[6] and medium and large companies[7] must have their statements audited.[8] The primary objective of these disclosures is to provide details to shareholders, potential investors and creditors in order to allow them to make informed decisions regarding their business dealings with the company. In other words, financial

[1] Directive 68/151/EEC of 9 March 1968 on co-ordination of safeguards which, for the protection of the interests of members and others, are required by Member States of companies within the meaning of the second paragraph of Article 58 of the Treaty, with a view to making such safeguards equivalent throughout the Community [1968] OJ L 65, arts 2 and 3 mandating all registered companies in the European Economic Community (EEC) to disclose basic information including the company's constitution, its balance sheet and profit and loss account for each financial year on to a public register.

[2] See N De Luca, *European Company Law*, 2nd edn (Cambridge, Cambridge University Press, 2021), 44–48 and ch 12.

[3] Directive 2013/34/EU of the European Parliament and of the Council of 26 June 2013 on the annual financial statements, consolidated financial statements and related reports of certain types of undertakings, amending Directive 2006/43/EC of the European Parliament and of the Council and repealing Council Directives 78/660/EEC and 83/349/EEC [2013] OJ L 182/19.

[4] For the sake of consistency, this chapter uses 'company' rather than the term 'undertaking' that is used in EU Regulations and Directives on disclosures. 'Undertaking' is broader than company but includes the public and private companies of the EU Member States. See Directive 2013/34/EU, Annex 1.

[5] ibid art 4.

[6] ibid arts 23 and 33 and as set out by Regulation (EC) No 1606/2002 of the European Parliament and of the Council of 19 July 2002 on the application of international accounting standards [2002] OJ L 243/1.

[7] As defined by Directive 2013/34/EU (n 3), art 3.

[8] ibid art 34.

disclosures facilitate and promote investment across the EU's common market by reducing information asymmetries and establishing 'economic reliability'.[9]

Information disclosure can also have a value beyond an economic context.[10] Companies reporting information on sustainability related issues such as their impact on human rights and environmental matters has long been viewed as a potentially useful tool in developing socially responsible business.[11] Many companies now voluntarily report information on such matters[12] to enhance their reputation within capital markets – particularly for environmental, social and governance (ESG) orientated investors[13] – and with customers and the public more generally. However, the difficulty with such voluntary disclosures is the incentives that exist for companies to report favourable information while misrepresenting or not disclosing unfavourable information.[14] A solution is to apply the legal rules of financial reporting to sustainability reporting ie impose mandatory reporting rules to be produced in accordance with detailed standards and auditing procedures. If companies are required to produce standardised and independently verified reports, the potential for greenwashing and cherry picking is reduced and companies will have to engage in an information gathering process on their external impact. This will make companies more aware of their external effects and companies that want positive information to report, in order to protect or enhance their reputation, will be more likely to take steps to improve their record on environmental and human rights issues.[15] In other words, the mandatory rules, the independent verification and the potential reputational effects provide the external stimulation necessary for a reflexive response where companies mobilise their internal resources to reduce their negative externalities.[16]

[9] Taking the term from Stefan Grundmann who regards economic reliability for shareholders and creditors as a core function of European company law: S Grundmann, 'European Company Law in Transformation – Striving for Participation and Sustainability' (2023) 42 *Yearbook of European Law* 210, 211–15.

[10] See A Lipton, 'Not Everything is About Investors: The Case for Mandatory Stakeholder Disclosure (2020) 37 *Yale Journal on Regulation* 499.

[11] See C Stone, *Where the Law Ends: The Social Control of Corporate Behaviour* (Harper & Row, 1975).

[12] See KPMG, 'Key Global Trends in Sustainability Reporting' (2022) available at https://kpmg.com/xx/en/our-insights/esg/survey-of-sustainability-reporting-2022/global-trends.html.

[13] See M Barzuza, Q Curtis and D Webber, 'Shareholder Value(s): Index Fund ESG Activism and the New Millennial Corporate Governance' (2020) 93 *Southern California Law Review* 1243 and J Macey, 'ESG Investing: Why Here? Why Now?' (2022) 19 *Berkeley Business Law Journal* 258.

[14] See D Ahern, 'Turning Up the Heat? EU Sustainability Goals and the Role of Reporting under the Non-Financial Reporting Directive' (2016) 4 *European Company and Financial Law Review* 599 noting that companies, left to their own devices, are inclined 'to report favourable aspects than less favourable aspects of their activities and policies.'

[15] See D Hess, 'Social Reporting: A Reflexive Law Approach to Corporate Social Responsiveness' (1999) 25 *The Journal of Corporation Law* 41.

[16] G Teubner, 'Corporate Fiduciary Duties and their Beneficiaries' in G Teubner and K Hopt (eds), *Corporate Governance and Directors' Liabilities: Legal, Economic and Sociological Analyses on Corporate Social Responsibility* (De Gruyter, 1985) 165 arguing that 'reflexion cannot be voluntary, but needs to be stimulated by powerful external forces'.

In 2014 the EU enacted the Non-Financial Reporting Directive (NFRD)[17] which sought to manage change toward 'social justice and environmental protection'[18] through disclosures by certain companies of their policies and principal risks regarding the environment, human rights, social and employee matters.[19] However, in accordance with the 'flexible' approach of European company law at the time,[20] the NFRD was not mandatory and instead followed a comply or explain model[21] with non-binding disclosure standards. This undermined the potential impact of the NFRD[22] and a review conducted by the Commission in 2021[23] found that many companies were failing to disclose material information and that there was a lack of consistency regarding the content and presentation of the information reported.[24]

In response to the NFRD's limitations and in line with the objectives of the European Green Deal[25] and Action Plan on Financing Sustainable Growth,[26] the EU began strengthening its rules on sustainability reporting. The first changes were introduced by the Sustainable Finance Disclosure Regulation (SFDR) in 2019[27] followed by the Taxonomy Regulation on facilitating sustainable investment[28] that was followed by the Corporate Sustainability Reporting Directive (CSRD).[29] The CSRD amended the NFRD, broadening the scope of application, widening the range of information to be disclosed, was mandatory subject to a 'double materiality' test, and requires adherence to a detailed and binding reporting standard. Given the strength of the CSRD rules, there is now a realistic prospect of reliable sustainability reporting and a reflexive response by

[17] Directive 2014/95/EU of the European Parliament and of the Council of 22 October 2014 amending Directive 2013/34/EU as regards disclosure of non-financial and diversity information by certain large undertakings and groups [2014] OJ L 330/1.

[18] ibid recital 3.

[19] ibid art 1.

[20] As discussed in ch 3.

[21] Directive 2014/95/EU (n 17), art 1 provided that companies that do not have a policy for the relevant non-financial matter must provide a 'reasoned explanation for not doing so.'

[22] See D Szabó and K Sorensen, 'New EU Directive on the Disclosure of Non-Financial Information' (2015) 12(3) *European Company and Financial Law Review* 307.

[23] Report from the Commission to the European Parliament, the Council and the European Economic and Social Committee on the review clauses in Directives 2013/34/EU, 2014/95/EU, and 2013/50/EU [2021] COM/2021/199 final, available at https://eur-lex.europa.eu/legal-content/EN/TXT/?uri=CELEX%3A52021DC0199.

[24] ibid 17.

[25] European Commission Communication on the European Green Deal (2019) see https://commission.europa.eu/strategy-and-policy/priorities-2019-2024/european-green-deal_en.

[26] European Commission, Action Plan: Financing Sustainable Growth available at https://eur-lex.europa.eu/legal-content/EN/TXT/?uri=CELEX:52018DC0097.

[27] Regulation (EU) 2019/2088 of the European Parliament and of the Council of 27 November 2019 on sustainability-related disclosures in the financial services sector [2019] OJ L 317/1.

[28] Regulation (EU) 2020/852 of the European Parliament and of the Council of 18 June 2020 on the establishment of a framework to facilitate sustainable investment, and amending Regulation (EU) 2019/2088 [2020] OJ L 198/13.

[29] Directive (EU) 2022/2464 of the European Parliament and of the Council of 14 December 2022 amending Regulation (EU) No 537/2014, Directive 2004/109/EC, Directive 2006/43/EC and Directive 2013/34/EU, as regards corporate sustainability reporting [2022] OJ L 322/15.

companies. However, the European Commission's Omnibus I proposal proposes an 80 per cent reduction in the scope of application plus a revised, less demanding reporting standard, which, if introduced, would undoubtedly weaken the effect of the CSRD.[30]

Section II briefly discusses European company law rules on financial disclosure and their role in providing economic reliability. Section III develops the relationship between reflexivity and corporate reporting and analyses the shortcomings of many existing reporting laws. Section IV sets out the recent EU legislative developments on mandatory reporting, including the requirements of the CSRD and the changes proposed by Omnibus I.

II. CORPORATE TRANSPARENCY AND FINANCIAL DISCLOSURES

One of the common dimensions of company law across all jurisdictions is that companies are required to disclose certain information through a public register. The most obvious example is financial disclosures, the basic rationale of which is to allow parties dealing with a company to take informed decisions and protect themselves against possible losses.[31] As described in the *Anatomy of Corporate Law*, modern financial reporting regimes developed along two different tracks.[32] In seventeenth century France, disclosure laws emerged primarily to protect creditors.[33] Because of the company's legal personality, the claims of creditors are, in general, limited to the assets of the company and cannot be asserted against the personal assets of the company's shareholders or directors.[34] Hence, should a company enter insolvent liquidation the creditor may not receive full satisfaction of their debt, depending on the degree of insolvency and level of security held by the creditor.[35] This risk of corporate insolvency increases the importance of corporate financial transparency which, assuming the information is reliable,

[30] See European Commission, 'Omnibus I' (2025) available at https://commission.europa.eu/publications/omnibus-i_en. The Omnibus is a proposal only and, at the time of writing, is going through the EU legislative process.

[31] See P Davies and S Worthington, *Gower's Principles of Moden Company Law*, 10th edn (Sweet and Maxwell, 2016) 689–691 and C Leuz and P Wysocki, 'The Economics of Disclosure and Financial Reporting Regulation: Evidence and Suggestions for Future Research' (2016) 54(2) *Journal of Accounting Research* 525.

[32] R Kraakman et al, *The Anatomy of Corporate Law: A Comparative and Functional Approach*, 3rd edn (Oxford, Oxford University Press, 2017) 249–54.

[33] ibid 252 but also to enable corporate taxation.

[34] Certain legislative provisions do allow creditors to take claims against company officers for harming the interests of creditors. One such example is 'Wrongful Trading' under the UK Insolvency Act 1986, s 214. For a broader discussion of the law's response to this issue see J Quinn and P Gavin, 'The Creditor Duty Post *Sequana*: Lessons for Legislative Reform' (2023) 23(1) *Journal of Corporate Law Studies* 271.

[35] See J Quinn, 'The Crystallisation of Floating Charges: Rethinking the Conceptual Framework' (2020) 20(1) *Journal of Corporate Law Studies* 179.

allows a creditor to make an informed decision on whether to advance credit to a company and if so, for what amount and at what rate of interest. In an Anglo-American context, financial disclosures developed along different lines, the principal objective being to offer transparency to investors and to enhance the capacity of existing shareholders to monitor their investments.[36]

Following these same rationales of reducing information asymmetries for creditors, investors and shareholders, corporate disclosure rules have been a central component of European company law since the First Company Law Directive.[37] The First Directive applied to all private and public companies and mandated the disclosure of the company's constitution, any amendments to the constitution and the appointment, termination and particulars of the persons authorised to represent the company.[38] Companies were also required to disclose the company's capital, balance sheet and the profit and loss account.[39] Under the Directive, Member States had to open a central register where the information was to be filed and access was to be given to the public for a fee not exceeding the administrative cost.[40] The First Directive has since been amended multiple times[41] and the rules on financial disclosures have been expanded and separated from more general disclosures regarding, for example, the company's constitution.[42] The Fourth Company Law Directive in 1978 began this expansion by providing rules on how annual accounts should be maintained and disclosed.[43] This process was continued by the Seventh Directive in 1983 which provided rules on consolidated accounts for corporate groups[44] while the Eighth Directive related to the approval of persons responsible for carrying out the statutory audits of

[36] See R Kraakman et al, *The Anatomy of Corporate Law* (n 32) 338–39. The authors note that periodic disclosure of financial information allows shareholders to determine whether they wish to invest further in the company or exit and also provides mechanisms to limit agency costs through, for example, disclosure requirements on third party transactions and where directors must disclose details of transactions to gain approval from shareholders.

[37] Council Directive 68/151/EEC (n 1).

[38] ibid art 2.

[39] ibid art 2(e) and (f).

[40] ibid art 3.

[41] First in 2003 by Directive 2003/58/EC of the European Parliament and of the Council of 15 July 2003 amending Council Directive 68/151/EEC, as regards disclosure requirements in respect of certain types of companies [2003] OJ L 221/13. This provided for the disclosure of information by electronic means.

[42] See arts 3, 4 and 16 of Directive (EU) 2017/1132 of the European Parliament and of the Council of 14 June 2017 relating to certain aspects of company law (codification) [2017] OJ L 169/46. Public companies are still required to disclose the 'statutes or the instrument of incorporation' which must include the type and name of the company, the objects of the company and its share capital.

[43] Fourth Council Directive 78/660/EEC of 25 July 1978 based on Article 54(3)(g) of the Treaty on the annual accounts of certain types of companies [1978] OJ L 222/11. For example, art 2(3) provided that the annual accounts shall give a true and fair view of the company's assets, liabilities, financial position and profit or loss.

[44] Seventh Council Directive 83/349/EEC of 13 June 1983 based on the Article 54(3)(g) of the Treaty on consolidated accounts [1983] OJ L 193/1.

accounting documents.[45] These Directives, and other more recent Directives,[46] are now part of the EU Accounting Directive[47] which consolidated the various accounting, audit and financial disclosure rules into a more accessible format.

Under the EU Accounting Directive, companies[48] must prepare annual financial statements which include, at a minimum, the balance sheet, the profit and loss account and supplementary notes.[49] The Accounting Directive also requires companies to prepare a management report which reviews the development and performance of the undertaking's business together with a description of the principal risks and uncertainties that it faces.[50] The guiding principle of the Accounting Directive is that the statements must present a true and fair view of the company's assets, liabilities, financial position and profit or loss,[51] true and fair view generally referring to accounts that are free from material misstatements, are factually correct and have been prepared in accordance with the relevant accounting standards.[52] Accordingly, the Accounting Directive includes detailed Annexes which outline what information must be included in both the balance sheets[53] and profit/loss accounts[54] while public-interest entities[55] and medium and large undertakings are required to have their financial statements audited by one or more statutory auditors.[56]

This very brief description of the EU financial reporting landscape demonstrates that a core part of European company law has been ensuring what Stefan Grundmann terms as 'economic reliability'.[57] Grundmann describes much of early European company law as being focused on 'outsider reliability' – 'outsider' meaning creditors and investors – who often give large, long-term investments and need a reliable basis on which to form a productive relationship.[58] Basic levels of harmonisation across jurisdictions helps provide such reliability but so does the requirement to disclose accounts in accordance with mandatory

[45] Eighth Council Directive 84/253/EEC of 10 April 1984 based on Article 54 (3) (g) of the Treaty on the approval of persons responsible for carrying out the statutory audits of accounting documents [1984] OJ L 126/20.

[46] For example, Directive 2006/43/EC of the European Parliament and of the Council of 17 May 2006 on statutory audits of annual accounts and consolidated accounts, amending Council Directives 78/660/EEC and 83/349/EEC and repealing Council Directive 84/253/EEC [2006] OJ L 157/87 (the Statutory Audit Directive).

[47] Directive 2013/34/EU (n 3).

[48] ibid art 3 divides undertakings into small, medium and large and imposes different regulatory burdens on each type of undertaking.

[49] ibid art 4(1). The notes are to provide additional context to the accounts.

[50] ibid art 19.

[51] ibid art 4.

[52] De Luca, *European Company Law* (n 2) 230–32.

[53] Directive 2013/34/EU (n 3) Annex III and IV allowing Member States to select either vertical or horizontal formats.

[54] ibid Annex V and VI.

[55] ibid defined by art 2 as all listed companies, credit institutions, insurance undertakings and other companies designated by Member States because of their activities, size or number of employees.

[56] ibid art 34.

[57] Grundmann, 'European Company Law in Transformation' (n 9) 215.

[58] ibid 211.

professional scrutiny.[59] However, Grundmann also notes that mandatory disclosures and auditing procedures are themselves insufficient to provide reliability and legal measures must also allow for information to be located in one place and be presented in an understandable format.[60] Accordingly, Grundmann highlights the importance of the European Register system, originally created in the First Company Law Directive,[61] which is now digitalised and linked into national registers through the Business Registers Interconnection System (BRIS).[62] BRIS connects the business registers of each Member State to a 'European Central Platform' to widen accessibility of the disclosed information.[63] While high profile corporate collapses[64] and the financial crisis[65] have demonstrated that legal rules on financial disclosures and mandatory auditing do not guarantee economic reliability, such measures remain important tools to reduce information asymmetries for investors and creditors.

III. REFLEXIVITY AND THE FAILURE OF REPORTING LAWS

Many companies voluntarily report information on sustainability related matters like human rights and environmental impacts.[66] Such reporting can be important from an economic perspective by reducing information asymmetries around sustainability risks that have potential financial consequences and by influencing the decisions of socially conscious shareholders, customers and investors.[67] However, the difficulty with voluntary reporting is its reliability

[59] ibid 212.

[60] ibid 213.

[61] Directive 68/151/EEC (n 1).

[62] See https://ec.europa.eu/digital-building-blocks/sites/pages/viewpage.action?pageId=533365899. Directive 2003/58/EC provided the first step toward digitisation followed by Directive 2012/17/EU which provided for the interconnection of central, commercial and companies registers.

[63] The EU have recently expanded and upgraded the use of digital tools and processes in company law through Directive (EU) 2025/25 of the European Parliament and of the Council of 19 December 2024 amending Directives 2009/102/EC and (EU) 2017/1132 as regards further expanding and upgrading the use of digital tools and processes in company law [2024] OJ L. See European Commission, 'Study on the Disclosure and Cross-Border use of Company Data, and Digital Developments Related to Company Law' (2023) available at https://op.europa.eu/en/publication-detail/-/publication/566b66da-e7cb-11ed-a05c-01aa75ed71a1/language-en.

[64] Most famously Enron, see J Coffee, 'Understanding Enron: It's about the Gatekeepers, Stupid' (2001) 57 Business Law 1403; and S Deakin and S Konzelmann, 'Learning from Enron' (2004) 12(2) *Corporate Governance: An International Review* 134.

[65] The underlying rationale for BRIS stemmed from the financial crisis and the EU's resultant belief that up-to-date, trustworthy information on companies would encourage greater confidence in the single market. See https://ec.europa.eu/digital-building-blocks/sites/pages/viewpage.action?pageId=533365899.

[66] Nearly all of the world's top 250 companies report on sustainability related issues and the number of companies producing sustainability reports is rising. See KPMG, 'Key Global Trends in Sustainability Reporting' (2022) available at https://kpmg.com/xx/en/our-insights/esg/survey-of-sustainability-reporting-2022/global-trends.html.

[67] As demonstrated by the rise of ESG investing. See D Esty and Q Karpilow, 'Harnessing Investor Interest in Sustainability' (2019) 36 *Yale Journal on Regulation* 625 and Macey, 'ESG Investing' (n 13).

given the potential for companies to fail to gather important information, fail to engage with stakeholders regarding risks and impacts as well as the incentives that exist to not report unfavourable information (cherry picking),[68] report false information (greenwashing),[69] or produce vacuous reports with non-material information (boilerplate reporting).[70] One method to solve this reliability issue is to adopt a legal framework similar to financial reporting where companies are under mandatory obligations to report information in accordance with detailed standards and auditing procedures.

If companies are required to produce detailed and independently verified reports, the potential for cherry picking and greenwashing is reduced and companies will have to engage in an information gathering process to develop an understanding of their external impact. This will include engagement with stakeholders[71] which in some cases may be itself sufficient for decision makers to take steps to mitigate their negative impacts. Such a process of information gathering and sharing may even highlight opportunities to reduce the company's negative externalities in a way that does not reduce or even improve its business performance.[72] Because such a process would need to be conducted by the various departments within a company, it has the potential to influence decision making across multiple levels of the organisation[73] rather than simply being limited to the board of directors.[74] Hence, the information gathering process can provoke a reflexive response by opening the company up to its external effects thereby shaping the company's 'internal discourse and their methods of coordination with other social systems'.[75]

Further, if reporting is mandatory, detailed and standardised, companies that want to have positive information to report in order to protect or enhance their reputation will be more likely to take steps to mobilise their internal resources to improve their impacts on environmental and human rights issues.[76] This effect is more likely in competitive markets where standardised reporting allows similar companies to be objectively compared on issues, especially

[68] See D Ahern, 'Turning Up the Heat?' (n 14).

[69] See E Yu, B Lu, and C Chen, 'Greenwashing in Environmental, Social and Governance Disclosures' (2020) 52 *Research in International Business and Finance* 1.

[70] See D Monciardini, 'Regulating Accounting for Sustainable Companies: Some Considerations on the Forthcoming Directive' (2014) 11(2) *European Company Law* 121.

[71] See D Ahern (n 14) 613.

[72] See S Zadek et al, *Building Corporate Accountability Emerging Practice in Social and Ethical Accounting and Auditing* (Routledge, 1997), ch 2 on 'Why Count Social Performance?'.

[73] Hess, 'Social Reporting: A Reflexive Law Approach to Corporate Social Responsiveness' (n 15) 82.

[74] See C Witting, 'The Place of Managers in the Corporate Governance Architecture' (2024) 24(1) *Journal of Corporate Law Studies* 1 highlighting the importance of mid-management in influencing how companies function.

[75] See G Teubner, 'Substantive and Reflexive Elements in Modern Law' (1983) 17(2) *Law and Society Review* 239, 255.

[76] See C Hill, 'Marshalling Reputation to Minimize Problematic Business Conduct' (2019) 99 *Boston University Law Review* 1193, 1208–1211 noting that the mere fact that companies go to significant effort to engage in greenwashing suggests that they are concerned with public perceptions.

in sectors that are sensitive to sustainability issues.[77] The potential for such a response becomes even more likely if sustainability reports begin to be regarded as a source of reliable information due to their external verification by auditors, and if presented in an understandable way in an easily accessible online format, a system which is provided at the EU level through BRIS.

Despite the potential of reporting of sustainability related information, legal frameworks to date have failed to introduce rules sufficiently strong to create reliability and have reflexive effects. An early example of sustainability reporting was the UK's Operating and Financial Review (OFR)[78] which was to function as part of the Enlightened Shareholder Value Framework[79] which provides for company directors to have regard to a wide range of stakeholder interests, such as employees, the community and the environment. The OFR was to include information about: (a) the company's impact on the environment; (b) the company's employees; and (c) about social and community issues,[80] and was to be audited and prepared in accordance with a reporting standard created by the Accounting Standards Board.[81] However, the OFR was withdrawn[82] and replaced by a much less demanding 'Business Review'[83] with no alignment with a reporting standard.[84] Reporting requirements in the UK have since been amended and expanded,[85] but in Johnstone's view, the more recent requirements have not resulted in high quality reporting.[86]

In 2001, the European Commission began exploring reporting obligations beyond financial information in a Green Paper on corporate social responsibility (CSR).[87] The Paper noted that many multinational companies were

[77] See R Breijer and R Orij, 'The Comparability of Non-Financial Information: An Exploration of the Impact of the Non-Financial Reporting Directive' (2022) 19(2) *Accounting in Europe* 332.

[78] UK Companies Act 1985 (Operating and Financial Review and Directors Report etc) Regulations 2005, SI 2005/1011.

[79] UK Companies Act 2006, s 172(1). See A Keay, *The Enlightened Shareholder Value Principle and Corporate Governance* (Routledge, 2012).

[80] Companies Act 1985 (Operating and Financial Review and Directors Report etc) Regulations 2005, SI 2005/1011, Part 3.

[81] ibid.

[82] See A Johnston, 'After the OFR: Will UK Shareholder Value Still Be Enlightened?' (2006) 7 (4) *European Business Organization Law Review* 817.

[83] Introduced by the Companies Act 2006, s 417.

[84] Davies has described the Business Review as providing scope to companies to produce a 'self-serving and vacuous narrative rather than analytical material which is of genuine use'. Paul Davies, *Gower and Davies Principles of Modern Company Law*, 8th edn (Sweet and Maxwell, 2008) 740.

[85] The most notable development is through the Modern Slavery Act 2015, s 54 which requires companies to produce an annual 'slavery and human trafficking statement' setting out 'the steps the organisation has taken during the financial year to ensure that slavery and human trafficking is not taking place'.

[86] See A Johnston, 'Market-Led Sustainability through Information Disclosure' in B Sjåfjell and C Bruner (eds), *The Cambridge Handbook of Corporate Law, Corporate Governance and Sustainability* (Cambridge, Cambridge University Press, 2020).

[87] European Commission, *Green Paper – Promoting a European Framework for Corporate Social Responsibility* (2001) available at https://eur-lex.europa.eu/legal-content/EN/TXT/?uri=celex%3A52001DC0366.

producing 'social responsibility' reports but that the content of such reports varied widely between companies. The Commission believed that to be useful the content and format of such reporting must be standardised and that there needed to be a reliable auditing procedure.[88] This Green paper was followed by a Commission Communication[89] which again emphasised the value of reporting social and environmental information.[90] In 2011, a European Commission Communication[91] acknowledged the importance of sustainable development, the need to protect the environment and fight climate change and recommended the development of a legislative proposal on the disclosure of social and environmental information by companies.[92] Later in 2011, the Commission released another communication on CSR[93] which was defined as 'the responsibility of enterprises for their impacts on society' including on human rights, employees, environmental issues and corruption.[94] The Commission regarded the disclosure of 'non-financial' information as important because of its capacity to cut across these different fields, help identify material risks and increase accountability.[95] These Communications led to the Commission's proposed Directive on the disclosure of non-financial and diversity information in 2013,[96] which ultimately became the NFRD, enacted in 2014.[97]

The NFRD was based on a view that the disclosure of non-financial information was vital for 'managing change towards a sustainable global economy' by helping the measurement, monitoring and management of the impact of business on society.[98] The NFRD applied to 'large' companies[99] or parent companies of a large corporate group with an average number of 500 employees during the

[88] ibid [66].

[89] Communication from the Commission concerning Corporate Social Responsibility: A business contribution to Sustainable Development (2002) COM/2002/0347 final, available at https://eur-lex.europa.eu/legal-content/EN/TXT/?uri=celex%3A52002DC0347.

[90] ibid [5.3].

[91] Communication from the Commission to the European Parliament, the Council, the Economic and Social Committee and the Committee of the Regions – 'Single Market Act Twelve levers to boost growth and strengthen confidence "Working together to create new growth"' (2011) COM/2011/206 final, available at https://eur-lex.europa.eu/legal-content/EN/ALL/?uri=CELEX%3A52011DC0206.

[92] ibid 5.

[93] Communication from the Commission to the European Parliament, the Council, the European Economic and Social Committee and the Committee of the Regions – 'A Renewed EU Strategy 2011–14 for Corporate Social Responsibility'(2011) COM/2011/0681 final, available at https://eur-lex.europa.eu/legal-content/EN/TXT/?uri=celex%3A52011DC0681.

[94] ibid [3].

[95] ibid [4.5].

[96] Proposal for a Directive of the European Parliament and of the Council amending Council Directives 78/660/EEC and 83/349/EEC as regards disclosure of non-financial and diversity information by certain large companies and groups (2013) COM/2013/0207 final, available at https://eur-lex.europa.eu/legal-content/EN/ALL/?uri=CELEX%3A52013PC0207.

[97] Directive 2014/95/EU (n 17) amending Directive 2013/34/EU.

[98] ibid Recital 3.

[99] Defined by art 3(4) of Directive 2013/34/EU as meeting two of three following criteria: (a) balance sheet total: EUR 20 000 000; (b) net turnover: EUR 40 000 000; (c) average number of employees during the financial year: with over 250 employees.

financial year.[100] These companies were to report, to the extent necessary for an understanding of its development, performance, position and impact, information relating to environmental, social and employee matters, respect for human rights and anti-corruption matters.[101] In producing the information, the company was to provide: (a) a brief description of the undertaking's business model; (b) a description of the policies pursued by the undertaking on the listed matters; (c) the outcome of those policies; (d) the principal risks related to the listed matters and how the undertaking manages those risks; and (e) non-financial key performance indicators relevant to the particular business.[102] Recital 7 provided further detail regarding what the EU believed should be reported. In relation to the environment, recital 7 provided that companies should include details of the current and foreseeable impact on the environment as well as information on health and safety, the use of renewable and/or non-renewable energy, greenhouse gas emissions, water use and air pollution. In relation to social and employee-related matters, recital 7 stated that the disclosures should include details on the actions taken to ensure gender equality, suitable working conditions, as well as the implementation of international labour-related conventions on the protection of employees. The recital also stated that the non-financial statement could include information on the prevention of human rights abuses and instruments in place to fight corruption and bribery.

The NFRD followed a 'comply or explain model'[103] such that if the undertaking did not pursue policies in relation to the listed matters, it was to provide 'a clear and reasoned explanation for not doing so'.[104] Similarly, the details provided for by recital 7 were recommendations only and the NFRD did not have any auditing requirement and did not include any standard for what information was to included or how it was to be presented. The Commission did publish non-mandatory guidelines in 2017[105] which set out a general expectation that companies should identify the material information to be disclosed in a fair, balanced and comprehensive manner.[106] The guidelines relied on the definition of 'material' set out in the Accounting Directive as 'the status of information where its omission or misstatement could reasonably be expected to influence decisions that users make on the basis of the financial statements'[107] but stated that the NFRD widened that definition to include information 'necessary for an

[100] ibid art 1.

[101] ibid.

[102] ibid.

[103] For analysis of comply or explain regulation see A Keay, 'Comply or Explain in Corporate Governance Codes: In Need of Greater Regulatory Oversight?' (2014) 34(2) *Legal Studies* 279.

[104] ibid.

[105] Communication from the Commission – 'Guidelines on non-financial reporting (methodology for reporting non-financial information)' [2017] OJ C 215/1, available at https://eur-lex.europa.eu/legal-content/EN/TXT/?uri=CELEX:52017XC0705(01).

[106] ibid [4].

[107] Directive 2013/34/EU (n 3), art 2(16).

understanding of the impact of [the company's] activity'.[108] Hence, the guidelines took a 'double materiality' approach to non-financial reporting based on the combined definition from the Accounting Directive and the NFRD.[109] The guidelines did provide a detailed outline of what information should be included under the various NFRD headings such as business model, policies, principal risks[110] and for the various subject matters such as the environment and respect for human rights[111] and included more context specific examples of the type of information companies should disclose.[112] However, the guidelines remained non-binding and companies could simply ignore them when preparing their reports.

The NFRD was a landmark piece of legislation as the first European Company Law Directive to extend beyond economic objectives and implement rules aiming to reduce the negative impact of companies on society. However, its potential impact was undermined by its comply or explain model, the lack of any auditing procedure and the non-binding nature of the guidelines.[113] At the time, Szábo and Sorensen argued that the NFRD without 'detailed rules and standards on the collection and processing of the information, is not likely to have a significant effect'.[114] Their analysis has been borne out and a 2021 Commission report on the NFRD[115] showed that many companies were failing to disclose material information while simultaneously reporting significant amounts of immaterial information making it harder for users to find the information sought.[116] The report also noted a lack of consistency in both the content and presentation of information[117] and that there was little evidence that the Commission's guidelines had addressed these issues given their voluntary nature.[118] The report included responses from an open consultation in which 73 per cent of respondents believed the reliability of the reports was a significant problem while 82 per cent of respondents believed that requiring companies to use common reporting standards would resolve the main problems with the NFRD.[119] The ultimate conclusion of the report was that the NFRD was not 'fit for purpose'.[120]

[108] Commission Guidelines on Non-Financial Reporting (n 105) [3.1].

[109] See F Mezzanotte, 'Corporate Sustainability Reporting: Double Materiality, Impacts, and Legal Risk' (2023) 23(2) *Journal of Corporate Law Studies* 633.

[110] ibid [4.1]–[4.5].

[111] ibid [4.6].

[112] For example, the guidelines provide that 'A bank may consider that its own water consumption in offices and branches is not a material issue' but 'the bank may assess that the social and environmental impacts of projects that it funds and its role in supporting the real economy of a city, a region or a country are material information' ibid [3.1].

[113] See J Quinn and B Connolly, 'The Non-Financial Information Directive: An Assessment of its Impact on Corporate Social Responsibility' (2017) 14(1) *European Company Law* 15.

[114] Szabó and Sorensen, 'New EU Directive on the Disclosure of Non-Financial Information' (n 22) 340.

[115] European Commission, Report on the review clauses in Directives (n 23).

[116] ibid 17.

[117] ibid.

[118] ibid 20.

[119] ibid 18.

[120] ibid 19.

Christopher Bruner has recently argued that disclosure-based rules are unlikely to result in companies becoming more sustainable or reducing their negative externalities.[121] He bases this argument on the fact that disclosures do not alter the incentives of shareholders, are often limited by the definition of materiality that determines what is to be disclosed and that inconsistent disclosure standards lead to greenwashing, generalisations and boilerplate reports.[122] To support this argument, Bruner highlights examples of 'weak and ineffective'[123] reporting regimes in operation in the US.[124] However, such criticisms, while wholly valid in the context of the UK, US and the NFRD, do not undermine a more general argument that sufficiently strong reporting rules, that have the potential to affect internal decision makers and the company's reputation, can move companies toward becoming more responsible and doing less harm.

IV. MANDATORY SUSTAINABILITY REPORTING IN EUROPEAN COMPANY LAW

Given the limitations of the NFRD and the commitments made in the European Green Deal on corporate transparency,[125] new rules on corporate transparency became a priority for the EU. The first reforms were introduced in 2019 by the Sustainable Finance Disclosure Regulation (SFDR).[126] The SFDR aimed to harness private funding to help Europe shift to a net-zero economy by increasing transparency on the sustainability of financial products[127] to allow ESG orientated investors to select companies and projects which support sustainability related activities.[128] The SFDR applies to 'financial market participants' which includes credit institutions, investment firms providing portfolio management and financial advisers.[129] These market participants must disclose their policies on 'sustainability risks' defined as 'an environmental, social or governance event or condition that, if it occurs, could cause a negative material impact on the

[121] See C Bruner, 'Corporate Governance Reform and the Sustainability Imperative' (2022) 131(4) *The Yale Law Journal* 1062.

[122] ibid 1253–54.

[123] ibid 1255.

[124] Eg, US Securities and Exchange Commission (SEC) rules on 'human capital reporting'. For analysis see G Georgiev, 'The Human Capital Management Movement in US Corporate Law' (2021) 95 *Tulane Law Review* 639 and J Artigues, 'Who Wins? Analyzing Global ESG Reporting through the EU's Corporate Sustainability Reporting Directive and the Evolving US Scheme' (2024) 32(1) *Tulane Journal of International and Comparative Law* 143.

[125] Commission Communication on the European Green Deal (2019) (n 25) fn.

[126] Regulation (EU) 2019/2088 (n 27). For analysis see E Partiti, 'Addressing the Flaws of the Sustainable Finance Disclosure Regulation: Moving from Disclosures to Labelling and Sustainability Due Diligence' (2024) 25 *European Business Organization Law Review* 299.

[127] Defined as managed portfolios, alternative investment funds, undertakings for collective investment in transferable securities, insurance-based investment products, or pension products.

[128] Regulation (EU) 2019/2088 (n 27), recital 9.

[129] ibid art 1.

value of the investment'.[130] In 2022, the European Commission enacted a delegated Regulation on regulatory technical standards which specifies the details of the content, methodologies, and presentation of disclosures.[131]

The next development was the Taxonomy Regulation[132] introduced in 2020 which creates a classification system for 'environmentally sustainable' economic activities. The Taxonomy Regulation applies to certain high impact sectors[133] and is based around six objectives: (1) climate change mitigation; (2) climate change adaptation; (3) the sustainable use and protection of water and marine resources; (4) the transition to a circular economy; (5) pollution prevention and control; and (6) the protection and restoration of biodiversity and ecosystems.[134] To qualify as 'environmentally sustainable' an economic activity must: substantially contribute to one or more of these objectives while doing no significant harm to the other objectives. The rules are mandatory and financial market participants must disclose how much of their activities are aligned with the Taxonomy Regulation.

The next development, and the one with the most far-reaching potential effects, was the CSRD which was originally proposed in 2021,[135] was enacted in 2022,[136] and entered into effect in January 2024. The CSRD amends the NFRD and follows a similar format by requiring certain companies to disclose information related to their impacts on environmental and human rights issues. The CSRD replaces the term 'non-financial information' used in the NFRD with 'sustainability information' in recognition of the fact that sustainability information can be financially material, through, for example, environmental risks that could create financial liabilities.[137] The CSRD's aim is to make public information that is of interest not just to investors but to citizens, trade unions, customers, civil society actors and environmental agencies.[138] This aim was based on a belief that high quality sustainability reporting could improve companies reputation, access to capital, help companies identify and manage their own sustainability risks and provide a formal basis for dialogue with stakeholders.[139]

[130] ibid art 3.

[131] Commission Delegated Regulation (EU) 2022/1288 of 6 April 2022 supplementing Regulation (EU) 2019/2088 of the European Parliament and of the Council with regard to regulatory technical standards specifying the details of the content and presentation of the information in relation to the principle of 'do no significant harm', specifying the content, methodologies and presentation of information in relation to sustainability indicators and adverse sustainability impacts, and the content and presentation of the information in relation to the promotion of environmental or social characteristics and sustainable investment objectives in pre-contractual documents, on websites and in periodic reports [2022] OJ L 196/1.

[132] Regulation (EU) 2020/852 (n 28).

[133] ibid art 9 including energy agriculture, transport, manufacturing.

[134] ibid, art 9. Articles 10–15 provide greater depth on these objectives.

[135] Proposal for a Corporate Sustainability Reporting Directive (CSRD) available at https://eur-lex.europa.eu/legal-content/EN/TXT/?uri=CELEX:52021PC0189.

[136] Directive (EU) 2022/2464 (n 29).

[137] ibid recital 8.

[138] ibid recital 9.

[139] ibid recital 12.

The scope of the CSRD expands over time in three waves. For the financial year 2024, it applies to the same companies as the NFRD, namely large[140] companies and parents of large groups[141] with an average number of over 500 employees during the year (wave 1).[142] For the financial year 2025, the CSRD applies to large companies and parent companies with an average number of over 250 employees during the year (wave 2).[143] For the financial year 2026, the CSRD expands to include small[144] and medium-sized undertakings[145] with securities listed on an EU regulated market (wave 3).[146] From 2028, the Directive will apply to companies registered outside the EU who generate more than €150 million in net income per year inside the EU and that has at least one subsidiary company that exceeds income of €40 million or a subsidiary that qualifies as a large, medium or a small company listed on an EU regulated Market.[147] This expansion in scope will result in an increase in reporting from approximately 11,700 companies under the NFRD to approximately 50,000 companies.[148]

The information required by the CSRD includes:

- a description of the company's business model and strategy, particularly for sustainability matters including plans to ensure they are compatible with the transition to a sustainable economy and are in line with the targets set by the Paris Agreement;[149]
- a description of time-bound sustainability-related targets, including potential greenhouse gas emission reductions, a description of progress made to achieve these targets, and specification of whether the targets are based on scientific evidence;[150]

[140] Defined by art 3(4) of Directive 2013/34/EU (n 3) as meeting two of three following criteria: (a) balance sheet total: EUR 20,000,000; (b) net turnover: EUR 40,000,000; (c) average number of employees during the financial year: with over 250 employees.

[141] Defined by art 3(7) of Directive 2013/34/EU (n 3) as meeting, on a consolidated basis, two of the three following criteria: (a) balance sheet total: €20,000,000; (b) net turnover: €40,000,000; (c) average number of employees during the financial year: 250.

[142] Directive (EU) 2022/2464 (n 29) art 5(2)(a).

[143] ibid art 5(2)(b).

[144] Defined by art 3(2) of Directive 2013/34/EU (n 3) as undertakings which meet two of the following criteria: (a) balance sheet total: EUR 4,000,000; (b) net turnover: €8,000,000; (c) average number of employees during the financial year: 50.

[145] Defined by Article 3(3) of Directive 2013/34/EU (n 3) as undertakings which meet two of the three following criteria: (a) balance sheet total: EUR 20,000,000; (b) net turnover: €40,000,000; (c) average number of employees during the financial year: 250.

[146] Directive (EU) 2022/2464 (n 29), art 5(2)(c). But not to 'micro undertakings' defined by Article 3(4) of Directive 2013/34/EU as undertakings which meet two of the three following criteria: (a) balance sheet total: €350,000; (b) net turnover: €700,000; (c) average number of employees during the financial year: 10.

[147] ibid recital 20.

[148] See K Hummel and D Jobst, 'An Overview of Corporate Sustainability Reporting Legislation in the European Union' (2024) *Accounting in Europe* 1, 15.

[149] Directive (EU) 2022/2464 amending Directive 2013/34/EU, art 29(2)(a).

[150] ibid art 29a(1), (2)(b).

- a description of the role of administrative, management, and supervisory bodies in sustainability matters and their expertise and skills to fulfil this role;[151]
- a description of the company's sustainability-related policies and how their strategy takes account of stakeholders;[152]
- a description of the due diligence processes,[153] the principal actual or potential adverse impacts in the company's own operations and 'value chain', actions taken to identify and track these impacts, and actions to mitigate these adverse impacts;[154]
- a description of sustainability-related risks and how these risks are managed;[155]

The CSRD further provides that reports include information regarding environmental factors such as: climate change mitigation;[156] resource use and the circular economy; pollution; and biodiversity.[157] In regard to human rights factors, the CSRD states the reports should specify the information to be disclosed regarding equal treatment and opportunities, including gender equality and equal pay for work of equal value, training and skills development, the employment and inclusion of people with disabilities and measures against violence and harassment in the workplace.[158] However, most detail is provided by an accompanying standard to which the CSRD delegates the details of what must be reported.[159]

To overcome the difficulties of the NFRD and its non-binding standards, the Commission tasked the European Financial Reporting Advisory Group (EFRAG) with developing a set of reporting standards that would set out in detail what was required to be reported under the above headings.[160] In response, EFRAG developed the European Sustainability Reporting Standards (ESRS) which are now the standards to which reports under the CSRD must comply.[161] The ESRS are divided across 12 sections, starting with ESRS 1 and 2 which set out general, cross cutting reporting requirements followed by 10 specific standards on

[151] ibid art 29a(2)(a), (c).
[152] ibid art 29a(1), (4).
[153] ibid recital 31, due diligence being defined as the process that undertakings carry out to identify, monitor, prevent, mitigate, remediate or bring an end to the principal actual and potential adverse impacts connected with their activities and the activities of their value chain.
[154] ibid art 29b(1), (2)(f), (4).
[155] ibid art 29b(1), (5)(g).
[156] ibid including as regards scope 1, scope 2 and, where relevant, scope 3 greenhouse gas emissions.
[157] ibid art 29b(2)(a).
[158] ibid art 29b(2)(b).
[159] Directive (EU) 2022/2464 (n 29), recital 39.
[160] Remarks by Executive Vice-President Dombrovskis at the conference on implementing the European Green Deal (2020) available at https://ec.europa.eu/commission/presscorner/detail/en/SPEECH_20_139.
[161] European Commission Delegated Regulation (EU) supplementing Directive 2013/34/EU and including European Sustainability Reporting Standards (ESRS) C/2023/5303 final, available at https://eur-lex.europa.eu/legal-content/EN/ALL/?uri=PI_COM:C(2023)5303.

environmental, social and governance matters: E1 Climate change; E2 Pollution; E3 Water and marine resources; E4 Biodiversity and ecosystems; E5 Resource use and circular economy; S1 Own workforce; S2 Workers in the value chain; S3 Affected communities; S4 Consumers and end-users; G1 Business conduct.[162] Under each of the headings, the ESRS provides a detailed account of what companies must report, subject to a double materiality test based on financial materiality and impact materiality.[163] A sustainability matter is material from a financial perspective if it triggers or could reasonably be expected to trigger material financial effects on the undertaking ie where the matter generates risks or opportunities that have a material influence, or could reasonably be expected to have a material influence, on the company's development, financial position or performance, cash flows, access to finance or cost of capital over the short-, medium- or long-term.[164] A sustainability matter is material from an impact perspective when it pertains to the company's material, actual or potential, positive or negative impacts on people or the environment over the short, medium- or long-term including from it upstream and downstream value chain, through its products and services, as well as through its business relationships that are not limited to direct contractual relationships.[165] It is this 'double materiality' standard that is the core metric for companies to determine what information should be disclosed and once a 'matter' meets the test, it is mandatory to disclose it.[166]

The CSRD requires the reports to be audited to ensure its compliance with the ESRS.[167] The standard of auditing is divided into 'limited assurance' which means that the auditor declares no matter has been identified to suggest that the object of the audit is materially misstated and 'reasonable assurance' which involves substantive procedures and tests, after which the auditor expresses a positive opinion on the company's declarations.[168] From 2024, reports are required to receive 'limited assurance'[169] with the verification extending to 'reasonable assurance' after 2028.[170] The opinion of the auditor must be published alongside the report and the qualifications of statutory auditors have been amended to ensure that auditors on sustainability matters have received specialised training and can perform their duties in an independent and professional way.[171]

[162] ibid s 3.

[163] See Directive (EU) 2022/2464 (n 29), recital 29.

[164] ESRS (n 161), s 3.5.

[165] ibid s 3.4.

[166] For a comprehensive analysis for what is likely to meet the double materiality see F Mezzanotte, 'Corporate Sustainability Reporting (n 109) and F Mezzanotte, 'Examining the Reasons for Impact Materiality in EU Corporate Sustainability Reporting' (2024) 35(7) *European Business Law Review* 925.

[167] Directive (EU) 2022/2464 (n 29), art 3(2).

[168] ibid recital 60.

[169] Which can be provided for by a statutory auditor or another accredited sustainability assurance provider.

[170] Directive (EU) 2022/2464 (n 29), art 26A.

[171] In imposing this requirement, the CSRD amends several Directives including Directive 2001/34/EC of the European Parliament and of the Council of 28 May 2001 on the admission of securities

In terms of enforcement, the CSRD legislative proposal included an amendment to Article 51 of the Accounting Directive under which Member States would be obliged to introduce effective, proportionate and dissuasive penalties, including specific measures for cases of non-compliance, such as a public statement on the person responsible for the disclosures and a cease and desist order.[172] However, this was not included in the final CSRD which makes no reference to enforcement or penalties. Enforcement of the CSRD now falls under the general EU enforcement provisions regarding annual financial statements and disclosure obligations.[173] For example, article 51 of the Accounting Directive, into which the CSRD is integrated, provides for the introduction of penalties at the national level that are 'effective, proportionate and dissuasive'.

This section presents only a very brief description of the requirements and detail contained in the SFDR, the Taxonomy Regulation, the CSRD and ESRS. The point it has aimed to demonstrate is that these rules place the disclosure of sustainability information in the EU within a similar framework to financial disclosure, where reporting is mandatory, standardised and independently verified. By doing so, the rules increase the reliability of information and its potential to create a reflexive response within companies.

A. The Proposed Omnibus Amendments

As part of the omnibus proposal, the European Commission has proposed several changes to the CSRD. Perhaps the most striking proposed change is to the thresholds of application, the Omnibus proposing to reduce the number of companies subject to the CSRD by around 80 per cent.[174] It proposes to do this by raising the thresholds of application to large undertakings with more than 1000 employees with a turnover above €50 million or a balance sheet above €25 million. This would remove some companies from the first and second wave and all small and medium sized listed companies from the third wave. The Omnibus also proposes a two-year delay for the entry of the CSRD's second and third wave. In addition, the Omnibus aims to revise the ESRS by bringing forward a new delegated Act which will reduce the number of mandatory datapoints, removing those deemed 'least important', prioritising quantitative datapoints over narrative text and further distinguishing between mandatory

to official stock exchange listing and on information to be published on those securities [2001] OJ L 184/1 (the Transparency Directive).

[172] CSRD proposal (n 135) 54.

[173] See T Pantazi, 'The Introduction of Mandatory Corporate Sustainability Reporting in the EU and the Question of Enforcement' (2024) 13(1) *European Business Organization Law Review* 510, 520–22 highlighting how the CSRD is integrated into other EU Directives that have enforcement provisions.

[174] Omnibus I (n 30) 4.

and voluntary datapoints.[175] The Omnibus also includes a proposal to remove the shift in the auditing requirement from a standard of limited assurance to reasonable assurance. The Omnibus does not propose amending the double materiality standard but it does state that clearer instructions will be provided on how to apply the materiality principle.

The ultimate aim of the Omnibus is to simplify the EU's corporate sustainability framework. This aim is understandable as the CSRD is a particularly complex piece of legislation which is integrated into both the NFRD and accounting legislative frameworks. The result is that the requirements, definitions and standards are split across many long and complex documents. At a very basic level, the CSRD could have been made considerably simpler if its requirements were set out in a new Directive, not based on the NFRD, with fewer cross references and amendments. At a broader level, the overall corporate sustainability framework could have been simplified if the reporting and due diligence rules were integrated into a single and complimentary framework. However, despite the aim of simplification being understandable, it is difficult to escape an impression that the Omnibus has created further uncertainty. The CSRD is already in effect for companies subject to wave 1, and many companies that were preparing for waves 2 and 3 were doing so on the basis of the ESRS standards. These companies are now left in limbo, unsure if the changes proposed by the Omnibus will be rejected, introduced or be further amended through the legislative process involving the European Council and Parliament.

V. CONCLUSION

The importance of financial disclosures in providing economic reliability has long been recognised by company law. Many attempts to introduce rules on corporate reporting that go beyond financial disclosures have lacked the strength necessary to provoke the type of reflexive response outlined in this chapter. For corporate reporting rules to have such an impact and provide reliability they must be subject to similar requirements to that of financial disclosures ie they must be mandatory, detailed, standardised and independently verified. The CSRD has these components and provides an example for what such a corporate reporting framework could look like.

[175] ibid 5.

5

Corporate Sustainability Due Diligence

I. INTRODUCTION

THE MOST SIGNIFICANT of the European Union's (EU) corporate sustainability reforms is the Corporate Sustainability Due Diligence Directive (CSDDD).[1] The modern globalised economy has seen businesses expand transnationally and fragment their operations into groups of companies[2] or supply chains that operate through contractual governance and codes of conduct.[3] This feature of globalisation[4] has created difficulties for legal systems as these business structures often operate outside of traditional legal frameworks of responsibility thereby encouraging the externalisation of costs leading to many human rights abuses and environmental harms. This reality is partly due to the company's legal personality whereby each company represents a separate boundary of liability that is 'individually' responsible for its conduct. This legal position does not change merely because the company forms part of a wider organisation and where harm is caused by the activities of one company within a group or chain, the default legal assumption is that liability lies with that company only.[5] For example, a 'lead firm' in a supply

[1] Directive (EU) 2024/1760 of the European Parliament and of the Council of 13 June 2024 on corporate sustainability due diligence and amending Directive (EU) 2019/1937 and Regulation (EU) 2023/2859 [2024] OJ L, 2024/1760. See M Bodie, 'Shareholders All the Way Down: EU Corporate Sustainability Reforms and the Structure of Corporate Governance' (2024) 52 *Georgia Journal of International and Comparative Law* 559, 566 describing the CSDDD as the most dramatic regulatory reform to date. See also L Enriques, M Gatti, R Shapira, 'How the EU's Sustainability Due Diligence Directive Could Reshape Corporate America' (2025) *European Corporate Governance Institute Working Paper* available at www.ecgi.global/publications/working-papers/how-the-eus-sustainability-due-diligence-directive-could-reshape.

[2] The defining characteristic of a corporate group is typically common ownership of shares, often where one parent owns shares in multiple subsidiaries. See J Dine, *The Governance of Corporate Groups* (Oxford, Oxford University Press, 2000) 40.

[3] See A Beckers, *Enforcing Corporate Social Responsibility Codes on Global Self-Regulation and National Private Law* (Oxford, Hart Publishing, 2018).

[4] While exacerbated by modern globalisation, the fundamental problem of multiple company organisations being used as vehicles to avoid liability and externalise costs is not new and many arguments for law reform have been advanced including 'enterprise liability' and unlimited liability for corporate torts. See A Berle, 'The Theory of Enterprise Entity' (1947) 47(3) *Columbia Law Review* 343 and H Hansmann and R Kraakman, 'Toward Unlimited Shareholder Liability for Corporate Torts' (1991) 100(7) *The Yale Law Journal* 1879.

[5] Transferring liabilities between companies is possible but only in very narrow circumstances that are not typically present in fragmented business structures. This point will be developed below.

chain may create the general conditions for human rights abuses or environmental harms to occur but where a company further down the chain is the direct cause of the harm there is no obvious legal avenue for a victim to transfer that company's liability up the chain and attribute it to the lead firm. Hence, an 'accountability gap'[6] emerges and the victim is left without recourse as the company directly responsible may be insolvent, poorly capitalised or located in a jurisdiction with comparatively low legal protections for employees, human rights or the environment.

To close this accountability gap, European states and the EU have looked to due diligence laws derived from the United Nations Guiding Principles on Business and Human Rights (UNGPs).[7] The UNGPs provide that to meet their responsibility to respect human rights[8] 'business enterprises' should identify, prevent, mitigate and account for how they address their impacts on human rights.[9] After several Member States introduced due diligence laws,[10] the European Commission published its proposed CSDDD[11] which was based on the UNGPs[12] and aimed to limit the environmental harms and human rights abuses caused by the operations of corporate groups and transnational supply chains.[13] However, the Commission's proposal did not attempt to create a new legal category of 'business enterprise' but rather the CSDDD was to be applied to individual companies that met financial and employee thresholds who could then be made civilly liable for a failure to conduct due diligence across their subsidiaries and supply chain. The finalisation of the CSDDD proved to be politically fraught with objections being raised in the European Council.[14] However, a final Directive was agreed and entered into force in July 2024.[15] The final CSDDD was weaker than the Commission's original proposal, increasing the thresholds of application, introducing a more complex model of civil liability[16] and excluding the activities of indirect, downstream business partners.[17] The CSDDD is now subject to further proposals to remove the model of civil liability and restrict

[6] See generally C Witting, *Liability of Corporate Groups and Networks* (Oxford, Oxford University Press, 2018).

[7] OHCHR, 'Guiding Principles on Business and Human Rights' (2011), available at www.ohchr.org/Documents/Publications/GuidingPrinciplesBusinessHR_EN.pdf.

[8] ibid Principle 11.

[9] ibid Principle 15.

[10] Including France, Germany and the Netherlands.

[11] Proposal for a Directive of the European Parliament and of the Council on Corporate Sustainability Due Diligence and amending Directive (EU) 2019/1937 [2022] COM/2022/71 final (Proposed Corporate Sustainability Due Diligence Directive) available at https://eur-lex.europa.eu/legal-content/EN/TXT/?uri=CELEX%3A52022PC0071.

[12] ibid recitals 5–7.

[13] ibid, explanatory memorandum [1–10].

[14] Germany and Italy leading the objections, see www.reuters.com/markets/europe/eu-postpones-decision-proposed-supply-chain-due-diligince-law-2024-02-09/. See N Bueno et al, 'The EU Directive on Corporate Sustainability Due Diligence (CSDDD): The Final Political Compromise' (2024) *Business and Human Rights Journal* (2024) 1.

[15] Directive (EU) 2024/1760 (n 1).

[16] ibid art 29.

[17] ibid art 3(g), downstream referring to distribution, transport and storage.

its application to direct partners under the European Commission's Omnibus I Proposal.[18] However, despite its dilution, the CSDDD remains a landmark piece of legislation that imposes a detailed mandatory process on companies focused on reducing human rights abuses and environmental harms caused and enabled by the operation of transnational business organisations. As such, it offers an important example of company law legislation with reflexive elements.

Section II sets out the basic individualistic framework of company law which regards companies as separate persons and goes on to discuss the conditions which warrant deviation from this default position and how they fail to map on to fragmented realities of corporate groups and supply chains. Section III examines the development of Human Rights Due Diligence through the work of John Ruggie and the UNGPs. Section IV discusses the requirements of the CSDDD and its model of civil liability. Section V offers some analysis from a reflexive law perspective.

II. THE ACCOUNTABILITY GAP

Today, the most economically successful companies tend to be those that have broken free of territorial boundaries, and regulatory law, have a global footprint and have created their own regimes of regulatory governance. These transnational corporations come in the form of corporate groups, where a parent company owns shares in several subsidiary companies or a supply chain where a 'lead firm' coordinates multiple companies through techniques of contractual governance.[19] Yet despite these ownership and contractual links,[20] from a legal perspective, corporate groups and supply chains remain comprised of a formally distinct set of legal persons.

The company's legal personality is a recognition by the legal system that a company is a distinct individual, ie a separate subject of rights and duties[21] with a formal boundary between it and the persons (legal and natural) associated with it. As non-corporeal entities, companies must effectuate their will through others, usually directors,[22] and, in this attenuated sense, the company is 'personally' responsible for its conduct. The company's formal boundary and individual

[18] European Commission, 'Omnibus I' (2025) available at https://commission.europa.eu/publications/omnibus-i_en.

[19] See L Cáta Backer, 'Theorizing Regulatory Governance Within Its Ecology: The Structure of Management in an Age of Globalization' (2018) 24(5) *Contemporary Politics* 607.

[20] See R Gilson et al, 'Contracting for Innovation: Vertical Disintegration and Interfirm Collaboration' (2009) 109 *Columbia Law Review* 431.

[21] See J Dewey, 'The Historic Background of Corporate Legal Personality' (1926) 35(6) *Yale Law Journal* 655 or in Maitland's terminology a 'right-and-duty bearing unit'. See F Maitland, 'Moral Personality and Legal Personality' (1905) 6 *Journal of the Society of Comparative Legislation* 192.

[22] The default position in company law is that directors are automatically delegated authority to act *as* the company while shareholders retain authority over fundamental decisions such as altering the company's constitutional documents. Third parties may be expressly granted authority by an

autonomy means that, in general, the actions of one company cannot be equated with another, including subsidiaries and companies connected through contract which form a broader business organisation. The most obvious expression of this legal reality is the rule of limited liability which provides that shareholders, be they natural persons or parent companies, are not responsible for the company's general liabilities.[23] This legal position reflects the general form of private law – into which the company has been 'assimilated'[24] – whereby a person is 'not responsible for the deeds of others'.[25] This default position restricts the aggregation of rights and duties into more comprehensive wholes and doing so requires special justification. What emerges from this picture are two models of liability: (1) the default model of individual liability where an individual person is responsible for their own actions; (2) and 'organisational' liability, where an individual can be held responsible for the actions of another due to specific circumstances which justifies deviation from the default position.[26] In company law, the precise justifications that allow for such a deviation vary across jurisdictions but it can be said that such examples are confined to narrow contexts only where there is either consent, impropriety or extensive economic and organisational integration.

A company's rights or liabilities can be extended to third parties where they have agreed to be so bound, for example, where a third party provides a contractual guarantee or security for a specific company liability or debt. Another example is where two companies form a principal–agent relationship which, depending on the scope of the agreement, may allow for the principal to be liable for the actions of its agent.[27] While common law agency is based on the concept of 'authority'[28] and civil law jurisdictions use the term 'mandate'[29] they

agency agreement. See R Kraakman et al, *The Anatomy of Corporate Law: A Comparative and Functional Approach*, 3rd edn (Oxford, Oxford University Press, 2017) ch 3.

[23] They can, of course, lose their investment but are liable only to the extent of that investment. Likewise, the debts of shareholders cannot be imposed on the company. See H Hansmann and R Squire, 'External and Internal Asset Partitioning: Corporations and their Subsidiaries' in J Gordon and WG Ringe, *The Oxford Handbook of Corporate Law and Governance* (Oxford, Oxford University Press, 2018).

[24] See P Muchlinski, *Multinational Enterprises and the Law*, 3rd edn (Oxford, Oxford University Press, 2021) 303.

[25] See H Collins, 'Ascription of Legal Responsibility to Groups in Complex Patterns of Economic Integration' (1990) *MLR* 731, 731. He continues: 'The law constructs an atomistic conception of social relations, delimiting our legal responsibilities to our own acts and omissions, absolving us from blame for our brother's wrongs'.

[26] For a discussion of various models of liability in EU law see A Beckers, 'Global Value Chains in EU Law' (2023) 42 *Yearbook of European Law* 322.

[27] See S Worthington, 'Corporate Attribution and Agency: Back to Basics' (2017) 133 *LQR* 118.

[28] Which may be express, implied or ostensible based on express contractual agreement or implied from behaviour. See P Watts, *Bowstead and Reynolds on Agency*, 22nd edn (Sweet and Maxwell, 2020) [1.001–1.035].

[29] Where the agent has direct or indirect powers of representation, see I Schiau, 'A Comparative Assessment of the Agency Concept: with Special Regard to the Romanian Approach' (2021) 11(2) *Juridicial Tribune* 219.

both rest on consent as the basis for transferring liabilities between persons. In European company law, the European Economic Interest Grouping (EEIG)[30] is a composite business organisation comprised of legal persons formally registered within EU Member States. The companies which form an EEIG have unlimited joint and several liability for the Grouping's debts and liabilities[31] but again, such persons consent to this group liability when entering the contract required to form the EEIG in the first instance.[32]

Company law also provides for liabilities to be extended beyond the company's boundary in instances of impropriety, for example, when an officer's actions warrant personal liability under statute[33] or where the courts decide to 'pierce the corporate veil' and impose a company's liability on to a shareholder.[34] In *Prest v Petrodel Resources Ltd*,[35] the UK Supreme Court provided a detailed examination of 'veil piercing' at common law with Lord Sumption concluding that only two grounds – concealment or evasion – justified piercing the veil.[36] Concealment involves using a company to hide illegality[37] while evasion involves interposing a company to prevent the enforcement of a pre-existing right against the appropriate individual or, in other words, using a company to evade existing legal obligations.[38] In continental European jurisdictions, veil piercing is also a narrow doctrine to be applied in 'extreme circumstances' where shareholders engage in fraud, misrepresentation or opportunism.[39] While the law on veil piercing is notoriously complex,[40] it is certain that veil piercing depends on

[30] Directive 2013/34/EU and briefly discussed in ch 3.

[31] ibid art 24.

[32] ibid arts 1 and 2. See N De Luca, *European Company Law*, 2nd edn (Cambridge, Cambridge University Press, 2021), 54–57.

[33] These examples vary across jurisdictions but frequently include failing to uphold corporate formalities such as non-compliance with financial recording and filing requirements and harming the interests of creditors when the company is insolvent. One well known example is 'wrongful trading' under the UK Insolvency Act 1986, s 214.

[34] See G Allan, 'To Pierce or not to Pierce? A Doctrinal Reappraisal of Judicial Responses to Improper Exploitation of the Corporate Form' (2018) 7 *Journal of Business Law* 559.

[35] [2013] UKSC 34. For an excellent conceptual analysis of the judgment, and an argument against a doctrine of disregarding the company's legal personality see E Micheler, 'Separate Legal Personality – An Explanation and a Defence (2024) 24(1) *Journal of Corporate Law Studies* 301.

[36] ibid *Prest v Petrodel* (n 35) [28]. Not all judges followed this dual characterization, for example, Lady Hale stated the doctrine may include a principle of 'unconscionable advantage' at [92].

[37] Eg, *Gencor ACP v Dalby* [2000] 2 BCLC 734 involved a director who breached his fiduciary duties by profiting personally at the plaintiff company's expense and then transferring the proceeds to a foreign company which conducted no legitimate business.

[38] Eg, *Jones v Lipman* [1962] 1 All ER 442 where the defendant transferred property to a company in an attempt to circumvent an order for specific performance under a previous agreement.

[39] This description is taken from Kraakman et al, *The Anatomy of Corporate Law* (n 22) 132–34, specifically referring to German, French and Italian law. Hopt similarly states that German and French courts 'lift the corporate veil only rarely and under very strict requirements': see K Hopt, 'Groups of Companies: A Comparative Study of the Economics, Law, and Regulation of Corporate Groups' (2024) *European Corporate Governance Institute Working Paper* available at www.ecgi.global/sites/default/files/working_papers/documents/groupsofcompanies.pdf, 49–50.

[40] For an attempt to clarify the US position see J Macey and J Mitts, 'Finding Order in the Morass: The Three Real Justifications for Piercing the Corporate Veil' (2014) 99 *Cornell Law Review* 100.

some form of impropriety or illegality[41] and does not apply where companies are merely part of a group, have contractual links with other companies, or even where companies are intentionally used as a shield from future, potential liability.[42]

Another basis for transferring rights and liabilities between companies is organisational in nature where formally separate companies are merged into a single 'enterprise' or 'economic entity'. The justification for applying the 'enterprise entity' doctrine is that the formal legal assumptions of corporate personality do not reflect the factual and economic realities, and to ignore those realities would result in injustice. The need for such a doctrine is most clearly articulated by Berle[43] who claimed a variety of problems in company law were caused by the 'divergence' between a company's distinct legal personality 'and the underlying economic facts'[44] and presented an argument for a reconceptualisation of the company as an 'enterprise bounded by economics'.[45] The doctrine was applied in a series of UK cases between 1950 and 1970,[46] the leading case being *DHN Food Distributors Ltd v Tower Hamlet London Borough Council*[47] which involved an application from a parent company seeking permission to initiate proceedings for a wrong committed against its two subsidiary companies. Lord Denning stated that the three companies 'should not be treated separately so as to be defeated on a technical point',[48] that the court 'is entitled to look at the realities of the situation'[49] and that the 'three companies should, for present purposes, be treated as one'.[50] The doctrine was also applied in an Irish case, where a non-compete clause entered into by a parent company was enforced against its subsidiary due to the economic connection between them and to avoid injustice on the contracting party.[51] Costello J stated 'a court may, if the justice of the case so requires, treat two or more related companies as a single entity so that the business notionally carried on by one will be regarded

[41] See A Dignam and P Oh, 'Rationalising Corporate Disregard' (2020) 40 *Legal Studies* 187, 189 stating that all judges in *Prest v Petrodel* (n 35) unanimously concluded that a company's legal personality could not be disregarded in the absence of impropriety.

[42] This was expressly stated in *Adams v Cape Industries plc* [1990] Ch 433, 544 where the English Court of Appeal held there was nothing illegal or improper in using a corporate group structure to ensure that future liabilities fell on one member of that group. This is no surprise given the fundamental rationale for the company is to reduce future risk. See R Posner, *Economic Analysis of Law*, 8th edn (Wolters Kluwer, 2011) 14–16.

[43] Berle, 'The Theory of Enterprise Entity' (n 4).

[44] ibid 344.

[45] ibid 345.

[46] See, *Scottish Cooperative Wholesale Society v Meye* [1962] 2 QB; *Wallersteiner v Moir* [1974] 1 WLR 991; *Littlewoods Mail Ltd v Inland Revenue Commissioners* [1969] 1 WLR 1241, CA (Civ Div) 324.

[47] [1976] 1 WLR 852.

[48] ibid 860.

[49] ibid 861.

[50] ibid 860.

[51] *Power Supermarkets Ltd v Crumlin Investments Ltd and Dunnes Stores (Crumlin) Ltd* (22 June 1981, unreported), HC.

as the business of the group or another member of the group if this conforms to the economic and commercial realities of the situation'.[52] However, in recent years the UK and Irish courts have rowed back on the enterprise entity doctrine. For example, in *Ord v Belhaven Pubs Ltd*,[53] the UK Court of Appeal held that in the absence of impropriety, there were no grounds to ignore the separateness of companies.[54] Since that case, English courts have repeatedly reiterated that economic reality will not take precedence over legal form and the separateness of legal persons will continue to be upheld.[55]

The single enterprise doctrine continues to be applied in the US,[56] with several state courts citing Berle's article.[57] For example, *Gartner v Snyder*[58] involved a real estate developer who owned shares and controlled three companies working a single housing project that failed to uphold separate corporate formalities.[59] Based on the high degree of integration, the Second Circuit in New York treated the three companies as one enterprise that was responsible for the liabilities of one of the companies. Many US states also apply a substantively similar 'alter ego' doctrine.[60] The specific elements of this doctrine differs across jurisdictions but, in general, there is a requirement of control to such a degree that there is no operational distinction between a parent and subsidiary.[61] In Germany,

[52] Eg, see *Adams v Cape Industries plc* [1990] Ch 433 discussed below. For an Irish example see *Allied Irish Coal Ltd v Powell Duffryn Ltd* [1998] 2 IR 519.

[53] [1998] 2 BCLC 447.

[54] The judgment directly overruled *Creasy v Breachwood* [1993] BCLC 480 which had involved an action for wrongful dismissal against a company. The company was subsequently taken over and the takeover company had assumed all liabilities except for the wrongful dismissal claim. The court allowed the plaintiff to transfer liability between companies 'so as to achieve justice' ibid 494.

[55] Eg, in *Linsen International Ltd v Humpuss Sea Transport Pte Ltd* [2011] EWHC 2339 the High Court held that 'it is not enough to show that a company or a group of companies is closely controlled by an individual or a family or by a holding company. If the element of control were sufficient in itself, the English courts would have accepted the concept of the "single economic unit"' at [19]. Indeed, the doctrine was never widely applied in English law. Robert Goff LJ stated in *Bank of Tokyo Ltd v Karoon* [1987] AC 45 at 64 that 'Counsel suggested beguilingly that it would be technical for us to distinguish between parent and subsidiary company in this context; economically, he said, they were one. But we are concerned not with economics but with law. The distinction between the two is, in law, fundamental and cannot here be bridged.'

[56] See S Presser, 'The Bogalusa Explosion, "Single Business Enterprise," "Alter Ego," and other Errors' (2006) 100 *Northwestern University Law Review* 405, 422.

[57] Eg, *State Dept of Envtl Prot v Ventron* 468 A 2d 150, 164 (NJ 1983) and *Walkovsky v Carlton* 223 NE 2d 6, 8–10 (NY 1966).

[58] 607 F 2d 582, 586 (NY 2d Cir 1979).

[59] Documents for all three companies were kept in a single file, all financial records were kept in a single account and letters were sent on the same letterhead.

[60] The doctrine was originally developed in California, see *Riddle v Leuschner* 335 P 2d 107, 110–11 (Cal 1959). See also S Bainbridge, 'Abolishing LLC Veil Piercing' (2005) 1 *University of Illinois Law Review* 77.

[61] The extent of control necessary is based on a broad range of factors which include: commingling of funds and other assets; the confusion of the records of the companies; the failure to adequately capitalise the subsidiary company; the disregard of legal formalities and both entities having the same controllers. See *Kinney Shoe Corp v Polan* 939 F 2d 209 (4th Cir 1991) and *Middendorf v Fuqua Indus Inc* 623 F 2d 13, 17 (6th Cir 1980).

the statutory regime for corporate groups (*Konzernrecht*)[62] provides that parent companies who have a 'control agreement'[63] must indemnify their subsidiaries for any losses suffered from acting in the group's interest and if they fail to do so, creditors of the subsidiary company may claim damages from the parent company.[64] In EU law, the clearest expression of the enterprise entity doctrine is under competition law which applies to 'undertakings',[65] defined in the case law as an 'economic unit' that can be comprised of several natural and legal persons.[66] A corporate group will be determined to be an undertaking where a parent exercises such control that the subsidiary has no real freedom to determine its course of action on the market.[67]

At a conceptual level, it may appear that the enterprise entity doctrine is applicable to corporate groups or a supply chain where there is a disparity between their classification in formal law as a set of completely separate companies and the practical realities of their operation as a single organisation. However, as evident from the above examples, the enterprise entity doctrine is dependent upon high degrees of economic and organisational integration, which exists only where a parent company is functionally in 'control' over its subsidiary such that there is no meaningful difference between the two. In the absence of such control and deep integration, fundamental difficulties emerge in drawing the boundaries of the enterprise.[68] Even competition law, which expressly overlooks legal personality in favour of economic realities, has rejected the notion that a supply chain comprised of different companies could be a single undertaking.[69] In this respect, company law mirrors UK tort law and the principle from *Vedanta v Lungowe* where the UK Supreme Court held that to impose liability on to a parent company it must '... take over, intervene in, control, supervise or advise the management of the relevant operations (including land use) of the subsidiary'.[70]

[62] See V Emmerich and M Habersack, *Konzernrecht*, 10th edn (CH Beck, 2016).

[63] As described by *Aktiengesetz* s 302.

[64] *Aktiengesetz* s 309. See A Scheuch, 'Konzernrecht: An Overview of the German Regulation of Corporate Groups and Resulting Liability Issues' (2016) 13 *European Company Law* 191.

[65] Articles 101–06 of the Treaty on the Functioning of the European Union (TFEU) prohibiting practices have the objective or effect of preventing, restricting or distorting competition within the internal market.

[66] See *Shell International Chemical Company Ltd v Commission* T-11/89, ECLI:EU:T:1992:33, [1992] ECR II-757, [311]; and *Mo Och Domsjö AB v Commission* T-352/94, ECLI:EU:T:1998:103, [1998] ECR II-1989, [87].

[67] *Corinne Bodson v Pompes Funèbres des Régions Libérées* Case 30/87, ECLI:EU:C:1988:225, [1988] ECR 2479, [19]; and *Michelin v Commission* T-203/01, ECLI:EU:T:2003:250, [2003] ECR II-4071, [290].

[68] See M Petrin and B Choudhury, 'Group Company Liability' (2018) 20 *European Business Organization Law Review* 1, 13–15.

[69] See *Établissements Consten SàRL and Grundigverkaufs-GmbH v Commission* Joined cases 56 and 58-64, ECLI:EU:C:1966:41, [1966] ECR 299.

[70] *Vedanta v Lungowe* [2019] UKSC 20, [49]. See also *HRH Okpabi v Royal Dutch Shell Plc* [2021] UKSC 3.

A. The Limitations of Company Law

The above discussion demonstrates that company law occasionally moves beyond individual liability to transfer liabilities between companies. This is an important feature of company law which prohibits the company being used as an engine of impropriety or, to the extent that the enterprise entity doctrine is applied, parent companies escaping liability for what is evidently within their control. However, these exceptions remain available in narrowly construed contexts, their doctrinal principles preventing them being mapped on to most corporate groups and supply chains which operate without the impropriety required for veil piercing or the directly controlled parent–subsidiary relationships required by the enterprise entity doctrine. Similarly, the mechanisms of contractual governance used to manage supply chains fall well short of a consensual agency agreement which could allow for the transfer of liabilities between companies. As such, parent companies or lead firms which influence standards across a fragmented transnational organisation, remain formally separate persons with no responsibility for harms accruing from activities further down the chain.

Perhaps the best illustration of the legal reality described above is the UK case of *Adams v Cape Industries plc*.[71] Cape Industries plc (Cape) was an English company with multiple subsidiaries that mined, supplied and marketed asbestos, one of which was the North American Asbestos Corporation (NAAC) based in Texas. Cape and some of its subsidiaries were subject to legal action in Texas arising from personal injuries suffered by employees from asbestos installation. Cape settled the case and subsequently restructured the group by selling most of the group's US assets, liquidating NAAC and effectively replacing it with an independently owned company Continental Products Corporation (CPC). The plaintiffs took a successful personal injuries claim against both NAAC and CPC in the US and sought to enforce the judgment against Cape in England. The critical question was whether Cape was 'present' in the US by virtue of its subsidiaries. The plaintiffs first argued that the court should ignore the separate legal personalities of companies in the group and treat them as a single economic unit when justice so demands.[72] However, the court in *Adams v Cape* rejected the single economic unit argument stating that the law 'recognises the creation of subsidiary companies, which though in one sense are creatures of their parent companies will nevertheless under the general law fall to be treated as separate legal entities'.[73] The court also explicitly stated that it is not free to disregard legal personality 'merely because it considers that justice requires it'.[74] The plaintiffs then argued that the court should pierce the corporate veil because the primary purpose of the US based companies was to shield Cape

[71] [1990] Ch 433.
[72] ibid 532.
[73] ibid 536.
[74] ibid 536.

from liability and so they were mere façades, concealing the true activities of Cape. The court agreed that the structuring of the group was for the purpose of shielding Cape from liability but held that there was nothing illegal or improper in using a corporate group structure to ensure that future liabilities fell on one member of that group.[75] The plaintiffs then argued that the American companies, NAAC and CPC, were agents of Cape and so Cape should be deemed present in the US. While NAAC had an express agency agreement with Cape, that agreement had strictly defined limits with no general authority to bind Cape or other members of the group while CPC had no agency agreement with Cape. The court held that the agency agreement did not establish a relationship sufficient to deem Cape present in the US.[76]

Adams v Cape is a particularly instructive example because it upheld the principles of separate legal personality and limited liability at what is, from a conceptual perspective, their weakest point: a claim of involuntary creditors – tort victims who were employees – against a closely connected corporate group.[77] The case, while limited to an English context, generally reflects the position across jurisdictions where the special justification necessary to transfer liability between formally separate companies does not exist in fragmented corporate groups and supply chains. Hence, it can be said that the doctrines of company law, on the one hand, provide the basis for the accountability gap to exist, while on the other hand offer no clear path to closing it. It is against this background where due diligence rules sought to move beyond these traditional doctrinal limitations and provide a basis through which responsibility and liability could be transferred between and across corporate groups and supply chains.

III. THE CONCEPT OF DUE DILIGENCE

In Europe, the continuing harms resulting from the operation of multi company organisations[78] and the limits of traditional company law doctrine to address these harms resulted in the introduction of due diligence laws derived from the UNGPs. In developing the UNGPs, John Ruggie, Special Representative of the UN Secretary-General, deliberately chose due diligence as a term already familiar

[75] ibid 544.

[76] ibid 458–59.

[77] Tort victims, unlike voluntary creditors, cannot adjust to the risks of dealing with companies. See Hansmann and Kraakman, 'Toward Unlimited Shareholder Liability for Corporate Torts' (n 4) and P Lipton, 'The Mythology of Salomon's Case and the Law Dealing with the Tort Liabilities of Corporate Groups: An Historical Perspective' (2014) 40 *Monash University Law Review* 452.

[78] For a detailed report highlighting many examples see British Institute of International and Comparative Law, 'Study on Due Diligence Requirements Through the Supply Chain' (2020) available at https://op.europa.eu/en/publication-detail/-/publication/8ba0a8fd-4c83-11ea-b8b7-01aa75ed71a1/language-en.

to the business[79] and legal communities.[80] Bonnitcha and McCorquodale[81] trace the legal origins of due diligence to Roman law where a person could be liable for accidental harm if it resulted from a failure to meet the standard of conduct expected of a *diligens paterfamilias* or 'prudent head of a household'.[82] This Roman standard of conduct, judged by reference to a hypothetical responsible person, influenced the development of the tort of negligence in several legal systems.[83]

In modern company law, most jurisdictions now impose a duty on company directors to act with due care and diligence.[84] For example, s 228(1)(g) of the Irish Companies Act 2014, which is substantively similar to s 174 of the UK Companies Act 2006, provides that a director of a company shall 'exercise reasonable care, skill and diligence' to a standard that would be expected of a reasonable person.[85] Despite the duty of diligence being assessed by an objective standard, compliance with the duty is assessed by reference to the process which led to a particular decision rather than an examination of the outcome.[86] For example, English courts have outlined an expectation that directors maintain sufficient knowledge and understanding of the company's business,[87] understand signed documents,[88] seek expert advice and supervise delegated tasks.[89] The duty of care and diligence is also evaluated by reference to the process in continental European jurisdictions.[90] For example, in Germany, §93 of the German Stock Corporation Act (*Aktiengesetz*)[91] imposes a duty of care and

[79] In business, due diligence is a process to establish information which helps identify and manage risk. See G Lawrence, *Due Diligence in Business Transactions* (Law Journal Press, 2023).

[80] See J Ruggie, *Just Business: Multinational Corporations and Human Rights* (Norton, 2013) 141–47.

[81] J Bonnitcha and R McCorquodale, 'The Concept of "Due Diligence" in the UN Guiding Principles on Business and Human Rights' (2017) 28(3) *European Journal of International Law* 899.

[82] Ibid, citing R Zimmerman, *The Law of Obligations: Roman Foundations of the Civilian Tradition* (Oxford, 1996), 1009 and C Lobingier, *The Evolution of the Roman Law: From Before the Twelve Tables to the Corpus Juris*, 2nd edn (Rothman, 1923), 105.

[83] See C Van Dam, 'Tort Law and Human Rights: Brothers in Arms: On the Role of Tort Law in the Area of Business and Human Rights' (2022) 2(3) *Journal of European Tort Law* 221, 237.

[84] See Kraakman et al, *The Anatomy of Corporate Law* (n 22) 69.

[85] This reasonable person having: (i) the knowledge and experience that may reasonably be expected of a person in the same position as the director; and (ii) the knowledge and experience which the director has. See B Clarke, 'Duty of Care Skill and Diligence – From Warm Baths to Hot Water' (2016) 56(56) *The Irish Jurist* 139.

[86] This principle follows the 'business judgment rule' applied across jurisdictions that courts will refrain from assessing the outcomes of decisions and instead review the process which led to the decision. See Kraakman et al (n 22) 69 and more generally A Keay and J Loughrey, 'The Concept of Business Judgment' (2019) 39(1) *Legal Studies* 36. For the German perspective see, G Deipenbrock, 'The 'Business Judgment Rule' and the Problem of Hindsight Bias – Observations from a German Company Law Perspective' (2016) 27(2) *European Business Law Review* 197.

[87] *Dorchester Finance Co Ltd v Stebbing* [1989] BCLC 498.

[88] *Re D'Jan London* [1994] 1 BCLC 561.

[89] *Re Barings plc (No 5)* [1999] 1 BCLC 433.

[90] Eg, Article 2381 of the Italian Civil Code referenced in Kraakman et al (n 22) 69.

[91] See Norton Rose, 'Translation of the German Stock Corporation Act' available at www.nortonrosefulbright.com/-/media/files/nrf/nrfweb/imported/german-stock-corporation-act.pdf.

diligence on directors but states that they will not breach the duty if they had good reason to assume that they were acting on the basis of adequate information. Hence, in company law, due diligence has traditionally meant a duty which must be followed to a reasonable standard.

A. The UNGPs

The foundations of the UNGPs lie in John Ruggie's 'conceptual and policy framework' which sought to address the relationship between business and human rights.[92] In the opening pages of the document, Ruggie articulates the same accountability gap described above:

> The root cause of the business and human rights predicament today lies in the governance gaps created by globalization … These governance gaps provide the permissive environment for wrongful acts by companies of all kinds without adequate sanctioning or reparation.[93]
>
> A parent company and its subsidiaries continue to be construed as distinct legal entities. Therefore, the parent company is generally not liable for wrongs committed by a subsidiary …[94]

Ruggie's starting point to find a solution was to revert to the principle of 'do no harm'.[95] In order to do no harm, a company must first become aware of their impact and in Ruggie's view, most companies had no system in place that could support a claim that they respected human rights and were doing no harm.[96] Ruggie therefore proposed a system of human rights due diligence whereby a company should take a series of steps to become aware of, prevent and address adverse human rights impacts and emphasised that comparable processes were already embedded in companies to assess and manage financial and other risks.[97] In describing the appropriate scope of a due diligence obligation, Ruggie emphasised that a company may contribute to harm through relationships connected to their activities such as with international business partners and suppliers as well as state agencies.[98]

The UNGPs, published in 2011, aimed to 'operationalise' and 'provide concrete and practical recommendations' for the implementation of Ruggie's framework document.[99] The UNGPs are organised around three pillars: (1) the

[92] OHCHR, 'Protect, Respect and Remedy: A Framework for Business and Human Rights' (2008) available at www2.ohchr.org/english/bodies/hrcouncil/docs/8session/a-hrc-8-5.doc.
[93] ibid [3].
[94] ibid [13].
[95] ibid [24].
[96] ibid [25].
[97] ibid [56].
[98] ibid [57].
[99] UNGPs (n 7) [9].

State duty to protect human rights; (2) the corporate responsibility to respect human rights; and (3) access to remedy for victims of business-related human rights abuses. Guiding Principle 13 reflected the principle of 'do no harm' in Ruggie's original framework and states that the responsibility to respect human rights requires business enterprises to avoid causing or contributing to adverse human rights impacts through their own activities and from their business relationships. Guiding Principle 15 introduces the subject of due diligence, defining it as a 'process' to identify, prevent, mitigate and account for human rights impacts while Guiding Principle 17 says the process should include assessing actual and potential human rights impacts, integrating the findings across their operations,[100] tracking the outcomes of their responses,[101] and communicating how the impacts are addressed.[102]

Ruggie's framework and the UNGP's are seminal contributions to the area of business and human rights,[103] have been endorsed by the OECD[104] and laid the conceptual foundations for legislative reform in Europe. The fact that the UNGPs were guidelines and not law, afforded Ruggie a scope to avoid the technical definitions required by legal instruments. In fact, Ruggie wanted to deliberately avoid precise definitions, instead aiming to ground the UNGP's on prevailing social norms, a business's 'social license to operate'[105] and a general moral perspective that business responsibility exists over and above compliance with law.[106]

IV. CORPORATE SUSTAINABILITY DUE DILIGENCE

While the UNGPs sought to close the accountability gap and reduce the incentive to externalise costs through norm setting and voluntary engagement, due diligence laws impose mandatory obligations to follow a due diligence process overseen by regulatory authorities backed by the threat of enforcement. In 2017, France became the first European country to impose legal obligations

[100] ibid. Principle 19 provides further detail on integration providing that businesses should integrate the findings from their impact assessments across relevant internal functions and processes and take appropriate action.

[101] ibid. Principle 20 provides further detail on tracking providing that business should monitor the effectiveness of their responses to human rights impact in order to drive continuous improvement.

[102] ibid. Principle 21 provides further detail on communication providing that business enterprises should be prepared to communicate how they address their human rights impacts externally.

[103] See P Muchlinski, 'The Impact of the UN Guiding Principles on Business Attitudes to Observing Human Rights' (2021) 6 *Business and Human Rights Journal* 212.

[104] OECD, 'OECD Guidelines for Multinational Enterprises on Responsible Business Conduct' (2023) at available at https://doi.org/10.1787/81f92357-en originally published in 2011.

[105] J Ruggie, 'The Future of Corporate Accountability for Violations of Human Rights American Society of International Law' (2009), 284 available at https://scholar.harvard.edu/files/john-ruggie/files/asil_2009.pdf.

[106] UNGPs Principle 11. See also J Ruggie, 'The Concept of "Due Diligence" in the UN Guiding Principles on Business and Human Rights: A Reply to Jonathan Bonnitcha and Robert McCorquodale' (2017) 28(3) *The European Journal of International Law* 921, 924.

on companies to conduct due diligence through their supply chain.[107] The *Loi de Vigilance* applies to French companies that employ 5000 employees in France, or 10,000 globally and requires them to implement a 'vigilance plan' which should include measures to identify and prevent human rights and environmental harms arising from the activities of the company itself, its subsidiaries or suppliers and subcontractors with whom the company has an established commercial relationship.[108] The Dutch Child Labour Due Diligence Law passed in 2019[109] applies to all companies operating in the Netherlands and requires them to issue a statement declaring that they have exercised due diligence to prevent their goods and services being made using child labour. This consists of an obligation to implement a proactive plan to prevent serious adverse impact resulting from company, subsidiary, supplier and subcontractor activities throughout the world.[110] In 2021, Germany introduced similar obligations in its Supply Chain Due Diligence Act[111] which applies to any company that has 1,000 employees.[112] It requires companies to conduct risk analysis on human rights and environmental risks and develop a policy to implement preventive measures against such risks arising from its own operations and across its supply chain.[113]

Prompted by these developments at Member State level and as part of the EU's corporate sustainability focus, due diligence was introduced on to the EU's legislative agenda in 2018 by the Commission's Action Plan on Financing Sustainable Growth.[114] The Action Plan committed to conduct analytical and consultative work to assess the need to require corporate boards to conduct due diligence throughout their supply chains.[115] Shortly after, the European Parliament Report on Sustainable Finance sought a legislative proposal for an 'overarching, mandatory due diligence framework including a duty of care' that would take into account the proportionality principle.[116] A 500-page study followed, conducted by the British Institute of International and

[107] French Law No 2017-399 *Loi de Vigilance*.

[108] See A Pietrancosta, 'Codification in Company Law of General CSR Requirements: Pioneering Recent French Reforms and EU Perspectives' (2022) Law Working Paper No 639/2022 *European Corporate Governance Institute* available at www.ecgi.global/sites/default/files/working_papers/documents/codificationfinal_0.pdf.

[109] Netherlands Kamerstukken I, 2016/17, 34 506, A.

[110] See L Enneking, 'Putting the Dutch Child Labour Due Diligence Act into Perspective: An Assessment of the CLDD Act's Legal and Policy Relevance in the Netherlands and Beyond' (2019) 4 *Erasmus Law Review* 20.

[111] *LkSG – Lieferkettensorgfaltspflichtengesetz* 2021.

[112] The threshold was reduced from 3,000 in January 2024.

[113] See A Rühmkorf, 'The German Supply Chain Law: A First Step Towards More Corporate Sustainability' (2023) 20(1) *European Company Law* 6.

[114] Communication from the Commission to the European Parliament, the European Council, the Council, the European Central Bank, the European Economic and Social Committee and the Committee of the Regions – Action Plan: Financing Sustainable Growth [2018] COM/2018/097.

[115] ibid, Action 10.

[116] European Parliament resolution of 29 May 2018 on sustainable finance (2018/2007(INI)) [2018] OJ C 76/23 available at https://eur-lex.europa.eu/legal-content/EN/TXT/?uri=CELEX%3A52018IP0215, [6].

Comparative Law in partnership with Civic Consulting and the London School of Economics[117] which recommended the introduction of mandatory due diligence obligations at the EU level.

The first basis for this recommendation was that environmental and human rights abuses were continuing to be caused by multiple company organisations despite the introduction of the UNGPs.[118] The second basis was that despite the UNGPs, many companies were still not conducting due diligence across their business activities.[119] The report surveyed 334 businesses of different sizes and 37.14 per cent of those respondents stated that their companies conducted due diligence across their human rights and environmental impacts,[120] a further one-third of respondents stated that they undertook more limited due diligence actions[121] while only 16 per cent of respondents conducted due diligence beyond a first-tier supplier. The report referred to other reports which also noted that human rights and environmental due diligence was not a widespread activity.[122] These included a study by the British Institute of International and Comparative Law and Norton Rose Fulbright which found that the majority of companies surveyed were not undertaking human rights due diligence[123] and a Corporate Human Rights Benchmark report which assessed 101 of the largest publicly traded companies across three industries: agricultural products; apparel; and extractives,[124] which found that 40 per cent of those companies had no human rights due diligence procedures.[125] The third basis for recommending mandatory due diligence rules was because of increasing fragmentation of due diligence rules within Europe due to the developments at Member State level as well as sector specific EU due diligence rules. For example, the EU Timber Regulation[126] requires operators who place timber and timber products on the EU market to develop or use a due diligence system to provide information about the source of the timber, to allow for risk assessment procedures, monitoring and mitigating the risk of illegally harvested timber being placed on the EU market. Similarly, the

[117] British Institute of International and Comparative Law et al, 'Study on Due Diligence Requirements Through the Supply Chain' (n 78).

[118] ibid. The report provided multiple examples throughout of the ongoing human rights and environmental harms related to business operations both within and outside of the EU.

[119] ibid 218.

[120] ibid 45–47.

[121] ibid 48.

[122] ibid 49.

[123] The study was published as R McCorquodale et al, 'Human Rights Due Diligence in Law and Practice: Good Practices and Challenges of Business Enterprises' (2017) 2 *Business and Human Rights Journal* 195. The company surveyed 152 major companies working across various sectors.

[124] Corporate Human Rights Benchmark, '2018 Key Finding – Apparel, Agricultural Products and Extractive Companies', 2018, available at: https://assets.worldbenchmarkingalliance.org/app/uploads/2021/03/CHRB2018KeyFindingsReport.pdf.

[125] ibid 13.

[126] Regulation (EU) 995/2010 of the European Parliament and of the Council of 20 October 2010 laying down the obligations of operators who place timber and timber products on the market [2010] OJ L 295/23.

EU Conflict Minerals Regulation[127] requires EU importers of tin, tantalum, tungsten and gold to: (1) establish strong company management systems; (2) identify and assess risk in the supply chain; (3) design and implement a strategy to respond to identified risks; (4) carry out an independent third-party audit of supply chain due diligence; and (5) report annually on supply chain due diligence.[128] A majority of respondents to the survey believed that an EU regulation on due diligence would provide legal certainty by providing a 'level playing field'.[129]

In 2022, the European Commission published its proposed Corporate Sustainability Due Diligence Directive (CSDDD).[130] The CSDDD followed the rationales set out in the report, namely that despite the UNGPs, 'negative externalities from EU production and consumption' continue to arise[131] and that the harmonisation of due diligence requirements would be beneficial.[132] The Commission, rather than developing a legal concept of the UNGPs 'business enterprise', sought to fit corporate sustainability due diligence within the individualistic framework of company law set out above. Hence, the proposed CSDDD would apply to individual companies registered in EU Member States with over 500 employees and a turnover of over €150 million.[133] Those thresholds would be reduced to 250 employees and a turnover of over €40 million if 50 per cent of that turnover was generated from a 'high risk' sector which included the manufacturing of textiles or metal products, the wholesale trade of clothing and footwear; agriculture, forestry and the extraction of minerals.[134]

Companies subject to the Directive would be required to identify actual and potential adverse human rights and environmental impacts arising from their own or their subsidiaries operations or from 'established business relationships', which included direct and indirect partners,[135] in their 'value chain'.[136] Once potential adverse impacts were identified, companies would be required to take 'appropriate measures' to bring an end to, or if that was not possible, to minimise the extent of the impact.[137] Companies would be required to prepare a due diligence policy and code of conduct[138] that would be applied to subsidiaries

[127] Regulation (EU) 2017/821 of the European Parliament and of the Council of 17 May 2017 laying down supply chain due diligence obligations for Union importers of tin, tantalum and tungsten, their ores, and gold originating from conflict-affected and high-risk areas [2017] OJ L 130/1.

[128] ibid arts 4, 6, 8 and recital 17.

[129] British Institute of International and Comparative Law et al 'Study on Due Diligence Requirements Through the Supply Chain' (n 78).

[130] Proposed CSDDD (n 11).

[131] ibid explanatory memorandum [6].

[132] ibid [3.2].

[133] Proposed CSDDD (n 11) art 2.

[134] ibid.

[135] ibid art 3(f) defined as 'a business relationship, whether direct or indirect, which is, or which is expected to be lasting, in view of its intensity or duration and which does not represent a negligible or merely ancillary part of the value chain'.

[136] ibid art 6.

[137] ibid art 8.

[138] ibid art 5.

and other companies throughout its value chain.[139] Companies would then be required to seek contractual assurances from business partners with whom it has 'established business relationships' that it will comply with the company's code of conduct, including by seeking corresponding contractual assurances from its partners, to the extent that their activities are part of the company's value chain. The Directive provided that where impacts could not be ended or minimised, the company shall refrain from entering into new or extending existing relations with the partner and either temporarily suspend commercial relationships with the partner in question, while pursuing efforts to bring to an end or minimise the impact or terminate the business relationship with respect to the activities concerned, if the adverse impact is considered severe.[140] The proposal also included a requirement to adopt a plan to ensure that the company's business model and strategy were compatible with the transition to a sustainable economy and with the limiting of global warming to 1.5°C in line with the Paris Agreement.[141] Hence, in accordance with its historical development, due diligence in European company law was focused on implementing processes, the difference being that the CSDDD was aiming to reduce negative external impacts.

Compliance would be overseen by national supervisory authorities[142] and a European Network of Supervisory Authorities which are to facilitate the alignment of regulatory, investigatory, sanctioning and supervisory practices.[143] A company within scope could be civilly liable for damages if it failed to comply with these due diligence obligations and if as a result of that failure, an adverse impact that should have been identified, prevented, mitigated and or ended led to damage.[144] The company could also be liable if it conducted due diligence actions but these actions were such that it would be unreasonable to expect them to be adequate to prevent, mitigate or end the adverse impact arising from the activities of a company with whom it had an established business relationship.[145] Hence, companies who conducted due diligence but to an insufficient level could still be held civilly liable.

A crucial component of the proposed CSDDD, given the globalised nature of the issue, was its extraterritorial effects. The CSDDD would apply to companies registered outside the EU if they met the turnover threshold from business conducted inside the EU.[146] More importantly, the entire design of the CSDDD was based around having an indirect 'territorial extension'[147] as companies subject

[139] ibid art 5.
[140] ibid art 8(6).
[141] ibid art 15. The plan was to identify, on the basis of information reasonably available to the company, the extent to which climate change is a risk for, or an impact of, the company's operations.
[142] ibid art 19.
[143] ibid arts 17 and 18 and 21.
[144] ibid art 22.
[145] ibid.
[146] ibid art 2.
[147] J Scott, 'Extraterritoriality and Territorial Extension in EU Law' (2014) 62 *American Journal of Comparative Law* 87 differentiating between direct application of law to parties outside a

to the CSDDD would be required to conduct due diligence across their entire value chain, regardless of the size or geographical location of the other companies in the chain. Hence, small and large companies alike, across different continents would, assuming appropriate due diligence measures were implemented, come under pressure to comply with the company's code of conduct and mitigate any human rights and environmental impacts. Given that EU employment and environmental standards are comparatively high, and that companies subject to the Directive were likely to abide by those standards, the CSDDD had the potential to improve practices throughout the companies' transnational value chain.[148]

A. The Amended CSDDD

After objections were raised in the European Council,[149] a period of renegotiation ensued between the EU's legislative bodies and an amended CSDDD was agreed in April 2024.[150] A revised version was published in the Official Journal in June 2024[151] which entered into force in July 2024.[152] The structure of the amended CSDDD remained the same: large EU companies must develop due diligence practices, codes of conduct and policies and implement them across their value chain,[153] including extraterritorially,[154] with a view to ending or mitigating adverse human rights and environmental impacts. Compliance remained to be overseen by national supervisory authorities[155] and a European Network of Supervisory Authorities.[156] The amended Directive continued to provide for the termination of business relationships[157] and the failure to carry out the due diligence practices created the potential for civil liability.[158]

jurisdiction and 'territorial extension' where a party within the jurisdiction is required to affect conduct or circumstances abroad.

[148] See L Enriques, M Gatti, R Shapira, 'How the EU's Sustainability Due Diligence Directive Could Reshape Corporate America' (2025) *European Corporate Governance Institute Working Paper* available at www.ecgi.global/publications/working-papers/how-the-eus-sustainability-due-diligence-directive-could-reshape. This issue of international effect will be taken up in ch 6.

[149] Germany and Italy leading the objections, see www.reuters.com/markets/europe/eu-postpones-decision-proposed-supply-chain-due-diligince-law-2024-02-09/.

[150] European Parliament legislative resolution of 24 April 2024 on the proposal for a directive of the European Parliament and of the Council on Corporate Sustainability Due Diligence and amending Directive (EU) 2019/1937 [2024] COM(2022)0071 available at https://eur-lex.europa.eu/legal-content/EN/TXT/?uri=ep:P9_TA%282024%290329.

[151] Final CSDDD (n 1).

[152] See https://commission.europa.eu/business-economy-euro/doing-business-eu/sustainability-due-diligence-responsible-business/corporate-sustainability-due-diligence_en#:~:text=On%2025%20July%202024%2C%20the,across%20their%20global%20value%20chains.

[153] Final CSDDD (n 1) art 5.

[154] ibid art 2(2).

[155] ibid art 24.

[156] ibid art 28.

[157] ibid art 10(6).

[158] ibid art 29.

Companies remained under an obligation to develop detailed due diligence procedures that required engagement with business partners and other stakeholders. For example, the CSDDD provides that where an adverse impact cannot be immediately brought to an end the company shall: (1) be required to implement a corrective action plan with reasonable and clearly defined timelines for the implementation of appropriate measures which should be developed in cooperation with industry or multi-stakeholder initiatives and adapted to the companies' operations and chains of activities;[159] (2) seek contractual assurances from a direct business partner that it will ensure compliance with the company's code of conduct and, as necessary, a corrective action plan, including by establishing corresponding contractual assurances from its partners;[160] (3) make necessary financial or non-financial investments in, adjustments or upgrades of, for example, facilities, production or other operational processes and infrastructures;[161] (4) make necessary modifications of, or improvements to, the company's business plan, overall strategies and operations; (5) provide targeted and proportionate support to business partners of the company.[162] The CSDDD also requires companies to take appropriate measures to carry out effective engagement with stakeholders, including providing them with relevant and comprehensive information and consulting them when gathering the necessary information on actual or potential adverse impacts and when developing prevention and corrective action plans.[163] It further requires a company to develop a complaints procedure,[164] to assess every 12 months the implementation, adequacy and effectiveness of their own, their subsidiaries and business partners due diligence process,[165] and for the matters covered by the CSDDD to be published on the company's website through an annual statement.[166] One aspect of the CSDDD that is not focused on processes, is the requirement that where an adverse impact could not be prevented or adequately mitigated the company shall, as a last resort, be required to refrain from entering into new or extending existing relations with a business partner.[167]

However, despite the structure and detailed processes being maintained, the thresholds of application were significantly raised and the CSDDD now applies to companies or parents of a corporate group with more than 1000 employees and a net worldwide turnover exceeding €450 million.[168] While there is now

[159] ibid art 11(3)(b).
[160] ibid art 11(3)(c).
[161] ibid art 11(3)(d).
[162] ibid art 11(3)(e).
[163] ibid art 13.
[164] ibid art 14.
[165] ibid art 15.
[166] ibid art 16.
[167] ibid art 10(6).
[168] ibid art 2.

provision for consolidated thresholds for the parents of corporate groups,[169] the amendments doubled the number of required employees, tripled the required turnover while the lower thresholds for high-risk activities were removed. A further change is a greater emphasis on risk management,[170] as exemplified by a new mapping requirement to identify where adverse impacts are most likely to occur and to be most severe.[171] As part of this focus on risk, companies must, where it is not feasible to prevent, mitigate, bring to an end or minimise all identified adverse impacts, prioritise impacts based on the severity and likelihood of occurrence.[172] While high-risk, high-severity impacts should be prioritised, companies may see it as an additional defence whereby they can claim that they only failed to conduct due diligence because of their prioritisation of other human rights or environmental impacts.[173] The terminology used was also altered, with 'value chain' being replaced by 'chain of activities'.[174] While 'value chain' included direct (contractual) and indirect (non-contractual) relationships in both upstream[175] and downstream[176] business operations, 'chain of activities' excludes indirect, downstream business partners.[177] In plain language, companies are now freed from obligations to conduct due diligence in second tier business partners involved in downstream operations such as distribution, transport and storage.

The model of civil liability also underwent fundamental change. The CSDDD now includes an element of fault such that the company can only be liable where it 'intentionally or negligently' fails to comply with its due diligence obligations and requires that the failure caused damage to a person's legal interest under national law.[178] The CSDDD also expressly states that a company cannot be liable if the damage was caused only by its business partners in its chain of activities[179] while it no longer includes the provision which allowed for the imposition of liability where it was unreasonable to expect the due diligence actions to

[169] ibid. A company will fall within the scope of the Directive where it did not reach the threshold but where it was the parent of a group that did reach the thresholds in the previous financial year.

[170] Eg, the fundamental obligation to conduct due diligence set out by art 5 was amended to include the words 'risk based'. The text now states 'Member States shall ensure that companies conduct *risk-based* human rights and environmental due diligence'.

[171] Final CSDDD (n 1) art 8(2).

[172] ibid art 9.

[173] For analysis of the relationship between civil liability and negative externalities see A Pacces, 'Civil Liability in the EU Corporate Sustainability Due Diligence Directive Proposal: A Law & Economics Analysis' (2023) Law Working Paper No 691/2023 *European Corporate Governance Institute* available at https://papers.ssrn.com/sol3/papers.cfm?abstract_id=4391121, 5.

[174] Final CSDDD (n 1) art 3(g).

[175] 'Upstream' relating to the production of goods or the provision of services by the company, including the design, extraction, sourcing, manufacture, transport, storage and supply of raw materials, products or parts of the products and development of the product or the service.

[176] 'Downstream' relating to distribution, transport and storage of the product.

[177] Final CSDDD (n 1) art 3(g) stating that a chain of activities extends to 'downstream' 'business partners' who carry out those activities *for* the company or *on behalf* of the company.

[178] ibid art 27.

[179] ibid.

be adequate. These amendments have undoubtedly reduced the potential scope of civil liability claims under the CSDDD. First, the increased threshold reduces the number of companies that will fall within its scope. Second, the requirement to establish an 'intentional or negligent' failure adds an additional burden for claimants and determining that standard will be left to Member States for interpretation. Third, the requirement that the damage must affect a person's interest under national law changes the reference point from the damage caused and the company's due diligence practices to the national law of Member States. While a company implementing a code of conduct across its international value chain may raise employment and human standards above national law, a victim will be unsuccessful in attempts to impose civil liability unless their interest under national law is harmed, regardless of the company's code of conduct or its failures to implement due diligence. Fourth, the provision that companies will not be responsible for damage caused *only* by its business partners adds a new layer of uncertainty by implying a need for a causal connection between the actions of the company subject to the Directive and the damage. It is unclear whether a failure to comply with due diligence obligations is sufficient to create that link as breaching due diligence requirements and *causing* damage are substantively different actions. Fifth, companies have now a defence of prioritisation, which, of course, would require the company to adduce evidence of their efforts to mitigate or end more severe impacts but nevertheless adds a further element to a claim for civil liability. A final issue is the burden of proof.[180] The CSDDD provides that national law should decide which party must prove the 'conditions for liability'.[181] Presumably, the burden will fall on claimants under national law and while the final CSDDD allows for courts to require disclosures from a company subject to a claim for damages,[182] successfully establishing the multiple elements required is still likely to prove onerous for claimants.

B. The Omnibus Proposal

As part of the Omnibus I proposal,[183] the European Commission has put forward substantial changes to the CSDDD. The Directive's commencement has been proposed to be delayed by one year, the deadline for Member State transposition being moved to July 2027 and the application to companies being postponed by one year to July 2028. Further, the proposed periodic monitoring of due diligence measures is changed from annually to every five years, removes

[180] For analysis see Pacces, 'Civil Liability in the EU Corporate Sustainability Due Diligence Directive' (n 173) 12–13.

[181] Final CSDDD (n 1) recital 81.

[182] ibid art 29(3)(e) where a claimant presents a reasoned justification containing reasonably available facts and evidence sufficient to support the plausibility of their claim for damages.

[183] Omnibus I proposal (n 18).

the requirement to terminate relations with a business partner and reduces the extent of stakeholder engagement. The most fundamental proposed changes are to remove the EU specific model of civil liability in the Directive entirely and limit the application of the due diligence process to the company, its subsidiaries and their direct business partners[184] greatly reducing the CSDDD's transnational effects.[185]

V. ANALYSING THE CSDDD

The CSDDD, despite its dilution, and potential further dilution, remains a landmark piece of legislation. It exemplifies the reorientation of European company law toward aiming to reduce human rights abuses and environmental harms through legally mandated processes. It also breaks new ground in company law – unlike the special justifications in national law which allow for the transfer of liability between companies – due diligence laws are specifically adapted to the dispersed and transnational realities of corporate groups and supply chains and are a bespoke attempt to close the resulting accountability gap.[186] Given this novelty, the CSDDD may appear to create a new form of organisational liability, whereby large companies can be held responsible for the actions of formally separate companies due to their subsidiary status or by virtue of being part of the company's 'chain of activities'. This would extend the organisational framework of liability under the enterprise entity doctrine which, as we have seen, requires deep economic and organisational integration evident only where a parent functionally controls a subsidiary. However, despite being specifically adapted to fragmented business structures, the CSDDD remains thoroughly individualistic, applying to individual companies that will not be liable for the harm caused by another legal person, regardless of the severity of the harm or the relationship between it and the company whose actions directly led to the harm. This adherence to company law's individualistic framework of responsibility is one of the reasons for the repeated objections to the inclusion of civil liability in the CSDDD as it creates inevitable difficulties of justifying the extension of liabilities beyond the individual and demarcating the new boundary of liability.[187] This is a fundamental difficulty in moving from voluntary frameworks

[184] ibid 18. The Omnibus does provide that a company may have obligations to extend its due diligence practices to indirect partners where there is 'plausible information' suggesting adverse impacts.

[185] This point is taken up in ch 6.

[186] See P Zumbanssen, 'Global Value Chain Legislation, Modern Slavery, Climate Change and Finance: Lessons from the European Corporate Sustainability Due Diligence Directive' (2024) *McGill SGI Research Paper in Business, Finance, Law and Society* available at https://papers.ssrn.com/sol3/papers.cfm?abstract_id=4784608.

[187] There are, of course, political reasons for the proposed amendments to the CSDDD as briefly discussed in ch 3 in relation to the Omnibus I proposal.

which use terms such as 'business enterprise' and legal standards which must fit with existing legal categories.[188] The CSDDD's model of civil liability is now best understood as creating a new special justification for transferring liabilities between companies, and, like the justifications in national law described above, it is only possible in narrowly construed circumstances.

However, it is important not to reduce the analysis of the CSDDD solely to its model of liability. At its core, the CSDDD requires companies to carry out a detailed process involving the identification of actual and potential adverse human rights and environmental impacts, take measures to end or mitigate these impacts, develop a diligence policy and extend this across its subsidiaries and supply chain. In this respect, the CSDDD is broadly similar the Teubner's 'duty to organise' in large scale, complex organisations.[189] Teubner acknowledged the difficulty of 'top management' responsible for problems that arose across the organisation beyond their 'personal sphere of action'[190] and so argued for a 'system' of coordination, supervision and monitoring' to help develop a sense of social responsibility.[191] The detailed and demanding processes required by the CSDDD still have the potential to create a reflexive response by opening the company to its external impact and developing an internal sense of societal responsibility within the company. However, this reflexive effect is still dependent upon sufficiently strong external stimulation before decision makers within a company will begin to respond to the processes and start taking measures to reduce their negative externalities. Hence, the mandatory, detailed nature of the CSDDD is important, as is supervision by national and European regulatory authorities[192] who have the capacity to issue fines for a failure to comply with its requirements.[193] This public supervision and enforcement, while not guaranteeing compliance,[194] increases the strength of the CSDDD above voluntary frameworks given that the possibility of private enforcement through civil

[188] Of course, it is possible to develop new legal categories. The EU have made such legal leaps before like the category of 'undertaking' in competition law (Treaty on the Functioning of the European Union, arts 101–06) and, more recently, 'platform' (see Regulation (EU) 2022/2065 – Digital Services Act) and many other examples in privacy law such as 'data processor' and 'data controller' (see Regulation (EU) 2016/679 – General Data Protection Regulation). For a deeper exploration of this point see J Quinn and R Condon, 'Beyond the Individual-Company: From Corporate Social Responsibilities to Corporate Social Liability' (2025) *Transnational Legal Theory* available at www.tandfonline.com/doi/full/10.1080/20414005.2025.2479318?src=exp-la#abstract.

[189] See G Teubner, 'Corporate Fiduciary Duties and their Beneficiaries' in G Teubner and K Hopt (eds), *Corporate Governance and Directors' Liabilities: Legal, Economic and Sociological Analyses on Corporate Social Responsibility* (De Gruyter, 1985) 171–172.

[190] ibid.

[191] ibid, citing C Stone, *Where the Law Ends: The Social Control of Corporate Behaviour* (Harper & Row, 1975) 199.

[192] Final CSDDD (n 1) art 27.

[193] ibid. The basis for these fines are to be set by national law although the Directive states that the maximum limit of pecuniary penalties shall be not less than 5% of the net worldwide turnover of the company in the financial year preceding that of the decision to impose the fine.

[194] It obviously depends on the funding and engagement of the national and European authorities, as well as the framework of imposing fines set by national law.

liability is remote. From this perspective, the most consequential effect of the CSDDD's redrafting was the increase in thresholds as now fewer companies are required to implement a corporate sustainability due diligence process.

VI. CONCLUSION

The CSDDD is the most significant development to date in the transformation of European company law. It is an ambitious piece of legislation which aims to address the difficult problem of closing the accountability gap created by multi-company organisations and reducing human rights and environmental harms caused and enabled by these fragmented business structures. Despite the dilution of the civil liability model, there remains reasons to think the CSDDD will have a significant impact due to its mandatory nature, its detailed process and public enforcement which make a reflexive effect possible. As such, it offers an important example of company law legislation with reflexive elements.

6

International Effects of European Company Law

I. INTRODUCTION

Given the extent to which modern companies operate transnationally, any attempt to limit the negative externalities of business must be adapted to the realities of corporate globalisation.[1] However, legal efforts to reduce such negative externalities are inevitably limited by territorial jurisdiction.[2] The disparity between the globalised nature of business and the jurisdictional nature of law has contributed to the creation of the accountability gap[3] discussed in chapter five. Hence, one of the most significant aspects of the Corporate Sustainability Reporting Directive (CSRD)[4] and the Corporate Sustainability Due Diligence Directive (CSDDD)[5] is their capacity to affect companies outside of the European Union's (EU) jurisdiction.[6]

The EU has developed a sophisticated framework to have legal effects beyond its borders.[7] One element of this framework is 'jurisdictional triggers' which are used to apply EU law to persons outside the EU that have effects within its territory. Both the CSRD and the CSDDD use a jurisdictional trigger of 'business

[1] As discussed in ch 5. For a discussion of how EU law attempts to deal with corporate globalisation see A Beckers, 'Global Value Chains in EU Law' (2023) 42 *Yearbook of European Law* 322.

[2] One of the advantages of non-legal frameworks, such as the United Nations Guiding Principles on Business and Human Rights, is that they are not bound by legal jurisdiction.

[3] Or 'governance gaps' in the language of John Ruggie. See J Ruggie, 'Protect, Respect and Remedy: A Framework for Business and Human Rights' (2008) available at www2.ohchr.org/english/bodies/hrcouncil/docs/8session/a-hrc-8-5.doc, 3.

[4] Directive (EU) 2022/2464 of the European Parliament and of the Council of 14 December 2022 amending Regulation (EU) No 537/2014, Directive 2004/109/EC, Directive 2006/43/EC and Directive 2013/34/EU, as regards corporate sustainability reporting [2022] OJ L 322/15.

[5] Directive (EU) 2024/1760 of the European Parliament and of the Council of 13 June 2024 on corporate sustainability due diligence and amending Directive (EU) 2019/1937 and Regulation (EU) 2023/2859 [2024] OJ L, 2024/1760.

[6] For example, Enriques, Gatti and Shapira argue that the CSDDD will affect virtually all large American corporations: see L Enriques, M Gatti and R Shapira, 'How the EU's Sustainability Due Diligence Directive Could Reshape Corporate America' (2025) *European Corporate Governance Institute Working Paper* available at www.ecgi.global/publications/working-papers/how-the-eus-sustainability-due-diligence-directive-could-reshape, 14.

[7] See J Scott, 'The New EU "Extraterritoriality"' (2014) 51 *Common Market Law Review* 1343 and J Scott, 'Extraterritoriality and Territorial Extension in EU Law' (2014) 62 *American Journal of Comparative Law* 87.

conducted within the EU' to bring non-EU based companies within their scope. Another element is 'territorial extension' which describes contexts in which EU law uses a territorial connection with the EU to influence conduct that takes place outside of its territory. The CSDDD uses territorial extension by requiring companies within its scope to conduct due diligence across all their subsidiaries and business partners regardless of their size or geographical location. The reason for these international effects is first to give effect to the objectives of the Directives and second to establish a level playing field such that EU companies are not at a competitive disadvantage.[8]

EU law can have a more indirect international impact through the 'Brussels effect',[9] a phenomenon whereby EU law shapes the global regulatory environment through market forces rather than the direct application of law. The de jure Brussels effect describes a situation where companies, in order to gain or maintain access to the EU's market, comply with EU regulations and then apply those standards across their international operations. A de facto Brussels effect sometimes occurs where other jurisdictions enact laws similar to those in the EU because they have become the standard practice through the de facto Brussels effect and jurisdictions regularly enact rules which reflect existing market practices and standards. In some contexts at least, it seems likely that the CSDDD will produce a Brussels effect due to the non-divisibility[10] of supply chains.

This chapter assesses the international effects of the CSRD and CSDDD. Section II discusses jurisdictional triggers in EU law and under the CSRD and CSDDD. Section III discusses the method of territorial extension under the CSDDD, paying particular focus to the potential effects in the US. Section IV explores the potential of a Brussels effect arising from the CSRD and CSDDD.

II. JURISDICTIONAL TRIGGERS

Jurisdiction can be defined as 'the limits of legal competence of a state or other regulatory authority … to make, apply, and enforce rules of conduct upon persons'.[11] One of these limits is geographical[12] as demonstrated by the

[8] It is worth noting that both 'jurisdictional triggers' and 'territorial extension' still rely on a territorial link with the EU. As Scott notes, pure extraterritorial effects – meaning EU law's application to persons with no territorial connection to the EU – are exceptionally rare. See Scott, 'Extraterritoriality and Territorial Extension in EU Law' (n 7) 94.

[9] A Bradford, *The Brussels Effect: How the European Union Rules the World* (Oxford, Oxford University Press, 2019).

[10] ibid 54. 'Non-divisibility' meaning that it is more profitable to apply standards from its most regulated market across its entire global operations rather than customising standards for different markets.

[11] V Lowe, 'Jurisdiction' in M Evans (ed), *International Law* (Oxford, Oxford University Press, 2003) 329.

[12] Geography not only defines the limits of the jurisdiction of nation states but also empires and other power structures. See S Elden, *The Birth of Territory* (University of Chicago Press, 2013).

nation state whose territory circumscribes the legitimate realm of its power.[13] The jurisdiction of the EU, as a supranational organisation, is also bounded by geography.[14] Once within its competencies,[15] the EU's jurisdiction is, in general, limited to the territories of its Member States.[16] The geographical limits of jurisdiction creates difficulties in the context of global phenomena. One such example is the internet and data which are 'un-territorial'[17] or 'post-territorial'.[18] Another example, as discussed throughout this book, are corporate structures that have broken free of national boundaries and have transnational effects. It is these global business operations that are a main driver of negative externalities where a parent or 'lead firm' facilitates, ignores or fails to detect instances of environmental damage or human rights abuses arising from the operation of its subsidiaries or contractual partners. The disparity between globalised phenomena and the territorial nature of law, sometimes justifies effects on persons that lie outside a jurisdiction's territory.[19] However, in the context of corporate externalities, few legal frameworks have been developed which are specifically adapted for the transnational realities of modern business.[20]

A fundamental question for issues of jurisdiction is where a person is located.[21] In the context of companies, this is not always a straightforward determination. As discussed in chapter three, the question of a company's jurisdictional location produced a series of European company law cases[22] which held that the location of a company is where it is legally registered

[13] See K Raustiala, 'The Geography of Justice' (2005) 73 *Fordham Law Review* 2501, 2508–09.

[14] See J Weinzierl, 'Territoriality Beyond the State: The EU's Territorial Claims and the Search for Their Legitimacy' (2021) 22 *German Law Journal* 650.

[15] Article 5 of the Treaty on the Functioning of the European Union (TFEU) sets out the principle of conferral which limits the EU's competencies to those conferred on it by the Member States in the EU Treaties. See I Govaere, 'To Give or to Grab: The Principle of Full, Crippled and Split Conferral of Powers Post-Lisbon' (2016) *College Of Europe Research Papers in Law* available at www.coleurope.eu/sites/default/files/research-paper/researchpaper_4_2016_inge_govaere_0.pdf.

[16] Article 52 of the TFEU identities the territorial scope of the EU as encompassing the Member States alongside the territories set out in art 355 of the TFEU which bring other territories including Guadeloupe, French Guiana and Martinique within the scope of the treaties.

[17] See J Daskal, 'The Un-Territoriality of Data' (2015) *The Yale Law Journal* 326.

[18] See P De Hert and J Thumfart, 'The Microsoft Ireland Case and the Cyberspace Sovereignty Trilemma: Post-Territorial Technologies and Companies Question Territorial State Sovereignty and Regulatory State Monopolies' (2018) 4 *Brussels Privacy Hub Working Paper* available at https://papers.ssrn.com/sol3/papers.cfm?abstract_id=3228388.

[19] For a full exploration of this issue in the data context, see F Fabbrini, E Celeste and J Quinn, *Data Protection Beyond Borders: Transatlantic Perspectives on Extraterritoriality and Sovereignty* (Oxford, Hart, 2021).

[20] See P Zumbanssen, 'Global Value Chain Legislation, Modern Slavery, Climate Change and Finance: Lessons from the European Corporate Sustainability Due Diligence Directive' (2024) *McGill SGI Research Paper in Business, Finance, Law and Society* available at https://papers.ssrn.com/sol3/papers.cfm?abstract_id=4784608.

[21] See V Lowe and C Staker, 'Jurisdiction' in M Evans (ed), *International Law* (Oxford, Oxford University Press, 2010).

[22] Such as Case C-212/97 *Centros Ltd v Erhvervs-og Selskabssyrelsen* ECLI:EU:C:1999:126, [1999] ECR I-1459; Case C-208/00 *Überseering BV v Nordic Construction Company Baumanagement GmbH (NCC)* ECLI:EU:C:2002:632, [2002] ECR I-9919; and Case C-411/03 *Sevic Systems AG*

(the incorporation approach) rather than where it conducts the majority of its operations (the real seat approach).[23] However, this straightforward method of determining the jurisdictional location of a company does not necessarily prevent other jurisdictions from applying their laws to that company. This is because a company may have effects in other jurisdictions by, for example, selling products or goods across borders or impacting the rights of citizens located in other jurisdictions. To address such situations, EU law has developed a series of 'jurisdictional triggers' which extend the application of EU law to non-EU based companies that have effects within the EU,[24] for example, by conducting business in the EU or affecting the rights of EU residents. One example of a jurisdictional trigger can be found in the General Data Protection Regulation[25] which applies to all companies processing personal data of 'data subjects' residing in the EU, regardless of where the data processing takes place or where the company processing the data is located.[26] In this context, it is the data subject's location within the EU that serves to legitimatise the application of EU law to non-EU companies.[27]

Both the CSRD and the CSDDD use a jurisdictional trigger of 'business conducted within the EU' to bring companies registered outside the EU within their scope. From 2028, the CSRD will apply to non-EU companies if they have a net turnover of more than €150 million from business conducted within the EU and have a subsidiary or branch within the EU that qualifies as a large, medium or a small company listed on an EU regulated market.[28] These companies will have to prepare corporate sustainability reports in accordance with the European Sustainability Reporting Standards (ESRS)[29] and will be subject to oversight in accordance with Directive 2006/43/EC.[30] The first stated rationale

ECLI:EU:C:2005:762, [2005] ECR I-10805. These cases invalidated Member State rules restricting the freedom of establishment.

[23] See W Ebke, 'The Real Seat Doctrine in the Conflict of Corporate Laws' (2001) 36(3) *International Lawyer* 1015; and M Siems, 'Convergence, Competition, Centros and Conflicts of Law: European Company Law in the 21st Century' (2002) 27 *European Law Review* 47.

[24] For a detailed description of these 'jurisdictional triggers' across various areas of EU law see Scott, 'The New EU "Extraterritoriality"' (n 7).

[25] Regulation (EU) 2016/679 of the European Parliament and of the Council of 27 April 2016 on the protection of natural persons with regard to the processing of personal data and on the free movement of such data, and repealing Directive 95/46/EC (General Data Protection Regulation) [2016] OJ L 119/1.

[26] See C-131/12 *Google Spain SL v Agencia Española de Protección de Datos* [2014] ECLI:EU:C:2014:317 and Case C-507/17.

[27] For an exploration of the question of legitimacy in EU law in the context of access to information, see J Quinn, 'Geo-Location Technology: Restricting Access to Online Content Without Illegitimate Extraterritorial Effects' (2021) 11(3) *International Data Privacy Law* 294.

[28] Directive (EU) 2022/2464 (n 4), Chapter 9(a). The thresholds being a subsidiary that qualifies as a large, medium or a small company listed on an EU regulated market as defined by the Accounting Directive 2013/34/EU.

[29] Commission Delegated Regulation (EU) supplementing Directive 2013/34/EU of the European Parliament and of the Council as regards sustainability reporting standards [2013] C/2023/5303 final available at https://eur-lex.europa.eu/legal-content/EN/ALL/?uri=PI_COM:C(2023)5303.

[30] That Directive relates to statutory audits of annual accounts and consolidated accounts.

for this application to non-EU companies is that it is necessary to ensure that large companies are accountable for their impacts on people and the environment. The second stated rationale was to ensure a level playing field exists for EU registered companies, ie that EU companies are not at a competitive disadvantage within the EU market.[31]

The CSDDD applies to non-EU companies if they, or their subsidiaries on a consolidated basis, generate a net turnover[32] of €450 million from business conducted inside the EU.[33] The CSDDD will also apply to companies that have net turnover of over €80 million and have franchising or licensing agreements in the EU that produce royalties of over €22.5 million.[34] Non-EU companies that fall within these criteria are required to appoint an 'authorised representative' within the EU to facilitate the effective oversight and enforcement of the Directive.[35] The stated rationale for this application to non-EU companies is that it is necessary to achieve the objective of addressing adverse human rights and environmental impacts that arise from the operation of companies.[36] The CSDDD's application to non-EU companies also supports the objective of creating a 'level playing field'[37] within the EU market by protecting EU companies from competition from non-EU companies subject to less stringent regulation and lower operational costs.[38] Extending application to non-EU companies also restricts the potential for 'regulatory arbitrage'[39] by preventing EU companies from registering outside the EU to avoid the CSDDD and continuing its business in the EU through branches or subsidiaries. While the CSDDD's application to non-EU companies increased the likelihood of achieving its objectives, the ultimate justification for the jurisdictional trigger was that the turnover criteria created a 'territorial connection' with the EU as turnover is a proxy for the effects that those companies could have on the EU market.[40]

[31] ibid recital 20.

[32] Directive (EU) 2024/1760 (n 5) recital 30. The definition of the term 'turnover' is based on Directive 2013/34/EU which has established methods for calculating net turnover for companies registered outside the EU based on international accounting frameworks.

[33] ibid art 2(2). Recital 30 states that the number of employees was removed as a threshold element because the definition of 'employee' in the Directive is derived from EU law and so could not be easily applied to companies registered outside the EU.

[34] Only if those agreements ensure a common identity, a common business concept and the application of uniform business methods.

[35] Directive (EU) 2024/1760 (n 5) recital 74.

[36] ibid recital 29.

[37] ibid recital 98 and art 36.

[38] For example, if the CSDDD did not apply to non-EU companies conducting business in the EU they would be free to exploit foreign workers or not invest in due diligence practices that would put EU companies at a competitive disadvantage.

[39] See J Armour, 'Who Should Make Corporate Law? EC Legislation versus Regulatory Competition' (2005) Law Working Paper No 54/2005 *European Corporate Governance Institute* available at www.ecgi.global/sites/default/files/working_papers/documents/ssrn-id860444.pdf, 8–11.

[40] Directive (EU) 2024/1760 (n 5) recital 30.

III. TERRITORIAL EXTENSION

The above jurisdictional triggers bring non-EU based companies within the scope of the CSRD and CSDDD due to their business activity within the EU's territory. A different mechanism which EU law uses to have international effects is 'territorial extension'[41] which describes contexts where EU law uses a territorial connection to the EU to influence conduct that takes place outside its territory. The main context where EU law's territorial extension effects international conduct is its control of access to its market or territory. For example, EU product standards apply to imported as well as domestically produced goods and so, to gain access to the EU's market, non-EU companies must produce their goods in compliance with EU law.[42] An example of territorial access is the EU's limitation on the access of aircraft to its territory based on the safety record of the relevant air carrier and on the overall safety performance of the regulatory authorities in the air carrier's home jurisdiction.[43] Hence, if an aircraft company wishes to fly into the EU's geographical territory, it must meet EU standards and therefore those EU standards influence the behaviour of many companies registered outside the EU.[44]

The CSDDD extends its effects outside the EU's territory through 'firm-level' extension[45] requiring companies within its scope to conduct due diligence across all their subsidiaries and business partners[46] regardless of their size or geographical location. The CSDDD provides that where there is no reasonable expectation that subsidiaries or partners will mitigate or end their adverse human rights and environmental impacts, or where efforts have already failed to do so, the company is required to terminate the business relationship if the impacts are severe.[47] Hence, small and large companies alike across different continents would, assuming appropriate due diligence measures were implemented, come under pressure to comply with the company's code of conduct and mitigate their human rights and environmental impacts.[48] The ultimate

[41] Scott, 'Extraterritoriality and Territorial Extension in EU Law' (n 7).

[42] See 'EU Product Requirements' at https://commission.europa.eu/business-economy-euro/doing-business-eu/eu-product-safety-and-labelling/eu-product-requirements_en.

[43] See Regulation (EC) 2111/2005 of the European Parliament and of the Council of 14 December 2005 on the establishment of a Community list of air carriers subject to an operating ban within the Community and on informing air transport passengers of the identity of the operating air carrier, and repealing Article 9 of Directive 2004/36/EC [2005] OJ L 344/15.

[44] Scott, 'The New EU "Extraterritoriality"' (n 7) 1343.

[45] Taking the term from Enriques, Gatti and Shapira, 'How the EU's Sustainability Due Diligence Directive Could Reshape Corporate America' (n 6). See also J Scott, 'The Global Reach of EU Law' in M Cremona and J Scott (eds), *EU Law Beyond EU Borders: The Extraterritorial Reach of EU Law* (Oxford, Oxford University Press, 2019) 25–28.

[46] In their chain of activities. Directive (EU) 2024/1760 (n 5) art 3(g) defining 'chain of activities' as including downstream business partners (being defined as those involved in distribution, transport and storage) who carry out activities for the company or on behalf of the company and upstream partners relating to the production of goods or the provision of services by the company, including the design, extraction, sourcing, manufacture, transport, storage and supply of raw materials, products or parts of the products and development of the product or the service.

[47] ibid art 10(6).

[48] ibid arts 5–8.

effect is that many non-EU companies will be held to standards that are over and above what is legally required in their jurisdictions, the incentive to comply being the potential termination of a profitable business relationship. Enriques, Gatti and Shapira use the example of Sonos, the audio equipment company, to demonstrate the CSDDD's potential impact on foreign companies.[49] Sonos does not meet the CSDDD's thresholds and so does not fall within the jurisdiction of the EU, but it does supply products to large European companies that are within the CSDDD's scope.[50] Sonos will not be subject to the Directive but will be affected as their European partners due diligence practices place pressure on companies further down their value chains to improve their human rights and environmental practices. This effect does not only apply to relatively large operations like Sonos, but also to the smallest of companies in the supply chain of companies within the CSDDD's scope. In this way, the CSDDD has the potential to improve human rights and environmental practices globally.

This method of firm-level extension represents a model whereby the EU is, in effect, outsourcing the achievement of its legal objectives to private actors.[51] Van Loo describes this phenomenon as 'conscripted enforcement',[52] under which the penalty is the termination of a business relationship that can be devastating for smaller companies.[53] Such 'conscripted enforcement' runs fundamentally contrary to the nexus of contracts description of the company as a set of private agreements[54] instead pushing companies toward a public interest regulatory role.[55] The inclusion of such conscripted enforcement at the EU level demonstrates the theoretical shift that has taken place in European company law under the heading of corporate sustainability.[56]

A. Transatlantic Effects of the CSDDD

Gatti, Enriques and Shapira believe that between the jurisdictional triggers and firm-level extension, the CSDDD will affect virtually all large US companies.[57]

[49] Enriques, Gatti and Shapira (n 6) 13–14.

[50] Such as Ikea and Spotify. See, Sonos Reports Fourth Quarter and Fiscal 2024 Results (2024) available at https://investors.sonos.com/news-and-events/investor-news/latest-news/2024/Sonos-Reports-Fourth-Quarter-and-Fiscal-2024-Results/ (reporting less than €450 million sales in Europe).

[51] See K Bamberger, 'Regulation as Delegation: Private Firms, Decisionmaking, and Accountability in the Administrative State' (2006) 56 *Duke Law Journal* 377.

[52] See R Van Loo, 'The New Gatekeepers: Private Firms as Public Enforcers' (2020) 106(2) *Virginia Law Review* 467. Van Loo analyses various examples of federal regulators requiring large companies to regulate their contractual partners.

[53] ibid 471.

[54] As described in F Easterbrook and D Fischel, *The Economic Structure of Corporate Law* (Harvard University Press, 1991).

[55] Van Loo, 'The New Gatekeepers: Private Firms as Public Enforcers' (n 52) 473.

[56] As discussed in detail in ch 3, European company law has traditionally focused on enabling the common market and cross border business rather than imposing rules focused on protecting the environment and upholding human rights standards.

[57] Enriques, Gatti, Shapira (n 6), 14.

They argue that the most significant effect for US companies is not the impact of the due diligence obligations themselves but how the CSDDD will interact US oversight duties. The 1996 Delaware case of *Caremark*[58] imposed oversight duties on company directors to take a proactive role by, at a minimum, implementing a system that collects information about potential problems and addressing issues or 'red flags' that emerge from this system. The oversight duties set out in *Caremark* were for many years viewed as 'irrelevant' due to procedural difficulties in taking a claim.[59] This position was altered by the 2019 *Marchand* decision[60] where a listeria outbreak occurred in the product line of an ice-cream manufacturer causing multiple deaths. The Delaware Supreme Court held that the fact that the board were not aware of the listeria issues indicated that the directors had failed to comply with their oversight duties. *Marchand* was followed by several other successful *Caremark* claims[61] demonstrating an increased willingness to apply heightened scrutiny to directors' oversight obligations.[62]

Gatti, Enriques and Shapira note that since *Caremark*, most large US companies have developed information monitoring systems but courts remain deferential to directors' decisions on how to design these information systems and what types of information needs to flow up to the board.[63] The main exception to this judicial deference, as demonstrated by *Marchand*, is where certain risks are deemed central to the company's operation and so are too important to lie outside the monitoring system leading to courts concluding that a lack of knowledge is evidence of a failure of oversight.[64] Hence, companies are likely to include human rights and environmental issues within these information frameworks in contexts where they are central to the company's operations, including where this reality is made clear by the company's disclosures or where the potential reputational damage is too big to not proactively monitor such risks.[65] The CSDDD's application to US companies may also result in more red flags being brought to directors regarding environmental and human rights issues.[66] Once such issues are flagged, the CSDDD requires directors to react by preventing, mitigating or ending their impact. If directors fail to take such measures, not only would they be in breach of the CSDDD, but also potentially in breach of their *Caremark* duties.[67]

[58] *In re Caremark Int'l* 698 A 2d 959 (Del Ch 1996).
[59] See M Bullard, 'Caremark's Irrelevance' (2013) 10 *Berkeley Business Law Journal* 15.
[60] *Marchand v Barnhill* 212 A 3d 805 (Del 2019).
[61] See *Clovis Oncology* WL 4850188 (Del Ch 2019); *Hughes v Hu* WL 1987029 (Del Ch 2020); *In Boeing Co* WL 4059934 (Del Ch 2021).
[62] See R Shapira, 'Max Oversight Duties: How Boeing Signifies a Shift in Corporate Law' (2022) 48 *Journal of Corporation Law* 119, 121.
[63] Enriques, Gatti, Shapira, 'How the EU's Sustainability Due Diligence Directive Could Reshape Corporate America' (n 6) 22 citing T Haugh, 'Caremark's Behavioural Legacy' 90 *Temple Law Review* 611, 621.
[64] ibid.
[65] ibid 23.
[66] ibid 25.
[67] ibid 26–27.

Gatti, Enriques and Shapira's ultimate argument is that the CSDDD's application to US companies raises the potential for *Caremark* claims regarding environmental harms and human rights abuses which in turn makes it more likely that top corporate decision-makers will take such issues more seriously.[68] They emphasise that the CSDDD-*Caremark* combination is unlikely to result in significant increases in successful law suits against directors, but is likely to result in companies changing their behaviour to reduce their negative impact on human rights and environmental issues, including across their supply chains.[69] In other words, Gatti, Enriques and Shapira believe the CSDDD-*Caremark* combination will provoke a reflexive response within US companies.

IV. THE BRUSSELS EFFECT

Another way in which the CSRD and CSDDD may have an international impact is through a 'Brussels effect'.[70] The Brussels effect describes a phenomenon where EU law shapes the global regulatory environment through market forces rather than the direct application of law.[71] The de jure Brussels effect describes a situation where in order to gain or maintain access to the EU's market, companies comply with EU regulations and then apply those standards to the rest of their international operations. In contexts where a Brussels effect has taken place, the EU has become a regulatory hegemon, not through jurisdictional triggers or territorial extension but through the voluntary actions of large companies.[72] For example, in the context of privacy, multinational companies often develop products that comply with EU privacy law and sell them globally, not because they are under a legal obligation to do so but because there is a prohibitive cost involved in developing one product for the EU and another for the rest of the world. Alongside the de jure Brussels effect, a secondary de facto Brussels effect sometimes occurs where jurisdictions enact laws that are similar to those in the EU. This occurs partly because the EU has created a new language or framework for legal intervention in a specific context but also because EU standards have become the accepted practice through the de facto Brussels effect and jurisdictions regularly enact rules which reflect existing market practices and standards.[73]

[68] ibid 32.

[69] ibid 35.

[70] See Bradford, *The Brussels Effect* (n 9).

[71] See M Patrin, 'The Brussels Effect: How the European Union Rules the World' (2021) 13 *European Journal of Legal Studies* 377.

[72] Bradford (n 9) 53.

[73] In this way, EU law is influencing the evolution of law in other jurisdictions. The evolutionary path of commercial and company law is discussed in ch 1. See B Benson, 'The Spontaneous Evolution of Commercial Law' (1989) 55(3) *Southern Economic Journal* 644; and S Watson, *The Making of the Modern Company* (Oxford, Hart, 2022).

The Brussels effect is dependent upon several factors[74] including that the relevant market is sufficiently large that companies adapt to the EU's rules.[75] Another factor is that the regulation must apply to inelastic markets. One such example is consumer markets where standards apply based on where a product or service is sold[76] and so are unavoidable if the company wishes to have access to the market.[77] Another factor is 'non-divisibility' which describes a choice made by companies to apply standards from its most regulated market across its entire global operations rather than customising standards for different markets. Companies do this where the economies of scale of adopting a single standard outweigh the benefits of dividing their operations to apply lower standards for less regulated markets.[78] These economies of scale flow from having a single production and supply line, a single compliance framework and preserving uniformity across the company's brand.

It seems unlikely that the CSRD will produce a Brussels effect due to the divisible nature of corporate reporting. For example, if a large US company that meets the CSRD's non-EU threshold is selling products in both the EU and China through different subsidiaries, there is no advantage, from an economies of scale perspective, for the company to produce ESRS standardised reports for their Chinese operations. The main reason such a company would produce detailed reporting for its Chinese subsidiary would be to boost its reputation with consumers or environmental, social, and governance (ESG) orientated investors. The fact that the company was required to meet high reporting standards for their European operations may make it easier to apply such standards elsewhere, but this would not amount to a Brussels effect in the classic sense described above. The CSDDD seems more likely to produce a Brussels effect, given that at least some supply chains will be non-divisible and there will be economy of scale advantages from maintaining a unified production and supply chain.

It is clear from the above analysis that the CSRD and CSDDD will affect many companies outside the EU's territory. The breadth of this influence may produce a de facto Brussels effect where corporate sustainabilty reporting and due diligence become standard market practices for companies and as a result other jurisdictions enact similar laws, reflecting the market practice.[79] Jurisdictions may be more likely to introduce such rules given that the EU – and

[74] See Bradford (n 9) ch 2.

[75] Eg, if a company only has a small percentage of its market in the EU, it is unlikely it will adapt to fit the EU's rules.

[76] Bradford (n 9) 56. In contrast, capital markets are elastic as capital can flow across jurisdictions more readily than consumers move location.

[77] ibid 48.

[78] ibid 54.

[79] ibid. Bradford cites many examples where this has already happened, including in data protection (ch 5) and consumer health and safety (ch 7). In the due diligence context, Thailand is in the process of adopting a mandatory supply chain due diligence law. See www.walkfree.org/news/2025/thailand-to-introduce-mandatory-supply-chain-due-diligence-law/. While it is not clear this is as a

in a due diligence context EU Member States[80] and the United Nations Guiding Principles on Business and Human Rights[81] – have developed a language and structure for what such rules could look like. One counter point to a claim that the CSRD and CSDDD could produce a de facto Brussels effect is the European Commission's 2025 Omnibus I Proposal.[82] The Omnibus proposes to reduce the companies within the CSRD's scope by 80 per cent and limit the application of the due diligence requirements under the CSDDD to subsidiaries and direct contractual partners.[83] Hence, if enacted[84] the Omnibus, would greatly reduce the CSRD's and CSDDD's application to non-EU companies, reducing the likelihood of a Brussels effect.

V. CONCLUSION

The disparity between the globalised nature of corporate activity and the jurisdictional nature of law has caused difficulties for legal efforts to limit the negative externalities of business. The CSRD and CSDDD have used methods that exist in other areas of EU law to extend their effects beyond the geographical boundary of the EU. This is an important development which demonstrates that the jurisdictional nature of law does not mean that it cannot be adapted to the realities of corporate globalisation and the externalities which ensue from it.

result of a Brussels effect, it does show that enacting due diligence laws are on the agenda of non-EU countries.

[80] For example, France's *Loi de Vigilance* (Law No 2017-399) and the German Supply Chain Due Diligence Act (*LkSG – Lieferkettensorgfaltspflichtengesetz* 2021).

[81] OHCHR, 'Guiding Principles on Business and Human Rights' (2011), available at www.ohchr.org/Documents/Publications/GuidingPrinciplesBusinessHR_EN.pdf.

[82] European Commission, 'Omnibus I' (2025) available at https://commission.europa.eu/publications/omnibus-i_en.

[83] ibid 18. The Omnibus does provide that a company may have obligations to extend its due diligence practices to indirect partners where there is 'plausible information' suggesting adverse impacts.

[84] The Omnibus, at the time of writing, is a proposal only and subject to the EU legislative process.

7

The Corporate Purpose

I. INTRODUCTION

THE FUNDAMENTAL QUESTION addressed by this book is how company law can best align the interests of large companies with the interests of society in order to further the goal of advancing the aggregate welfare of all who are affected by a company's activities.[1] At its core, this is a question about the corporate purpose, ie for whose interests is the company managed? As set out in chapter one, the existing default position is one of shareholder value, where companies are managed for the benefit of shareholders.[2] Chapters one and two then set out an argument that shareholder value is not the optimal method of advancing aggregate welfare and instead argued that companies should directly aim to advance the interests of society. Of course, the difficult question is how to create such a shift in the corporate purpose. Any such attempt will necessarily focus on directors, who, as managers of the company, are responsible for delivering on the company's purpose.

The seminal debate on the corporate purpose took place in the 1930s between Adolf Berle and Merrick Dodd.[3] Berle argued that directors should exercise their powers for the benefit of shareholders because it would curb corporate managers from serving their own interests and thereby reduce agency costs.[4] Dodd replied by arguing that directors' should have broader responsibilities, emphasising that the company had a social function as well as a profit-making function.[5] Berle's response was that removing responsibility to shareholders would amount to handing unlimited power to directors and hoping 'something nice will come out of it all'.[6] The debate on the corporate purpose continued after Berle and Dodd's

[1] R Kraakman et al, *The Anatomy of Corporate Law: A Comparative and Functional Approach*, 3rd edn (Oxford, Oxford University Press, 2017) 22.

[2] See S Bainbridge, *The Profit Motive: Defending Shareholder Value Maximization* (Cambridge, Cambridge University Press, 2023).

[3] See J Macintosh, 'The Issues, Effects and Consequences of the Berle-Dodd Debate' (1999) 24 *Accounting, Organizations and Society* 139.

[4] See A Berle, 'Corporate Powers as Powers in Trust' (1930) 44 *Harvard Law Review* 1049, 1049 arguing that the powers granted to management 'are necessarily and at all times exercisable only for the ratable benefit of all the shareholders'.

[5] See M Dodd, 'For Whom are Managers Trustees?' (1932) 45 *Harvard Law Review* 1145, 1148.

[6] A Berle, 'For Whom Corporate Managers are Trustees: A Note' (1932) 45 *Harvard Law Review* 1365, 1368. Interestingly, B Cheffins has noted that both parties subsequently

exchange[7] and has increased in intensity in recent times,[8] however, the central question still revolves around the aims and responsibilities of directors.

Company law requires directors to subordinate their personal interests in favour of being loyal to the company. This expectation is most clearly expressed by the duty to act in the interests of the company. Once directors comply with this duty, they are afforded a wide discretion to exercise their business judgement and decide what is in the interests of the company in any given context. However, despite law granting directors a wide discretion, a combination of pressure from shareholders and financial markets, the influence of the nexus of contracts model as well as the structural features of company law[9] has created a corporate culture where shareholder value is the default expectation and where negative externalities are normalised.[10] As a result, many scholars now argue that company law should evolve and should clarify and provide guidance to directors on the corporate purpose.[11]

Several jurisdictions have already made efforts to clarify that directors are permitted to 'have regard to' or 'take into account' stakeholders or wider public concerns.[12] The EU sought to introduce a similar duty to take into account sustainability matters including human rights, climate change and environmental consequences[13] but the proposal was abandoned after objections from the EU's Regulatory Scrutiny Board.[14] Yet, duties 'to have regard' do little to displace

reevaluated their position and seemed to acknowledge the strengths of the other party's position: see B Cheffins, 'The Past, Present and Future of Corporate Purpose' (2023) Law Working Paper No 713/2023 *European Corporate Governance Institute* available at https://papers.ssrn.com/sol3/papers.cfm?abstract_id=4420800, 14–19.

[7] See M Jensen, 'Value Maximisation, Stakeholder Theory and the Corporate Objective Function' (2001) 7(3) *European Financial Management* 297; A Keay, *The Corporate Objective: Corporations, Globalisation and the Law* (Edward Elgar Publishing, 2011); D Attenborough, 'Giving Effect to the Corporate Purpose Debate: An Equitable Maximisation and Viability Principle' (2012) 32(1) *Legal Studies* 4.

[8] This was provoked by C Mayer's book *Prosperity: Better Business Makes The Greater Good* (Oxford, Oxford University Press, 2018) which prompted a series of responses that reinvigorated the debate. This point is taken up in Section IV below.

[9] For example, shareholders elect directors and have an exclusive or majority of voting rights as discussed in ch 2.

[10] See B Sjåfjell et al, 'Shareholder Primacy: The Main Barrier to Sustainable Companies' in B Sjåfjell and B Richardson (eds), *Company Law and Sustainability: Legal Barriers and Opportunities* (Cambridge, Cambridge University Press, 2015) arguing that the discretion afforded to directors has created a vacuum that has been filled by a 'social norm' of shareholder value.

[11] Eg, see B Sjåfjell, 'Beyond Climate Risk: Integrating Sustainability into The Duties of the Corporate Board' (2018) 23(2) *Deakin Law Review* 1; J Winter, 'Addressing the Crisis of the Modern Corporation: The Duty of Societal Responsibility of the Board' (2020) available at https://papers.ssrn.com/sol3/papers.cfm?abstract_id=3574681. A Johnston et al, 'Corporate Governance for Sustainability' available at https://papers.ssrn.com/sol3/papers.cfm?abstract_id=3502101.

[12] Some notable examples being the UK's Enlightened Shareholder Value, France's *Loi Pacte* and the US Constituency Statutes.

[13] Article 25 of the draft Corporate Sustainability Due Diligence Directive (CSDDD) (2022) available at https://eur-lex.europa.eu/legal-content/EN/TXT/?uri=CELEX%3A52022PC0071.

[14] Available at https://eur-lex.europa.eu/legal-content/EN/TXT/PDF/?uri=PI_COM:SEC(2022)95&from=EN. The main objections being that the proposed duty failed to provide clarity and

shareholder value as they merely permit directors to consider other interests, there is no requirement to do so or penalties for a failing to do so. Hence, scholars who argue that company law should provoke a shift in the corporate purpose argue for stronger measures such as mandatory purpose statements, a duty to do no harm or to sacrifice profits, or a positive duty to promote sustainable value creation. This chapter acknowledges the importance of proposals to change the corporate purpose, but emphasises the importance of supporting procedural rules to give effect to shifts.

Section II sets out the existing position of directors' duties, how it provides directors with extensive discretion and how this discretion has enabled a pursuit of shareholder value. Section III discusses the EU's attempt to reform the duties of directors and the issues revealed by their attempts to do so. Section IV engages with the debate on the corporate purpose, arguing that while setting a new corporate purpose is important, a supplementary framework of procedural rules plus enforcement are more likely to achieve the ultimate goal of reducing the harms caused by companies and better promoting the aggregate welfare of society.

II. DIRECTORS' DUTIES

Delegation of a company's management to a board of directors is a fundamental feature of company law.[15] This delegation reduces managerial costs for shareholders by limiting their involvement to the most fundamental of decisions.[16] However, granting powers of management creates the agency problem, namely the difficulty of ensuring the delegated powers of management are properly exercised.[17] The growth of the public company[18] and the complete separation between share ownership and managerial control[19] made it more difficult to prevent directors from acting opportunistically[20] or being wasteful.[21] As noted above, Berle's solution to this problem was for directors to manage the company for, and be accountable to, shareholders.[22]

what the duty offered in addition to directors' duties at national law and the duty of due diligence proposed by the CSDDD.

[15] See Kraakman et al, *The Anatomy of Corporate Law* (n 1) 12.

[16] Eg, electing directors and changing the company's constitution.

[17] For seminal works see E Fama, 'Agency Problems and the Theory of the Firm' (1980) 88 *Journal of Political Economy* 228 and M Jensen and W Meckling, 'Theory of the Firm: Managerial Behaviour, Agency Costs and Ownership Structure' (1976) 3 *Journal of Economics* 305.

[18] As first discussed in A Berle and G Means, *The Modern Corporation and Private Property* (Transaction, 1932).

[19] See M Blair, *Ownership and Control: Rethinking the Corporate Governance for the Twenty First Century* (Brookings Institute, 1996); and B Clarke, 'Corporate Responsibility in Light of the Separation of Ownership and Control' (1997) 19 *Dublin University Law Journal* 50.

[20] For example, by increasing their own salary or long-term job security.

[21] As discussed in O Williamson, *The Economics of Discretionary Behaviour: Managerial Objectives in a Theory of the Firm* (Prentice-Hall, 1964).

[22] Berle, 'Corporate Powers as Powers in Trust' (n 4).

However, under company law, directors owe their legal duties to the company as a legal person rather than to shareholders. These duties generally require directors to subordinate their personal interests in favour of being loyal to the company,[23] the most obvious demonstration being the duty, in operation across all European and common law jurisdictions, to act in the interests of the company.[24] To comply with this duty, directors must not act in their own personal interests and must have a reasonable basis for their belief that they were acting in the company's interests.[25] For example, in Ireland, like most common law jurisdictions,[26] this standard of reasonable belief is set by a requirement of good faith[27] that can be called into question where there are no reasonable grounds for the claim that the director was acting in the company's interest.[28] The same is true in continental European jurisdictions, for example, in Germany, directors must 'reasonably believe, based on appropriate information, that they were acting in the best interest of the company'.[29] Once directors satisfy this base standard, they are afforded a wide discretion to decide what is in the company's interests in any given context. These decisions, once compliant with their other duties[30] and the wider legal framework, are protected from legal review by the business judgment rule.[31] This rule, while varying in form across jurisdictions, generally provides that directors cannot be held liable for exercising their business judgment, even where a decision has negative consequences for the company or its shareholders.[32]

[23] Several duties exist aimed at ensuring loyalty, for example, directors must avoid a conflict of interests and must not divert corporate opportunities to themselves. The contours of these duties vary across jurisdictions but they are owed to the company and only the company can enforce them. For an exploration of the European context see R Dotevall, 'Is a Common Structure of Company Directors' Duties Evolving in EU?' (2016) 27(2) *European Business Law Review* 1.

[24] For a cross jurisdictional study of this duty, see Sjåfjell et al, 'Shareholder Primacy: The Main Barrier to Sustainable Companies' (n 10).

[25] See J Quinn, 'The Duty to Act in Good Faith in Light of the Business Judgment Principle' (2016) 27(4) *International Company and Commercial Law Review* 120.

[26] For the UK perspective see R Langford and I Ramsey, 'Directors' Duties to Act in the Best Interests of the Company – Subjective or Objective' (2015) 2 *Journal of Business Law* 173.

[27] Section 228(1)(a) of the Irish Companies Act 2014 provides that directors are required to 'act in good faith in what the director considers to be the interests of the company'.

[28] Eg, in the Irish case of *Bloxham (in Liquidation) v The Irish Stock Exchange Ltd* [2014] IEHC 93. Charleton J stated 'Thus, it seems that the test for the exercise of directors' duties must involve a scrutiny of … whether the presence or absence of reasonable grounds enables what is said subjectively to be an honest decision to stand as being in the best interests of the company as a whole'.

[29] See H Merkt, 'Germany: Internal and External Corporate Governance' in A Fleckner and K Hopt (eds), *Comparative Corporate Governance: A Functional and International Analysis* (Cambridge, Cambridge University Press, 2013) 543.

[30] Eg, the duty of care.

[31] See Kraakman et al (n 1) 69.

[32] See A Keay and J Loughrey, 'The Concept of Business Judgment' (2019) 39(1) *Legal Studies* 36. The primary rationales for the business judgment rule are that courts often lack the information and expertise necessary to accurately substitute their views in place of directors and that it would be unduly inhibiting for directors if their decisions were subject to review by the courts.

Despite being a core legal duty across all common law and European jurisdictions, the phrase to 'act in the interests of the company' is attributed a variety of meanings. First, the duty has been interpreted by several common law courts to mean a duty to act in the interests of the shareholders.[33] Perhaps the most well-known example of this interpretation comes from the US case of *Dodge v Ford*[34] where the Michigan court stated 'the business corporation is organised and carried on primarily for the profit of stockholders. The powers of directors are to be employed for that end'.[35] Second, a variety of this interpretation is 'enlightened shareholder value' where acting in the company's interests means prioritising shareholders while at the same time considering stakeholders or societal concerns.[36] The United Kingdom follows this approach[37] where directors are required to promote the success of the company for the 'benefit of its members as a whole' but, in doing so, they are to have regard to stakeholder interests including employees, customers, suppliers, and the local community. Enlightened shareholder value is also followed by most US States via constituency statutes[38] as well as in Portugal, Spain and Poland.[39] This 'enlightened' approach permits directors to consider interests beyond shareholders but does not mandate such consideration and is unenforceable by stakeholders.[40] The primary legal effect is that shareholders are prevented from taking legal action against directors who have deviated from the prioritisation of shareholders.[41]

A different, third, approach is to see the duty to act in the interests of the company as one which requires the company as a legal person to be prioritised over both shareholders and stakeholders.[42] Hopt describes this as the

[33] An English example is the Court of Appeal case, *Greenhalgh v Ardene Cinemas Ltd* [1951] 2 All ER 1120, 1126 where Lord Evershed stated that the 'phrase, the company as a whole does not mean the company as a commercial entity as distinct from the corporators. It means the corporators as a general body'. One Irish example is *G&S Doherty Ltd v Doherty* (19 June 1969, unreported), HC, 22 where Hency J stated that 'directors are in a fiduciary position, and must exercise their power bona fide for the benefit of the company as a whole, that is to say, the shareholders as a whole'. The Irish codification of directors' duties has not followed this case law, instead the Companies Act 2014, s 228(1)(a) imposes a general duty on directors to act in 'the interests of the company'.

[34] *Dodge v Ford Motor Co* 204 Mich 459; 170 NW 668 (Mich 1919).

[35] ibid 22.

[36] See A Keay, *The Enlightened Shareholder Value Principle and Corporate Governance* (Routledge, 2013).

[37] UK Companies Act 2006, s 172(1).

[38] See E Orts, 'Beyond Shareholders: Interpreting Corporate Constituency Statutes' (1993) 61 *George Washington Law Review* 14; and K Hale, 'Corporate Law and Stakeholders; Moving Beyond Stakeholder Statutes' (2003) 45 *Arizona Law Review* 823.

[39] See Sjåfjell et al (n 10) 100.

[40] Duties to 'have regard to' stakeholder interests are owed to the company and so cannot be directly enforced by any of the interest groups, see R Williams, 'Enlightened Shareholder Value in UK Company Law' (2009) 35 *University of New South Wales law Journal* 360, 369.

[41] P Davies, *Gower and Davies Principles of Modern Company Law*, 8th edn (Sweet and Maxwell, 2008) 519.

[42] This interpretation fits with an entity theory of the company briefly discussed in ch 1. See E Micheler, *Company Law: A Real Entity Theory* (Oxford, Oxford University Press, 2021).

'decisive factor' in German company law[43] and both the Canadian[44] and Dutch Supreme Courts[45] have followed this interpretation. A variety of this interpretation can be found in legislation which requires directors to act in the interests of the company but makes clear that this includes taking into account matters of the public interest.[46] For example, in France the 2019 *Loi Pacte*[47] provides that the 'company shall be managed in the corporate interest, taking into account the social and environmental concerns linked to its activity'.[48] Similarly, in New Zealand, directors must act in the best interests of the company but are expressly granted permission to 'consider matters other than the maximisation of profit (for example, environmental, social, and governance matters)'.[49] However, much like under an enlightened shareholder value interpretation, duties to have regard to these wider social issues are not mandated or legally enforceable and for the most part, directors remain free to ignore such interests.

The above discussion demonstrates that different interpretations exist for the duty to act in the interests of the company, all of which provide directors with extensive discretion. Even in jurisdictions which require the prioritisation of shareholders, directors still retain a broad managerial discretion to decide what that means in a given context, to determine time horizons and the general strategy to be pursued. Similarly, the other interpretations of the duty merely permit directors to consider stakeholders or wider social concerns rather than mandating that they do so or providing them with guidance or a procedure for how to do so. This lack of positive guidance is unsurprising given that the aim of the duty to act in the interests of the company is to ensure loyalty rather than setting a positive purpose for directors to pursue.

[43] Hopt, 'Corporate Purpose and Stakeholder Value Corporate Purpose and Stakeholder Value – Historical, Economic and Comparative Law Remarks on the Current Debate, Legislative Options and Enforcement Problems' (2024) Law Working Paper No 690/2023 *European Corporate Governance Institute* available at https://papers.ssrn.com/sol3/papers.cfm?abstract_id=4390119, 36.

[44] In *Peoples Department Stores Inc v Wise* [2004] 3 SCR 461 the Supreme Court held that the 'statutory duty to act in the best interests of the corporation should not be simply read as the best interests of the shareholders. From an economic perspective, the best interests of the corporation means the maximisation of the value of the corporation', 481.

[45] See Dutch case *ABN Amro* (JOR 2007, 178). For a discussion of further case law supporting this description see M Lokin and J Veldman, 'The Potential of the Dutch Corporate Governance Model for Sustainable Governance and Long Term Stakeholder Value' (2019) 12 *Erasmus Law Review* 50.

[46] The difference between this and an enlightened shareholder value approach is that there is no explicit requirement to prioritise the interests of shareholders.

[47] *Plan d'Action pour la Croissance et la Transformation des Entreprises* (2019).

[48] The meaning of this phrase continues to be the subject of intense debate in France. See A Pietrancosta, 'Codification in Company Law of General CSR Requirements: Pioneering Recent French Reforms and EU Perspectives' Law Working Paper No 639/2022 *European Corporate Governance Institute* available at https://www.ecgi.global/sites/default/files/working_papers/documents/codificationfinal_0.pdf, 47-59.

[49] Companies (Directors' Duties) Amendment Act 2023, s 131(5). See L Buckley, 'Directors' Duty of Loyalty and ESG Considerations: Aotearoa New Zealand's Controversial Companies (Directors' Duties) Amendment Act 2023' (2024) 39 *Australian Journal of Corporate Law* 323.

III. DIRECTORS' DUTIES AND EUROPEAN COMPANY LAW

Alongside the proposals to expand corporate reporting and introduce due diligence obligations, the EU also proposed to reform the duties of directors. In the European Green Deal, the European Commission set out a view that 'sustainability should be further embedded into the corporate governance framework, as many companies still focus too much on short-term financial performance compared to their long-term development and sustainability aspects'.[50] To take action on this policy position, the European Commission hired Ernst and Young (EY) to produce a report on 'Directors' Duties and Sustainable Corporate Governance'.[51]

EY's report focused extensively on the damaging nature of short termism, the abstract stating that the 'focus of corporate decision-makers on short-term shareholder value' reduced 'the long-term economic, environmental and social sustainability of European businesses'.[52] Relying on academic literature and empirical studies, the report identified seven major drivers of short term shareholder value, which included: that corporate governance frameworks failed to give sufficient voice to the long-term interests of stakeholders; and that there was a lack of enforcement of directors' duties.[53] The report also stated that the duty to act in the company's interest was widely understood by directors to mean the maximisation of short term shareholder value, even though this was not prescribed in the national law of Member States.[54] The report provided that even where national law made clear that shareholders should not be prioritised over other interests, citing the Netherlands as an example, the law failed to clarify what is meant by the 'company interest'.[55] The report concluded that EU law reform was necessary to challenge shareholder value[56] and that the reform of directors' duties at EU level could clarify misconceptions regarding the corporate purpose and make directors more accountable.[57] The report recommended a new EU directive requiring directors to 'properly balance the following interests, alongside the interest of shareholders, when acting in the interest of the company: long-term interests of the company (beyond 5–10 years); interests of employees; interest of customers; interest of local and global environment;

[50] Communication from the Commission to the European Parliament, the European Council, the Council, the European Economic and Social Committee and the Committee of the Regions – The European Green Deal [2019] COM/2019/640 final, available at https://eur-lex.europa.eu/legal-content/EN/TXT/?uri=celex:52019DC0640, 17.

[51] EY report for the European Commission, 'Study on Directors' Duties and Sustainable Corporate Governance' (2020) available at https://op.europa.eu/en/publication-detail/-/publication/e47928a2-d20b-11ea-adf7-01aa75ed71a1/language-en.

[52] ibid abstract.

[53] ibid vi.

[54] ibid 32.

[55] ibid 32.

[56] ibid vi.

[57] ibid vii.

interest of society at large'.[58] EY also recommended a new directive requiring corporate boards to integrate sustainability aspects (risks, opportunities, impacts) into the company's business strategy.[59]

The report's publication was met with extensive criticism from across academia on the basis that it used a flawed methodology due to its reliance unsupported assertions and a biased use of literature.[60] For example, Bassen, Lopatta and Ringe, in a response to the EU, stated the report 'randomly collects empirical findings without filtering by qualitative criteria'.[61] Similarly, a group of Nordic company law scholars described the report as displaying 'a lack of understanding of the nature of legal discourse' and presenting a 'biased, unrepresentative and highly politically motivated survey of literature and empirics'.[62] Beyond its methodological flaws, the primary substantive criticism was regarding the report's focus on time horizons. As Roe et al point out, the report failed to conceptually distinguish between problems of short termism and problems of negative externalities.[63] Roe et al argue that while short termism can lead to negative externalities, it is not problematic in and of itself[64] and is not suited to legal regulation while negative externalities are clearly problematic and are much more suited to legal intervention.[65]

Despite the criticisms, the European Commission seemed to broadly agree with EY's report stating in an impact assessment that though national company law requires 'corporate boards to act in the interest of the company as a whole, the company interest and directors duties are interpreted narrowly favouring maximisation of short-term financial value'.[66] However, the Commission did not bring forward new directives as recommended by the report but rather incorporated aspects of the recommendations into the proposal for the Corporate Sustainabilty Due Diligence Directive (CSDDD).[67] Article 25 of the proposed

[58] ibid 73–79. The report also recommended multiple other reforms including directors' remuneration and board composition which lie outside the scope of this chapter.

[59] ibid 104–09.

[60] Eg see response to the EY report by the Group of European Company Law Experts available at www.ecgi.global/events/directors-duties-and-sustainable-corporate-governance.

[61] A Bassen, K Lopatta and WG Ringe, 'Feedback Statement' available at https://www.ecgi.global/events/directors-duties-and-sustainable-corporate-governance.

[62] Nordic Company Law Scholars, 'Response to the Study on Directors' Duties and Sustainable Corporate Governance' (2021) *Nordic & European Company Law Working Paper* available at https://papers.ssrn.com/sol3/papers.cfm?abstract_id=3709762, 2.

[63] See M Roe et al, 'The Sustainable Corporate Governance Initiative in Europe' (2021) 7 *Yale Journal on Regulation Online Bulletin* 133, 136.

[64] ibid, using the example of the mafia to show that just because an organisation takes a long term approach does not mean it is good for society. Similarly, the group of Nordic company law scholars describe the notion of short termism as a 'vague notion' that is 'inapt for analytical purpose': Nordic Company Law Scholars, 'Response to the Study on Directors' Duties' (n 62) 6.

[65] Ibid 144.

[66] DG Justice, 'Inception Impact Assessment on Sustainable Corporate Governance' (2020) Ares 4034032 available at https://ec.europa.eu/info/law/better-regulation/have-your-say/initiatives/12548-Sustainable-corporate-governance_en, 2.

[67] Draft CSDDD (n 13).

CSDDD provided that company directors, when fulfilling their duty to act in the interests of the company, must take into account the consequences of their decisions for sustainability matters, including where applicable, human rights, climate change and environmental consequences in the short, medium and long term. The recommendations regarding the need to integrate sustainability risks into the business strategy were included, but limited to the company's duty to conduct due diligence rather than the proposed directors' duty.[68] In an accompanying impact assessment report of the CSDDD, the Commission again emphasised that the legal discretion afforded to directors resulted in an 'an almost exclusive focus on short-term financial value maximisation'[69] and that reform of European company law was necessary to clarify that directors of companies had broader responsibilities.[70]

The proposed duty was the subject of objections by the Regulatory Scrutiny Board[71] and was not included in the enacted version of the CSDDD. The Regulatory Scrutiny Board stated that the Commission had failed to make clear why a reform of directors' duties was necessary in addition to a duty of due diligence.[72] The Regulatory Scrutiny Board also criticised the proposed duty for lacking clarity, noting that the recommended change failed to specify whether directors should prioritise the long-term interest of the company over the particular interests of stakeholders or sustainability considerations.[73]

IV. THE CORPORATE PURPOSE

Ultimately, the European Commission failed in its objective to introduce a new directors' duty to take into account sustainability matters including, human rights, climate change and environmental consequences. If the Regulatory Scrutiny Board's opinion is taken as the reason for this failure, it was because the Commission's proposal lacked clarity and failed to describe what a new directors' duty would add over and above a duty of due diligence and the duties that

[68] These elements of the CSDDD are discussed in ch 5.

[69] European Commission, Impact Assessment Report for the proposed CSDDD available at https://ec.europa.eu/info/law/better-regulation/have-your-say/initiatives/12548-Sustainable-corporate-governance_en, 21–24.

[70] Ibid 47.

[71] European Commission Regulatory Scrutiny Board, Proposal for a Directive of the European Parliament and of the Council on Sustainable Corporate Due Diligence and amending Directive (EU) 2019/1937 (Impact Assessment on Sustainable Corporate Governance) available at https://eur-lex.europa.eu/legal-content/EN/TXT/PDF/?uri=PI_COM:SEC(2022)95&from=EN. The Regulatory Scrutiny Board was created in 2015 as an oversight body to assess the quality of draft impact assessments, fitness checks, and major evaluations within the Commission. See B Pircher, 'The EU's Commission Regulatory Scrutiny Board: Better Regulation or Biased Influence on Legislation' (2023) available at www.diva-portal.org/smash/get/diva2:1753934/FULLTEXT01.pdf.

[72] Regulatory Scrutiny Board, Impact Assessment on Sustainable Corporate Governance (n 71), 2.

[73] ibid 3.

exist at the national level. One reason for these shortcomings was due to the Commission's framing of the problem as one of short-term time horizons – a framing originating in the European Green Deal[74] – instead of the issue on which the other corporate sustainability reforms were focused, namely the reduction of negative impacts of companies on human rights and the environment. Had EY and the Commission focused on those issues they would have likely arrived at a different proposal as duties that permit directors to have regard to societal issues have had little if any impact in jurisdictions where they have been introduced. As Roe et al argue, simple exhortations in the form of directors' duties are unlikely to address the problem of externalities, using the US constituency statutes as an example.[75] Roe et al, instead argue that negative externalities are best regulated by sector specific law.[76] To use the language of chapter one of this book, their argument is that company law best advances aggregate welfare by being facilitative and other areas of law are best equipped to address negative externalities. However, many other scholars argue that redefining the corporate purpose and new directors' duties does have the capacity to better align the interests of companies with that of society and reduce the negative externalities of business. However, they must go beyond duties that merely permit directors to consider societal issues.

A. Purpose Statements

Colin Mayer has been at the forefront of arguing for the importance of the corporate purpose. His 2018 book *Prosperity*[77] begins by acknowledging that while companies are important creators of wealth, sources of employment and creators of new technologies, they are also sources of deprivation and environmental degradation.[78] Mayer argues that as our society becomes increasingly dependent on companies, we need to ensure that they can bear this responsibility.[79] Mayer is critical of Friedman's doctrine of 'make money for shareholders'[80]

[74] European Green Deal (n 50) stating that 'many companies still focus too much on short-term financial performance compared to their long-term development and sustainability aspects' [2.2.1].

[75] Roe et al, 'The Sustainable Corporate Governance Initiative in Europe' (n 63) 146.

[76] ibid.

[77] Mayer, *Prosperity* (n 8) 9. The book produced a series of responses from leading scholars including M Ventoruzzo, 'On Prosperity by Colin Mayer: Brief Critical Remarks on the (Legal) Relevance of announcing a Multi-Stakeholders Corporate Purpose' (2020) *Bocconi Legal Studies Research Paper* available at https://papers.ssrn.com/sol3/papers.cfm?abstract_id=3546139; G Ferrarini, 'An Alternative View of Corporate Purpose: Colin Mayer on Prosperity' (2020) *Genoa Centre for Law and Finance Working Paper* available at https://papers.ssrn.com/sol3/papers.cfm?abstract_id=3552156; P Davies, 'Shareholder Voice and Corporate Purpose: The Purposeless of Mandatory Corporate Purpose Statements' (2022) Law Working Paper No 666/2022 *European Corporate Governance Institute* available at https://ssrn.com/abstract=4285770.

[78] Mayer (n 8) 1.

[79] ibid.

[80] ibid 5.

or 'profit within the rules of the game',[81] which he regards as the 'seed of nature's destruction' and as having the potential 'to threaten our existence'.[82] He believes as the company's purpose is the source of its conduct and performance[83] that a reorientation away from Friedman's doctrine to a purpose of finding 'profitable solutions to the problems of people and the planet'[84] has the capacity to change how large companies operate. He is not alone in this view, for example, a group of high profile scholars have argued that a 'corporate purpose may exert a profound influence in shaping and directing every business decision'.[85]

Mayer has more recently developed his argument in *Prosperity*, through his work with the British Academy[86] and in his latest book,[87] to argue that the purpose of companies should be to 'produce profitable solutions for the problems of people and planet, not profiting from producing problems for either'.[88] The core of this argument is that shareholders should remain as the sole beneficiary of the company's residual success but that this success should be conditional on the avoidance of harm to others.[89] He argues that if companies are prevented from profiting from harm, then the only way they can produce profit is by creating value for society.[90]

Mayer's proposed method to implement this corporate purpose of 'profit while doing no harm' is through purpose statements, commitment techniques and public and private enforcement. The first element of this model, expressed in *Prosperity*, is a legal requirement for companies to articulate their purpose in their constitutional documents.[91] Hence, his argument is along similar lines to France's *Loi Pacte*[92] which provides that a company may define in its constitution its *raison d'être* alongside its core principles or values.[93] However, unlike France's *Loi Pacte*, Mayer argues that stating a company's purpose should be mandatory, stating that 'corporate law … should require companies to articulate their

[81] As expressed in M Friedman, 'The Social Responsibility of Business is to Increase Its Profits' (1970) New York Times, 13 September available at https://www.nytimes.com/1970/09/13/archives/a-friedman-doctrine-the-social-responsibility-of-business-is-to.html. See also, M Friedman, *Capitalism and Freedom* (The University of Chicago Press, 1962).

[82] Mayer (n 8) 2.

[83] ibid 12.

[84] ibid.

[85] B Deffains et al, 'A European Corporate Governance Model: Integrating Corporate Purpose into Practice for a Better Society' (2023) *Nordic and European Company Law LSN Research Paper* available at: https://ssrn.com/abstract=4632353.

[86] British Academy, 'Principles for Purposeful Business' (2019) available at www.thebritishacademy.ac.uk/publications/future-of-the-corporation-principles-for-purposeful-business/.

[87] C Mayer, *Capitalism and Crises: How to Fix Them* (Oxford, Oxford University Press, 2024).

[88] ibid. See also C Mayer, 'Success, Law and ESG' (2024) Law Working Paper No 725/2024 *European Corporate Governance Institute* available at https://papers.ssrn.com/sol3/papers.cfm?abstract_id=4939931.

[89] Mayer, *Capitalism and Crises* (n 87) ch 4; Mayer, 'Success, Law and ESG' (n 88) 5.

[90] Mayer, 'Success, Law and ESG' (n 88) 8.

[91] See Mayer (n 8).

[92] *Plan d'Action pour la Croissance et la Transformation des Entreprises* (2019).

[93] See Pietrancosta, 'Codification in Company Law of General CSR Requirements' (n 48).

purposes, incorporate them in their articles of association'.[94] However, Mayer does not think that law should direct what companies actually define as their purpose, instead that it should be left to companies themselves to decide their purpose, stating that the law should not seek to prescribe the positive problem-solving activities of companies and describing his approach as 'enabling not prescriptive or restrictive'.[95]

His more recent work sets out proposals for how to ensure companies do no harm. The first element of this is through governance and commitment to the company's purpose. He summarises these as follows: (1) the corporate purpose should be formally approved by the board and supported by the corporations' shareholders; (2) there should be a process of consulting with stakeholders about the requirements associated with achieving this purpose; (3) there must be a set of metrics to evaluate performance against delivery of the company's purpose, including a system of external reporting; (4) companies must set out how their internal governance, culture, values, and incentives aligned with its purpose; (5) companies should set out the current and capital costs involved in fulfilling its purpose; (6) companies should set out a compelling business case for how their objectives will be profitable and value enhancing once account is taken of the risks and costs; (7) corporations should determine the party who will be responsible for holding their boards to account for delivery of its commitments; (8) companies will report on the detriments they have and might cause in the future, how they will avoid, mitigate, remedy and rectify them, the costs involved in doing that now and in the future, the potential revenues that might result and the effect on their profitability and value creation.[96]

Mayer recommends for this framework to be upheld by a public regulatory authority[97] whose ultimate role would be to ensure that companies 'have the culture, values, strategies, processes and procedures in place to profit without harm and the systems for accounting, auditing and reporting to record that is the case'.[98] He also sees a role for private enforcement, stating that companies should incur the costs of rectifying, remedying, or mitigating the harm they inflict on others.[99] Mayer also recommends that directors should be under a duty of care to ensure that their companies have systems and processes in place to avoid detriments being imposed on other parties.[100]

[94] Mayer (n 8) 23.

[95] C Mayer, 'The Purpose of Corporate Purpose Statements: A Response to "Shareholder Voice and Corporate Purpose: The Purposeless of Mandatory Corporate Purpose Statements" by Paul Davies' (2023) Law Working Paper No 694/2023 *European Corporate Governance Institute* available at http://ssrn.com/abstract_id=4397435.

[96] ibid 8 and Mayer, 'Success, Law and ESG' (n 88) 14–16.

[97] Mayer (n 88) 11 referring to the proposed 'The Audit, Reporting and Governance Authority' in the British context, see www.accountancyage.com/2024/07/31/the-draft-audit-reform-and-corporate-governance-bill-landmark-legislation-in-the-making/.

[98] ibid 12.

[99] ibid 5–6.

[100] ibid 6.

B. Sustainable Value within Planetary Boundaries

Beate Sjåfjell is also at the forefront of arguments for a change to the corporate purpose. The starting point for her argument is that the discretion afforded to directors by the duty to act in the interests of the company has created a vacuum that has been filled by a 'social norm' of shareholder value which is now the main barrier to sustainable companies.[101] Her argument emphasises that the behaviour of corporate managers is not only shaped by law but also the norms within corporate culture,[102] which are driven by pressure from shareholders, financial markets and the corporate structure.[103] She argues that reforming directors' duties can alleviate the real or perceived pressure to pursue shareholder value and make clear that directors have wider responsibilities.

Her proposal is for directors to be under a legal duty to create 'sustainable value within planetary boundaries'.[104] She conceptualises sustainable value as being: (a) environmentally sustainable in that it ensures the long-term stability and resilience of the ecosystems that support human life; (b) socially sustainable in that it facilitates good governance, the respect and promotion of human rights and other fundamental social rights; and (c) economically sustainable in that it generates wealth and work in a way that satisfies the economic needs necessary for stable and resilient societies.[105] She defines the second aspect of the duty, 'planetary boundaries', as 'the scientifically recognised processes that regulate the stability and resilience of the Earth system within which humanity can continue to develop and thrive for generations to come'.[106] Hence, the duty is grounded in environmental science which aims to set out the ecological limits

[101] See B Sjåfjell et al, 'Shareholder Primacy: The Main Barrier to Sustainable Companies' (n 10). See also D Lund and E Pollman, 'The Corporate Governance Machine' (2021) 121 *Columbia Law Review* 2563, 3630 arguing that 'the shareholder primacy viewpoint has become enmeshed in our cultural and institutional understanding of good governance'.

[102] See J Hill, 'Shifting Contours of Directors' Fiduciary Duties and Norms in Comparative Corporate Governance' (2020) 5 *Journal of International, Transnational, and Comparative Law* 163; and J Coffee, 'Do Norms Matter? A Cross-Country Evaluation' (2001) 149 *University of Pennsylvania Law Review* 2151.

[103] Eg, shareholders elect directors and have an exclusive or majority of voting rights which, as discussed in ch 2, can influence the decision making of directors. Leo Strine Jr has argued that directors will naturally favour and be loyal to those who choose them: see L Strine Jr, 'Corporate Power is Corporate Purpose II: An Encouragement for Future Consideration from Professors Johnson and Millon' (2017) 74 *Washington and Lee Law Review* 1165, 1177. See also a study by Tomlinson et al, finding that representatives make decisions favouring the groups which they were told had selected them: See Tomlinson et al, 'A Participatory Simulation of the Accountable Capitalism Act' (2020) *Proceedings of the 2020 CHI Conference on Human Factors in Computing Systems* 1 available at https://dl.acm.org/doi/abs/10.1145/3313831.3376326.

[104] B Sjåfjell and J Mähönen, 'Upgrading the Nordic Corporate Governance Model for Sustainable Companies' (2014) 11(2) *European Company Law* 58. See also B Sjåfjell, 'Sustainable Value Creation Within Planetary Boundaries – Reforming Corporate Purpose and Duties of the Corporate Board' (2020) 12 *Sustainability* 6245.

[105] See B Sjåfjell and M Taylor, 'A Clash of Norms: Shareholder Primacy vs Sustainable Corporate Purpose' (2019) 13(3) *International and Comparative Corporate Law Journal* 40, 62.

[106] Sjåfjell, 'Sustainable Value Creation Within Planetary Boundaries' (n 104) 6251.

of the planet.[107] Sjåfjell and Taylor[108] see planetary boundaries as analogous to Lessig's concept of 'architecture' as a fixed constraint imposed by existing structures which serves as a 'modality of regulation'.[109] In other words, planetary boundaries as defined by the scientific literature serves as the outer boundary within which companies must develop their own individual understanding of sustainable value creation.

Sjåfjell argues that the value of this duty is first to definitively clarify that the duty of the board is not to maximise returns for shareholders and thereby relieve directors from the pressures of the shareholder value norm.[110] Alongside this declaratory value, Sjåfjell argues for the duty to be operationalised[111] through: (1) the development and publication of a business model that integrates sustainable value creation within planetary boundaries throughout the business; (2) internal control and risk management systems; and (3) a stringent sustainability assessment to be carried out every three years which includes information on stakeholder impacts.[112]

Sjåfjell's work informed a statement by over 60 high-profile company law scholars to argue that directors should be subject to a legally-binding obligation to develop, disclose and implement, a forward-looking corporate sustainability strategy that identifies and addresses material environmental and social issues, the purpose of which is to ensure respect for the planetary boundaries and human rights.[113] The group recommends a series of mechanisms through which this obligation should be implemented, including the publication of verifiable targets, the production of an annual progress report and the supervision by a non-executive committee. They also recommend that a failure to implement the corporate sustainability strategy should be a breach of the duty to act in the interests of the company and that a public regulatory authority should have the capacity to bring proceedings against companies where the non-implementation of the strategy caused serious harm to third parties or unlawful harm to the environment.[114]

[107] First developed by J Rockström et al, 'Planetary Boundaries: Exploring the Safe Operating Space for Humanity' (2009) 14(2) *Ecology and Society* 1 and subsequently built upon by W Steffen et al, 'Planetary Boundaries: Guiding Human Development on a Changing Planet' (2015) 347(6223) *Science* 736.

[108] See Sjåfjell and Taylor, 'A Clash of Norms' (n 105) 62.

[109] See L Lessig, *Code, and Other Laws of Cyberspace* (Basic Books, 1999); and L Lessig, 'The Law of the Horse: What Cyber Law Might Teach' (1999) 113 *Harvard Law Review* 501 the other modalities discussed by Lessig being law, social norms and markets.

[110] B Sjåfjell, 'Reforming EU Company Law to Secure the Future of European Business' (2021) 2 *European Company and Financial Law Review* 190, 209.

[111] B Sjåfjell, 'Beyond Climate Risk' (n 11). This is grounded in the work conducted by the Sustainable Market Actors for Responsible Trade (SMART) project available at https://www.smart.uio.no/.

[112] Sjåfjell, 'Reforming EU Company Law' (n 110) 212–15.

[113] A Johnston et al, 'Corporate Governance for Sustainability' available at https://papers.ssrn.com/sol3/papers.cfm?abstract_id=3502101.

[114] ibid.

C. Moral Responsibility

A different perspective on the corporate purpose comes from Elhauge[115] and Winter[116] who see the problem of the negative externalities of business as a result of the company's ability to interrupt society's normal interpersonal moral responsibility. Elhauge, Like Teubner,[117] rejects the idea that regulatory law can force companies to be socially responsible because it can never be sufficiently precise to deter or sanction all undesirable activity.[118] He argues that law, to promote the 'public interest', must create a framework of moral responsibility for directors through 'social and moral' sanctions which encourages them to sacrifice profits and consider their effects on others.[119] He describes social sanctions as including the embarrassment of bad publicity, the reproach of family and friends or being disdained or shunned by the wider community. Moral sanctions include the guilt from violating moral norms, the loss of feelings of inner peace or satisfaction which may make us reject certain choices, regardless of how much they benefit us personally. Elhauge's fundamental point is that the company has become a vehicle to insulate humans from the normal social and moral sanctions that exist in society.[120] He regards the company as providing this insulation permanently to shareholders[121] but that directors, as decision makers, can still be made subject to moral and social sanctions through 'pressures and processes' which: (1) counteract their sense of responsibility to shareholders; and (2) make clear that their decisions cause ill effects to others.[122]

Winter sees the problem in broadly similar terms, describing the company as a vehicle of alienation which can only be overcome by re-humanising the company.[123] To do this, Winter argues that legal reforms should focus on directors as the company's human agents in order to activate emotional responsibility through feelings of empathy, remorse and guilt. Winter's argument is to define the corporate purpose in terms of 'societal responsibility'[124] which involves understanding the way that human capital (employees), social capital (the communities in which the corporation operates) and natural capital (natural

[115] E Elhauge, 'Sacrificing Corporate Profits in the Public Interest' (2005) 80(3) *New York University Law Review* 733.

[116] Winter, 'Addressing the Crisis of the Modern Corporation' (n 11).

[117] See G Teubner, 'Substantive and Reflexive Elements in Modern Law' (1983) 17(2) *Law and Society Review* 239; and G Teubner, 'Corporate Fiduciary Duties and their Beneficiaries' in G Teubner and K Hopt (eds), *Corporate Governance and Directors' Liabilities: Legal, Economic and Sociological Analyses on Corporate Social Responsibility* (De Gruyter, 1985) and as discussed in ch 2.

[118] Teubner, 'Corporate Fiduciary Duties' (n 117) 748.

[119] ibid 744 and 752.

[120] ibid 758.

[121] ibid given that they have delegated the actual decision making to directors.

[122] ibid 800.

[123] See J Winter, 'The Dehumanisation of the Large Corporation' (2020) available at https://papers.ssrn.com/sol3/papers.cfm?abstract_id=3517492.

[124] See Winter, 'Addressing the Crisis of the Modern Corporation' (n 11).

resources and environmental and climate degradation) are used, maintained and compensated. He argues that understanding such elements will clarify the impact of directors' decision and claims that this will fundamentally change the deliberation and decision-making practices in boards.[125]

D. Advancing Societal Interests

The above proposals argue that redefining the corporate purpose can play a role in companies better advancing aggregate welfare. Hence, they aim to replace shareholder value with objectives of doing good while doing no harm, creating sustainable value creation or for companies to act with moral responsibility. These proposals also have in common a reliance on processes and procedures to give effect to their new vision of the corporate purpose. It is this dimension that elevates these proposals above permissive duties to 'have regard to' which in Roe's words, are little more than aspirational statements. It is not enough to allow directors to have regard to societal interests, they must be given guidance on what that means at a practical level (ie processes to follow) and must be incentivised to comply through enforcement mechanisms. This book is based on an argument for the importance of such procedures and processes and has argued that such rules can provoke a relieve effect which can establish the societal company which has an internal sense of responsibility to do no harm.

It is useful to clarify the argument for reflexive law against objections to legal interventions raised by Winter who argues that building new 'compliance bureaucracies' that attempt to control people will fail[126] as society cannot be engineered.[127] He further argues that after every crisis new rules are introduced that give a false sense of control coupled with new regulatory authorities that supervise organisations. He maintains that this combination of regulatory creep and external supervision has led to enormous, stultifying compliance bureaucracies the paradoxical consequence being that people's sense of responsibility is usurped by a focus on complying with the rules that protect them from having to take responsibility for their own judgements.[128] This is an entirely accurate description of the failures of regulatory law which attempts to control and achieve specific outcomes.[129] However, as set out in chapter two, reflexive law is different to regulatory law and rather than attempting to control the decision making of company directors, it mandates companies and directors to follow processes focused on their external impact. The aim of these processes is to bring to light the external effects of their decisions and in turn provoke a reflexion within the

[125] ibid 6.
[126] ibid 14.
[127] Winter, 'The Dehumanisation of the Large Corporation' (n 123) 4.
[128] ibid.
[129] See Teubner, 'Substantive and Reflexive Elements in Modern Law' (n 117).

board room and the company more broadly to develop 'economic self-restraint' regarding actions which cause harm to the non-economic environment.[130] Reflexive laws should not form a compliance bureaucracy but establish companies that exercise an informed and regulated autonomy, leaving directors with the final responsibility for the executive decisions made.

V. CONCLUSION

The corporate purpose is one of the main debates in company law. It has been ongoing since at least the Berle-Dodd debate in the 1930s and will continue being debated long into the future. This chapter, and indeed book, has argued that company law must evolve in order to better advance the interests of society by reducing the harms caused by companies. While redefining the corporate purpose away from shareholder value is an important part of this, this book argues that it is best achieved though reflexive laws focused on the company's external impacts.

[130] Teubner, 'Corporate Fiduciary Duties and their Beneficiaries' (n 117) 164–65.

Conclusion

LARGE COMPANIES HAVE a crucial role to play in addressing the most difficult challenges in our society. The role of company law is to provide the optimal set of rules to ensure companies help address these challenges and advance the interests of society. The traditional view is that the best way for company law to do this is by providing a set of rules that facilitates the economically efficient organisation of business while the negative externalities of business are dealt with by other areas of regulatory law. This book's central argument has been that the harms caused by companies cannot be adequately addressed through a patchwork of regulatory law and that a company law with reflexive elements provides a better framework to ensure large companies advance the interests of society.

The first basis for this argument is that the power of companies, their globalised operations and their reach across all aspects of society has meant it has become increasingly difficult for sector specific regulation to address all contexts where economically productive business is generating negative externalities and so should be subject to regulation. The second basis for this argument is grounded in systems theory which views society as being comprised of differentiated systems that are 'self-referential' in the sense that they function according to their own logic, values, norms, and language. This differentiation between systems makes it difficult for any single system to influence other systems. Hence, even if regulatory law could address every context where economically productive business should be regulated, it is not clear that legal interventions would be able to achieve its objectives of reducing or ending negative externalities.[1]

One response to these difficulties of sector specific regulation would be to argue for a regulatory company law, which alters the company's core characteristics[2] or imposes mandatory rules that constrain or direct the decisions of company managers. However, altering the company's evolved structure threatens its capacity to be efficient and productive while direct regulation reduces the company's capacity to be autonomous and responsive to specific challenges. Such interventions have the potential to produce a net negative effect

[1] This is the argument presented in G Teubner, 'Substantive and Reflexive Elements in Modern Law' (1983) 17(2) *Law and Society Review* 239.

[2] As described by the authors of *The Anatomy of Corporate Law* as: (1) legal personality; (2) limited liability of shareholders; (3) transferable shares; (4) delegated management to a board of directors; and (5) shareholders having ultimate control and access to net earnings. See R Kraakman et al, *The Anatomy of Corporate Law: A Comparative and Functional Approach*, 3rd edn (Oxford, Oxford University Press, 2017) 5–15.

on society by reducing the ability of companies to offer economic benefits. The challenge is to develop a framework that continues to enable the company's economic productivity while at the same time reducing the resulting harms.

The solution to this challenge put forward in this book is for company law to develop reflexive elements that are neither facilitative nor regulatory. A reflexive approach looks to law's ability to structure processes and procedures within systems to make them responsive to outside interests. In a company law context, the aim of new reflexive elements would be to prevent large companies operating as closed systems singularly focused on economic success and instead stimulate their internal resources in a way that develops 'economic self-restraint' regarding actions which cause harm to the non-economic environment.[3] Hence, it aims to achieve a balance between the need for companies to be both economically productive and socially responsible. This book has argued that a company law with reflexive elements can create the 'societal company' which possesses an internal sense of responsibility to do no harm that extends transnationally. However, in order to have this effect, such elements must possess the coercive power of law and be mandatory, sufficiently detailed and backed by the potential of legal enforcement.

The book has outlined a case for three such elements: (1) shared governance where a public interest director is appointed by the state or a regulatory authority to improve the inward and outward flow of information, links with stakeholders and allow for the public interest to be represented in the company board room;[4] (2) a duty on the company to gather and disclose detailed information related to its environmental and human rights impact – such a duty could produce a reflexive effect[5] by creating a new internal awareness of the company's external effects, limiting the company's ability to engage in greenwashing or cherry picking in their disclosures and by making companies reflect on the importance of their reputation and, in order to have positive information to report, take steps to reduce their negative externalities; and (3) a duty of due diligence requiring companies to develop a due diligence policy, a code of conduct and a corrective action plan for their negative externalities and apply these policies across their transnational operations while also investigating and taking steps to end their negative externalities.

The European Union (EU) has already introduced rules with many of these reflexive elements. The EU's Corporate Sustainability Reporting

[3] See G Teubner, 'Corporate Fiduciary Duties and their Beneficiaries' in G Teubner and K Hopt (eds), *Corporate Governance and Directors' Liabilities: Legal, Economic and Sociological Analyses on Corporate Social Responsibility* (De Gruyter, 1985) 164–65.

[4] As recommended by C Stone, *Where the Law Ends: The Social Control of Corporate Behaviour* (Harper & Row, 1975) and as discussed in ch 2.

[5] See D Hess, 'Social Reporting: A Reflexive Law Approach to Corporate Social Responsiveness' (1999) 25 *The Journal of Corporation Law* 41.

Directive (CSRD)[6] introduces reporting rules that are mandatory, detailed, standardised and independently verified and so is likely to result in corporate reporting that is accurate, reliable and potentially provoke a response within companies to reduce their negative externalities. The EU's Corporate Sustainability Due Diligence Directive (CSDDD)[7] requires companies within its scope to develop a due diligence policy, a code of conduct, a corrective action plan where an adverse external impact cannot be immediately ended, to engage with stakeholders in the development of these policies, plans and codes and requires a further process to monitor the adequacy and effectiveness of the company's due diligence practices. It also extends the application of due diligence to the company's subsidiaries and contractual partners both inside and outside the EU. The CSRD and CSDDD are by far the most ambitious pieces of company law legislation that focus on environmental and human rights matters and provide an example for what a company law with reflexive elements could look like. The EU's corporate sustainability framework also provides lessons on potential pitfalls, for example, the focus on short termism as a basis to reform the duties of directors, the complexity of the CSRD and the difficulties of introducing a model of civil liability for corporate groups and supply chains.

[6] Directive (EU) 2022/2464 of the European Parliament and of the Council of 14 December 2022 amending Regulation (EU) No 537/2014, Directive 2004/109/EC, Directive 2006/43/EC and Directive 2013/34/EU, as regards corporate sustainability reporting [2022] OJ L 322/15.

[7] Directive (EU) 2024/1760 of the European Parliament and of the Council of 13 June 2024 on corporate sustainability due diligence and amending Directive (EU) 2019/1937 and Regulation (EU) 2023/2859 [2024] OJ L, 2024/1760.

Bibliography

BOOKS

Addison J, *The Economics of Codetermination* (Springer, 2009)
Ahern D, *Directors' Duties: Law and Practice* (Roundhall, 2009)
Ayres I and Braithwaite J, *Responsive Regulation: Transcending the Deregulation Debate* (Oxford, Oxford University Press, 1992)
Bainbridge S, *The New Corporate Governance in Theory and Practice* (Oxford, Oxford University Press, 2008)
Bainbridge S, *The Profit Motive: Defending Shareholder Value Maximization* (Cambridge, Cambridge University Press, 2023)
Barnard C, *The Substantive Law of the EU: The Four Freedoms* (Oxford, Oxford University Press, 2022)
Beckers A, *Enforcing Corporate Social Responsibility Codes on Global Self-Regulation and National Private Law* (Oxford, Hart Publishing, 2018)
Berle A and Means G, *The Modern Corporation and Private Property* (Transaction, 1932)
Blair M, Ownership and Control: Rethinking the Corporate Governance for the Twenty First Century (Brookings Institute, 1996)
Bradford A, *The Brussels Effect: How the European Union Rules the World* (Oxford, Oxford University Press, 2019)
Bruner C, *The Corporation as Technology: Re-calibrating Corporate Governance for a Sustainable Future* (Oxford, Oxford University Press, 2022)
Condon R, *Network Responsibility: European Tort Law and the Society of Networks* (Cambridge, Cambridge University Press, 2022)
Craig P and G de Búrca G, *EU Law: Text, Cases, and Materials* (Oxford, Oxford University Press, 2020)
Davies P, *Gower and Davies Principles of Modern Company Law*, 8th edn (Sweet and Maxwell, 2008)
De Luca N, *European Company Law*, 2nd edn (Cambridge, Cambridge University Press, 2021)
Dine J, *The Governance of Corporate Groups* (Oxford, Oxford University Press, 2000)
Easterbrook F and Fischel D, *The Economic Structure of Corporate Law* (Harvard University Press, 1991)
Edwards V, *EC Company Law* (Oxford, Oxford University Press 1999)
Elden S, *The Birth of Territory* (University of Chicago Press, 2013)
Freeman RE, et al, *Stakeholder Theory: The State of the Art* (Cambridge, Cambridge University Press, 2010)
Freeman RE, *Strategic Management: A Stakeholder Approach* (Pitman, 1984)
Friedman M, *Capitalism and Freedom* (The University of Chicago Press, 1962)
Goode R, *Commercial Law in the Next Millennium: The Hamyln Lectures* (Sweet and Maxwell, 1998)
Greenfield K, *The Failure of Corporate Law: Fundamental Flaws and Progressive Possibilities* (Oxford, Oxford University Press, 2006)
Grundmann S, *European Company Law* (Intersentia, 2007)
Hayden G and Bodie M, *Reconstructing the Corporation: From Shareholder Primacy to Shared Governance* (Cambridge, Cambridge University Press, 2020)
Horwitz M, *The Transformation of American Law 1870–1960: The Crisis of Legal Orthodoxy* (Oxford, Oxford University Press, 1992)

Keay A, *The Corporate Objective: Corporations, Globalisation and the Law* (Edward Elgar Publishing, 2011)
Keay A, *The Enlightened Shareholder Value Principle and Corporate Governance* (Routledge, 2013)
Kraakman R et al, *The Anatomy of Corporate Law: A Comparative and Functional Approach*, 3rd edn (Oxford, Oxford University Press, 2017)
Lessig L, *Code, and Other Laws of Cyberspace* (Basic Books, 1999)
Luhmann N, *Law as a Social System* (Oxford, 2008)
Luhmann N, *Social Systems* (Stanford University Press, 1995)
Lynch-Fannon I and Murphy G, *Corporate Insolvency and Rescue*, 2nd edn (Bloomsbury, 2016)
Lynch-Fannon I, *Working Within Two Kinds of Capitalism: Corporate Governance and Employee Stakeholding – US and EC Perspectives* (Oxford, Hart Publishing, 2003)
Mayer C, *Capitalism and Crises: How to Fix Them* (Oxford, Oxford University Press, 2024)
Mayer C, *Prosperity: Better Business Makes the Greater Good* (Oxford, Oxford University Press, 2018)
Micheler E, *Company Law: A Real Entity Theory* (Oxford, Oxford University Press, 2021)
Micklitz HW, *The Politics of Justice in European Private Law: Social Justice, Access Justice, Societal Justice* (Cambridge, Cambridge University Press, 2018)
Moore M, *Corporate Governance in the Shadow of the State* (Oxford, Hart Publishing, 2013)
Muchlinski P, *Multinational Enterprises and the Law*, 3rd edn (Oxford, Oxford University Press, 2021)
Murphy D, *The Structure of Regulatory Competition* (Oxford, Oxford University Press, 2004)
Murphy JB, *The Philosophy of Customary Law* (Oxford, Oxford University Press, 2014)
Orts E, *Business Persons: A Legal Theory of the Firm* (Oxford, Oxford University Press, 2013)
Parkinson J, Gamble A, and Kelly G (eds) *The Political Economy of the Company* (Oxford, Oxford University Press, 2000)
Parkinson J, *Corporate Power and Responsibility: Issues in the Theory of Company Law* (Clarendon Press, 1993)
Posner R, *The Economic Analysis of Law*, 8th edn (Wolters Kluwer, 2010)
Rogers J and Streeck W (eds), *Works Councils: Consultation, Representation, and Cooperation in Industrial Relations* (University of Chicago Press, 2009)
Ruggie J, *Just Business: Multinational Corporations and Human Rights* (Norton, 2013)
Sjåfjell B and Bruner C (eds), *The Cambridge Handbook of Corporate Law, Corporate Governance and Sustainability* (Cambridge, Cambridge University Press, 2019)
Sjåfjell B, *Towards a Sustainable European Company Law: A Normative Analysis of the Objectives of EU Law, with the Takeover Directive as a Test Case* (Wolters Kluwer, 2009)
Stone C, *Where the Law Ends: The Social Control of Corporate Behaviour* (Harper & Row, 1975)
Teubner G, *Critical Theory and Legal Autopoiesis: The Case for Societal Constitutionalism* (Manchester, Manchester University Press, 2019)
Teubner G, *Law as an Autopoietic System* (Blackwell, 1993)
Teubner G, and Hopt K (eds), *Corporate Governance and Directors' Liabilities: Legal, Economic and Sociological Analyses on Corporate Social Responsibility* (De Gruyter, 1985)
Toth O, *The Lex Mercatoria in Theory and Practice* (Oxford, Oxford University Press, 2017)
Watson S, *The Making of the Modern Company* (Oxford, Hart Publishing, 2022)
Williamson O, *The Economics of Discretionary Behaviour: Managerial Objectives in a Theory of the Firm* (Prentice-Hall, 1964)
Witting C, *Liability of Corporate Groups and Networks* (Oxford, Oxford University Press, 2018)

BOOK CHAPTERS

Donnelly S, 'The Public Interest and the Company in Germany' in Parkinson J, Gamble A and Kelly G (eds), *The Political Economy of the Company* (Oxford, 2000)

Fabbrini F, 'The Principle of Subsidiarity' in Schütze R and Tridimas T (eds), *Oxford Principles of European Union Law* (Oxford, Oxford University Press, 2018)
Hart HLA, 'Definition and Theory in Jurisprudence' in Hart HLA, *Essays in Jurisprudence and Philosophy* (Clarendon Press, 1983)
Hayek F, 'The Corporation in a Democratic Society: In Whose Interest Ought It and Will It Be Run?' in H Ansoff (ed), *Business Strategy* (Penguin, 1969)
Johnston A, 'Integrating Sustainability into Corporate Governance' in Bruner C and Moore M (eds), *A Research Agenda for Corporate Law* (Edward Elgar Publishing, 2023)
Merkt H, 'Germany: Internal and External Corporate Governance' in Fleckner A and Hopt K (eds), *Comparative Corporate Governance: A Functional and International Analysis* (Cambridge, Cambridge University Press, 2013)
Millon D, 'Communitarianism in Corporate Law: Foundations and Law Reform Strategies' in L Mitchell (ed), *Progressive Corporate Law: New Perspectives on Law, Culture, and Society* (Westview Press, 1995)
Scott J, 'The Global Reach of EU Law' in Cremona M and Scott J (eds), *EU Law Beyond EU Borders: The Extraterritorial Reach of EU Law* (Oxford, Oxford University Press, 2019)
Sjåfjell B et al, 'Shareholder Primacy: The Main Barrier to Sustainable Companies' in Sjåfjell B and Richardson B (eds), *Company Law and Sustainability: Legal Barriers and Opportunities* (Cambridge, Cambridge University Press, 2015)
Stokes, M, 'Company Law and Legal Theory' in W Twining (ed), *Legal Theory and Common Law* (Blackwell Publishing, 1986)
Teubner G, 'Corporate Fiduciary Duties and their Beneficiaries' in G Teubner and K Hopt (eds), *Corporate Governance and Directors' Liabilities: Legal, Economic and Sociological Analyses on Corporate Social Responsibility* (De Gruyter, 1985)
Teubner G, 'Social Order from Legislative Noise? Autopoietic Closure as a Problem for Legal Regulation' in Teubner G and Fabbrajo A (eds), *State, Law, And Economy as Autopoietic Systems: Regulation and Autonomy in a New Perspective* (Giuffrè, 1992)

JOURNAL ARTICLES

Ahern D, 'Turning Up the Heat? EU Sustainability Goals and the Role of Reporting under the Non-Financial Reporting Directive' (2016) 4 *European Company and Financial Law Review* 599
Ahern D, 'The Mythical Value of Voice and Stewardship in the EU Directive on Long-term Shareholder Engagement: Rights Do Not an Engaged Shareholder Make' (2018) 20 *Cambridge Yearbook of European Legal Studies* 88
Alchian A and Demsetz H, 'Production, Information Costs, and Economic Organization' (1972) 62 *American Economic Review* 777
Allan G, 'To Pierce or not to Pierce? A Doctrinal Reappraisal of Judicial Responses to Improper Exploitation of the Corporate Form' (2018) 7 *Journal of Business Law* 559
Armour J and Ringe WG, 'European Company Law 1999–2010: Renaissance and Crisis' (2011) 48 *Common Market Law Review* 125
Attenborough D, 'Giving Purpose to the Corporate Purpose Debate: An Equitable Maximisation and Viability Principle' (2012) 32(1) *Legal Studies* 4
Bainbridge S, 'In Defence of the Shareholder Wealth Maximisation Norm: A Reply to Professor Green' (1993) 50 *Washington and Lee Law Review* 1423
Bainbridge S, 'Interpreting Nonshareholder Constituency Statutes' (1991) 19 *Pepperdine Law Review* 971
Bamberger K, 'Regulation as Delegation: Private Firms, Decisionmaking, and Accountability in the Administrative State' (2006) 56 *Duke Law Journal* 377
Bebchuck L and Roe M, 'A Theory of Path Dependence in Corporate Ownership and Governance' (2000) 52 *Stanford Law Review* 127

Bebchuck L, 'Federalism and the Corporation: The Desirable Limits on State Competition in Corporate Law' (1992) 105(7) *Harvard Law Review* 1435

Beckers A, 'Global Value Chains in EU Law' (2023) 42 *Yearbook of European Law* 322

Benson B, 'The Spontaneous Evolution of Commercial Law' (1989) 55(3) *Southern Economic Journal* 644

Berle A, 'Corporate Powers as Powers in Trust' (1930) 44 *Harvard Law Review* 1049

Berle A, 'For Whom Corporate Managers are Trustees: A Note' (1932) 45 *Harvard Law Review* 1365

Berle A, 'The Theory of Enterprise Entity' (1947) 47(3) *Columbia Law Review* 343

Blair M and Stout L, 'A Team Production Theory of Corporate Law' (1999) 85 *Virginia Law Review* 247

Bodie M, 'Shareholders All the Way Down: EU Corporate Sustainability Reforms and the Structure of Corporate Governance' (2024) 52 *Georgia Journal of International and Comparative Law* 559

Bonnitcha J and McCorquodale R, 'The Concept of "Due Diligence" in the UN Guiding Principles on Business and Human Rights' (2017) 28(3) *European Journal of International Law* 899

Bruner C, 'Corporate Governance Reform and the Sustainability Imperative' (2024) 131 *Yale Law Journal* 1217

Bruner C, 'The Enduring Ambivalence of Corporate Law' (2007) 59 *Alabama Law Review* 1385

Buckley L, 'Directors' Duty of Loyalty and ESG Considerations: Aotearoa New Zealand's Controversial Companies (Directors' Duties) Amendment Act 2023' (2024) 39 *Australian Journal of Corporate Law* 323

Bueno N et al, 'The EU Directive on Corporate Sustainability Due Diligence (CSDDD): The Final Political Compromise' (2024) *Business and Human Rights Journal* 1

Catá Backer L, 'Are Supply Chains Transnational Legal Orders: What We Can Learn From the Rana Plaza Factory Building Collapse' (2016) 1 *UC Irvine Journal of International, Transnational and Comparative Law* 11

Cáta Backer L, 'Theorizing Regulatory Governance Within its Ecology: The Structure of Management in an Age of Globalization' (2018) 24(5) *Contemporary Politics* 607

Clarke B, 'Corporate Responsibility in Light of the Separation of Ownership and Control' (1997) 19 *Dublin University law Journal* 50

Clarke B, 'Duty of Care Skill and Diligence – From Warm Baths to Hot Water' (2016) 56(56) *The Irish Jurist* 139

Coase R, 'The Nature of the Firm' (1937) 4 *Economica* 387

Coase R, 'The Problem of Social Cost' (1960) 3 *Journal of Law and Economics* 1

Dammann J, 'A New Approach to Corporate Choice of Law (2005) 38 *Vanderbilt Journal of Transnational Law* 51

Daskal J, 'The Un-Territoriality of Data' (2015) *The Yale Law Journal* 326

Deakin S, 'Reflexive Governance and European Company Law' (2009) 15(2) *European Law Journal* 224

Deipenbrock G, 'The "Business Judgment Rule" and the Problem of Hindsight Bias – Observations from a German Company Law Perspective' (2016) 27(2) *European Business Law Review* 197

Dewey J, 'The Historic Background of Corporate Legal Personality' (1926) 35(6) *Yale Law Journal* 655

Dodd M, 'For Whom are Managers Trustees?' (1932) 45 *Harvard Law Review* 1145

Dorf M, 'The Domain of Reflexive Law' (2023) 103 *Columbia Law Review* 384

Dotevall R, 'Is a Common Structure of Company Directors' Duties Evolving in EU?' (2016) 27(2) *European Business Law Review* 1

du Plessis J and Dine J, 'The Fate of the Draft Fifth Directive on Company Law: Accommodation Instead of Harmonisation' (1997) *Journal of Business Law* 23

Dworkin R, 'Is Wealth a Value?' (1980) 9(2) *The Journal of Legal Studies* 191

Dworkin R, 'Why Efficiency – A Response to Professors Calabresi and Posner' (1979) 8 *Hofstra Law Review* 563

Ebke W, 'The European Conflict-of-Corporate-Laws Revolution: *Überseering*, *Inspire Art* and Beyond' (2005) 16(1) *European Business Law Review* 9

Ebke W, 'The Real Seat Doctrine in the Conflict of Corporate Laws' (2001) 36(3) *International Lawyer* 1015

Eisenberg M, 'The Conception that the Corporation is a Nexus of Contracts and the Dual Nature of the Firm' (1998) 24 *Journal of Corporation Law* 819

Eisenberg M, 'The Structure of Corporation Law' (1989) 89 *Columbia Law Review* 1461

Enriques L, 'A Harmonized European Company law: Are We There Already?' (2017) 66(3) *International and Comparative Law Quarterly* 763

Enriques L, 'EC Company Law and the Fears of a European Delaware' (2004) 15 *European Business Law Review* 1259

Enriques L, 'EC Company Law Directives and Regulations: How Trivial Are They?' (2006) 27 *University of Pennsylvania Journal of International Economic Law* 1

Fama E, 'Agency Problems and the Theory of the Firm' (1980) 88 *Journal of Political Economy* 228

Ferran E and Schilling de Carvalho P, 'Reconciling Shareholder Primacy and the Interests of People and Planet' (2025) *Law Quarterly Review* (forthcoming)

Gelter M, 'The Structure of Regulatory Competition in European Corporate Law' (2005) 5 *Journal of Corporate Law Studies* 247

Gordon J, 'The Mandatory Structure of Corporation Law' (1989) 89 *Columbia Law Review* 1549

Grundmann S, 'European Company Law in Transformation – Striving for Participation and Sustainability' (2023) 42 *Yearbook of European Law* 210

Hackett C, 'The Challenge of MNCs and Development: Oil Extraction, CSR, Nigeria and Corruption' (2016) 2(2) *Journal of Human Rights in the Commonwealth* 1

Hale K, 'Corporate Law and Stakeholders; Moving Beyond Stakeholder Statutes' (2003) 45 *Arizona Law Review* 823

Hansmann H and Kraakman R, 'The End of History for Corporate Law' (2001) 89 *Georgetown Law Review* 440

Hansmann H and Kraakman R, 'Toward Unlimited Shareholder Liability for Corporate Torts' (1991) 100(7) *The Yale Law Journal* 1879

Hansmann H, Kraakman R and Squire R, 'Law and The Rise of The Firm' (2005) 119 *Harvard Law Review* 1335

Hardman J, 'Fixing the Misalignment of the Concession of Corporate Legal Personality' (2023) 43(3) *Legal Studies* 443

Hardman J, 'Tensions in Corporate Contractarianism: Rhetoric Rather than Logic' (2025) *International Journal for the Semiotics of Law* 1

Hayden G and Bodie M, 'The Corporation Reborn: From Shareholder Primacy to Shared Governance' (2020) 61 *Boston College Law Review* 2419

Hess D, 'Social Reporting: A Reflexive Law Approach to Corporate Social Responsiveness' (1999) 25 *The Journal of Corporation Law* 41

Hill J, 'Shifting Contours of Directors' Fiduciary Duties and Norms in Comparative Corporate Governance' (2020) 5 *Journal of International, Transnational, and Comparative Law* 163

Hübler O and Jirjahn U, 'Works Councils and Collective Bargaining in Germany: The Impact on Productivity and Wages' (2003) 50(4) *Scottish Journal of Political Economy* 471

Ireland P, 'Company Law and the Myth of Shareholder Ownership' (1999) 62 *Modern Law Review* 32

Iwai K, 'Persons, Things and Corporations: The Corporate Personality Controversy and Comparative Corporate Governance' (1999) 47(4) *The American Journal of Comparative Law* 583

Jensen M and Meckling W, 'Theory of the Firm: Managerial Behaviour, Agency Costs and Ownership Structure' (1976) 3 *Journal of Economics* 305

Jensen M, 'Value Maximisation, Stakeholder Theory and the Corporate Objective Function' (2001) 7(3) *European Financial Management* 297

Jungman C, 'The Effectiveness of Corporate Governance in One-Tier and Two-Tiered Board Systems' (2006) 4 *European Company and Financial Law Review* 426
Keay A and Loughrey J, 'The Concept of Business Judgment' (2019) 39(1) *Legal Studies* 36
Keay A, 'An Assessment of Private Enforcement Actions for Directors' Breaches of Duty' (2014) 33(1) *Civil Justice Quarterly* 76
Keay A, 'Ascertaining the Corporate Objective: An Entity Maximisation and Sustainability Model' (2008) 71(5) *The Modern Law Review* 663
Keay A, 'Good Faith and Directors' Duty to Promote the Success of Their Company' (2011) 35(2) *Company Lawyer* 138
Keay A, 'Stakeholder Theory in Corporate Law: Has it Got What it Takes?' (2010) 9 *Richmond Journal of Global Law and Business* 249
Keay A, 'The Public Enforcement of Directors' Duties: A Normative Inquiry' (2014) 43 *Common Law World Review* 89
La Porta R, 'The Economic Consequences of Legal Origins' (2008) 46(2) *Journal of Economic Literature* 285
Langford R and Ramsey I, 'Directors' Duties to Act in the Best Interests of the Company – Subjective or Objective' (2015) 2 *Journal of Business Law* 173
Lessig L, 'The Law of the Horse: What Cyber Law Might Teach' (1999) 113 *Harvard Law Review* 501
Licht A, 'The Mother of all Path Dependencies: Towards a Cross-Cultural Theory of Corporate Governance Systems' (2001) 26 *Delaware Journal of Corporate Law* 147
Lipton A, 'Not Everything is About Investors: The Case for Mandatory Stakeholder Disclosure (2020) 37 *Yale Journal on Regulation* 499
Lipton P, 'The Mythology of Salomon's Case and the Law Dealing with the Tort Liabilities of Corporate Groups' (2014) 40 *Monash University Law Review* 452
LoPucki L, 'Systems Approach to Law' (1997) 80 *Cornell Law Review* 479
Lord Devlin, 'The Relation Between Commercial Law and Commercial Practice' (1951) 14(3) *Modern Law Review* 249
Lowry J, 'Eliminating Obstacles to Freedom of Establishment: The Competitive Edge of UK Company Law' (2004) 63 *Cambridge Law Journal* 332
Lowry J, 'The Duty of Loyalty of Company Directors; Bridging the Accountability Gap Through Efficient Disclosure' (2009) 68 *Cambridge Law Journal* 607
Luhmann N, 'Differentiation of Society' (1977) 2 *Canadian Journal of Sociology* 29
Lynch-Fannon I, 'The Corporate Social Responsibility Movement and Law's Empire: Is There a Conflict? (2007) 58(1) *Northern Ireland Legal Quarterly* 1
Macey J, 'ESG Investing: Why Here? Why Now?' (2022) 19 *Berkeley Business Law Journal* 258
Macey J, 'Fiduciary Duties as Residual Claims: Obligations to Nonshareholder Constituencies from a Theory of the Firm Perspective' (1999) 84 *Cornell Law Review* 1266
Machen A, 'Corporate Personality' (1911) 24 *Harvard Law Review* 253
Macintosh J, 'The Issues, Effects and Consequences of the Berle-Dodd Debate' (1999) 24 *Accounting, Organizations and Society* 139
Maitland F, 'Moral Personality and Legal Personality' (1905) 6 *Journal of the Society of Comparative Legislation* 192
Maitland F, 'The Corporation Sole' (1900) 16(4) *Law Quarterly Review* 335
McGaughey E, 'The Codetermination Bargains: The History of German Corporate and Labor Law' (2016) 23(1) *Columbia Journal of European Law* 135
Mezzanotte F, 'Corporate Sustainability Reporting: Double Materiality, Impacts, and Legal Risk' (2024) 23(2) *Journal of Corporate Law Studies* 633
Mezzanotte F, 'Examining the Reasons for Impact Materiality in EU Corporate Sustainability Reporting' (2024) 35(7) *European Business Law Review* 925
Michales R, 'The True Lex Mercatoria: Law Beyond the State' (2007) 14 *Indiana Journal of Global Legal Studies* 447

Micheler E, 'Separate Legal Personality – An Explanation and a Defence' (2024) 24(1) *Journal of Corporate Law Studies* 301
Millon D, 'Communitarians, Contractarians, and the Crisis in Corporate Law' (1993) 50 *Washington and Lee Law Review* 1373
Millon D, 'Default Rules, Wealth Distribution, and Corporate Law Reform: Employment at Will' (1998) 146(4) *University of Pennsylvania Law Review* 975
Millon D, 'New Game Plan or Business as Usual? A Critique of the Team Production Model of Corporate Law' (2000) 86 *Virginia Law Review* 1001
Monciardini D, 'Regulating Accounting for Sustainable Companies: Some Considerations on the Forthcoming Directive' (2014) 11(2) *European Company Law* 121
Muchlinski P, 'The Development of German Corporate Law Until 1990: An Historical Reappraisal' (2013) 14(2) *German Law Journal* 339
Muchlinski P, 'The Impact of the UN Guiding Principles on Business Attitudes to Observing Human Rights' (2021) 6 *Business and Human Rights Journal* 212
O'Kelly C, 'History Begins: Shareholder Value, Accountability and the Virtuous State' (2009) 60(1) *Northern Ireland Law Quarterly* 35
O'Sullivan M, 'The Innovative Enterprise and Corporate Governance' (2000) 24 *Cambridge Journal of Economics* 393
Orts E, 'Beyond Shareholders: Interpreting Corporate Constituency Statutes' (1993) 61 *George Washington Law Review* 14
Orts E, 'Reflexive Environmental Law' (1994) 89(4) *Northwestern University Law Review* 1227
Orts E, 'The Complexity and Legitimacy of Corporate Law' (1993) 50(4) *Washington and Lee Law Review* 1565
Pantazi T, 'The Introduction of Mandatory Corporate Sustainability Reporting in the EU and the Question of Enforcement' (2024) 13(1) *European Business Organization Law Review* 510
Pargendler M, 'State Ownership and Corporate Governance' (2011) 80 *Fordham Law Review* 2917
Pargendler M, 'The Grip of Nationalism on Corporate Law' (2020) 95 *Indiana Law Journal* 533
Partiti E, 'Addressing the Flaws of the Sustainable Finance Disclosure Regulation: Moving from Disclosures to Labelling and Sustainability Due Diligence' (2024) 25 *European Business Organization Law Review* 299
Petrin M and Choudhury B, 'Group Company Liability' (2018) 20 *European Business Organization Law Review* 1
Raustiala K, 'The Geography of Justice' (2005) 73 *Fordham Law Review* 2501
Reynolds S, Schultz F and Hekman D, 'Stakeholder Theory and Managerial Decision Making: Constraints and Implications of Balancing Stakeholder Interests' (2006) 64 *Journal of Business Ethics* 285
Ribstein L, 'Why Corporations?' (2004) 1 *Berkeley Business Law Journal* 183
Rockström J et al, 'Planetary Boundaries: Exploring the Safe Operating Space for Humanity' (2009) 14(2) *Ecology and Society* 1
Roe M et al, 'The Sustainable Corporate Governance Initiative in Europe' (2021) *Yale Journal on Regulation* 7
Roe M, 'Chaos and Evolution in Law and Economics' (1996) 109(3) *Harvard Law Review* 641
Roe M, 'The Shareholder Wealth Maximisation Norm and Industrial Organisation' (2001) 149 *University of Pennsylvania Law Review* 2063
Ruggie J, 'The Concept of "Due Diligence" in the UN Guiding Principles on Business and Human Rights: A Reply to Jonathan Bonnitcha and Robert McCorquodale' (2017) 28(3) *The European Journal of International Law* 921
Rühmkorf A, 'The German Supply Chain Law: A First Step Towards More Corporate Sustainability' (2023) 20(1) *European Company Law* 6
Salminen J et al, 'Digital Platforms as Second-Order Lead Firms: Beyond the Industrial/Digital Divide in Regulating Value Chains' (2022) 6 *European Review of Private Law* 1059

Scott J, 'Extraterritoriality and Territorial Extension in EU Law' (2014) 62 *American Journal of Comparative Law* 87

Scott J, 'The New EU "Extraterritoriality"' (2014) 51 *Common Market Law Review* 1343

Sharpe N, 'Volkswagen's Bad Decisions & Harmful Emissions: How Poor Process Corrupted Codetermination in Germany's Dual Board Structure' (2017) 7 *Michigan Business and Entrepreneurial Law Review* 49

Siems M, 'Convergence, Competition, *Centros* and Conflicts of Law: European Company Law in the 21st Century' (2002) 27 *European Law Review* 47

Sjåfjell B and Mähönen J, 'Upgrading the Nordic Corporate Governance Model for Sustainable Companies' (2014) 11 *European Company Law* 58

Sjåfjell B and Taylor M, 'A Clash of Norms: Shareholder Primacy vs Sustainable Corporate Purpose' (2019) 13(3) *International and Comparative Corporate Law Journal* 40

Sjåfjell B, 'Beyond Climate Risk: Integrating Sustainability into the Duties of the Corporate Board' (2018) 23(2) *Deakin Law Review* 1

Sjåfjell B, 'Reforming EU Company Law to Secure the Future of European Business' (2021) 2 *European Company and Financial Law Review* 190

Sjåfjell B, 'Sustainable Value Creation Within Planetary Boundaries – Reforming Corporate Purpose and Duties of the Corporate Board' (2020) 12 *Sustainability* 6245

Steffen W et al, 'Planetary Boundaries: Guiding Human Development on a Changing Planet' (2015) 347(6223) *Science* 736

Stewart F, 'Berle's Conception of Shareholder Primacy: A Forgotten Perspective for Reconsideration During the Rise of Finance' (2011) 34 *Seattle University Law Review* 1457

Stoney C and Winstanley D, 'Stakeholding: Confusion or Utopia? Mapping the Conceptual Terrain' (2001) 38(5) *Journal of Management Studies* 603

Teubner G, 'Autopoiesis in Law and Society: A Rejoinder to Blankenburg' (1984) 18 *Law and Society Review* 291

Teubner G, 'Company Interest the Public Interest of the Enterprise in Itself (1986) 94 *Journal of Political Economy* 691

Teubner G, 'Enterprise Corporatism: New Industrial Policy and the "Essence" of the Legal Person' (1988) 36(1) *The American Journal of Comparative Law* 130

Teubner G, 'Substantive and Reflexive Elements in Modern Law' (1983) 17(2) *Law and Society Review* 239

Van Dam C, 'Tort Law and Human Rights: Brothers in Arms: On the Role of Tort Law in the Area of Business and Human Rights' (2022) 2(3) *Journal of European Tort Law* 221

Van Loo R, 'The New Gatekeepers: Private Firms as Public Enforcers' (2020) 106(2) *Virginia Law Review* 467

Watson S, 'The Corporate Legal Person' (2019) 19(1) *Journal of Corporate Law Studies* 137

Weinzierl J, 'Territoriality Beyond the State: The EU's Territorial Claims and the Search for Their Legitimacy' (2021) 22 *German Law Journal* 650

Williamson O, 'Transaction Cost Economics: The Governance of Contractual Relations' (1979) *Journal of Law and Economics* 22

Witting C, 'The Place of Managers in the Corporate Governance Architecture' (2024) 24(1) *Journal of Corporate Law Studies* 1

Worthington S, 'Corporate Attribution and Agency: Back to Basics' (2017) 133 *Law Quarterly Review* 118

Wymeersch E, 'The Transfer of Company Seat in European Company Law' (2003) 40 *Common Market Law Review* 661

Zingales L, 'In Search of New Foundations' (2000) 55 *Journal of Finance* 1623

Zumbanssen P, 'Law After the Welfare State: Formalism, Functionalism and the Ironic Turn of Reflexive Law' (2008) 56(3) *American Journal of Comparative* Law 769

REPORTS, STATEMENTS AND WORKING PAPERS

Armour J, 'Who Should Make Corporate Law? EC Legislation versus Regulatory Competition' (2005) *European Corporate Governance Institute Working Paper*

British Academy, 'Principles for Purposeful Business' (2019)

British Institute of International and Comparative Law et al, 'Study on Due Diligence Requirements Through the Supply Chain' (2020)

Cheffins B, 'The Past, Present and Future of Corporate Purpose' (2023) *European Corporate Governance Institute Working Paper*

Davies P, 'Shareholder Voice and Corporate Purpose: The Purposeless of Mandatory Corporate Purpose Statements' (2022) *European Corporate Governance Institute Working Paper*

Enriques L, Gatti M, Shapira R, 'How the EU's Sustainability Due Diligence Directive Could Reshape Corporate America' (2025) *European Corporate Governance Institute Working Paper*

European Commission, Action Plan: Financing Sustainable Growth (2018)

European Commission, Communication from the Commission concerning Corporate Social Responsibility: A Business Contribution to Sustainable Development (2002) COM/2002/0347 final

European Commission, Communication from the Commission to the Council and the European Parliament – Modernising Company Law and Enhancing Corporate Governance in the European Union – A Plan to Move Forward (2003) COM/2003/0284 final

European Commission, Communication from the Commission to the European Parliament, the Council, the European Economic and Social Committee and the Committee of the Regions – 'A Renewed EU Strategy 2011–14 for Corporate Social Responsibility' (2011) COM/2011/0681 final

European Commission, Communication from the Commission to the European Parliament, the European Council, the Council, the European Economic and Social Committee, the Committee of the Regions and the European Investment Bank – 'A Clean Planet for all – A European strategic long-term vision for a prosperous, modern, competitive and climate neutral economy' (2018) COM/2018/773 final

European Commission, Communication on a Simplified Business Environment for Companies in the Areas of Company Law, Accounting and Auditing (2007) COM 394

European Commission Communication on the European Green Deal (2019)

European Commission, Consultation on the Future of European Company Law (2012)

European Commission, Green Paper – Promoting a European Framework for Corporate Social Responsibility (2001)

European Commission, Study on the Disclosure and Cross-Border use of Company Data, and Digital Developments Related to Company Law (2023)

EY, Study on Directors' Duties and Sustainable Corporate Governance (2020)

Ferrarini G, 'An Alternative View of Corporate Purpose: Colin Mayer on Prosperity' (2020) *Genoa Centre for Law and Finance Working Paper*

Govaere I, 'To Give or to Grab: The Principle of Full, Crippled and Split Conferral of Powers Post-Lisbon' (2016) *College of Europe Research Papers in Law*

Governance Center for Firms' Sustainability, 'A European Corporate Governance Model: Integrating Corporation' (2023) *Nordic & European Company Law Working Paper*

Hopt K, 'Corporate Governance in Europe: A Critical Review of the European Commission's Initiatives on Corporate Law and Corporate Governance' (2015) *European Corporate Governance Institute Working Paper*

Hopt K, 'Corporate Purpose and Stakeholder Value – Historical, Economic and Comparative Law Remarks on the Current Debate, Legislative Options and Enforcement Problems' (2024) *European Corporate Governance Institute Working Paper*

Hopt K, 'Groups of Companies: A Comparative Study of the Economics, Law, and Regulation of Corporate Groups' (2024) *European Corporate Governance Institute Working Paper*

Lafarre A, 'Mandatory Corporate Sustainability Due Diligence in Europe: The Way Forward' (2022) *European Corporate Governance Institute Blog*
Nordic Company Law Scholars, 'Response to the Study on Directors' Duties and Sustainable Corporate Governance' (2021) *Nordic & European Company Law Working Paper*
Pacces A, 'Civil Liability in the EU Corporate Sustainability Due Diligence Directive Proposal: A Law & Economics Analysis' (2023) *European Corporate Governance Institute Working Paper*
Pargendler M, 'The EU Proposal on Corporate Sustainability Due Diligence and the Mystique of Complete Corporate Separateness' (2022) *Oxford Business Law Blog*
Pietrancosta A, 'Codification in Company Law of General CSR Requirements: Pioneering Recent French Reforms and EU Perspectives' (2022) *European Corporate Governance Institute Working Paper*
Rock E, 'For Whom is the Corporation Managed in 2020?: The Debate over Corporate Purpose' (2020) *European Corporate Governance Institute Working Paper*
Stout L et al, 'The Modern Corporation Statement on Company Law Summary: Fundamental Rules of Corporate Law' (2016) *SSRN Working Paper*
Teubner G, 'Corporate Responsibility as a Problem of Company Constitution' (1983) *European University Institute Working Paper*
Ventoruzzo M, 'On "Prosperity" by Colin Mayer: Brief Critical Remarks on the (Legal) Relevance of announcing a Multi-Stakeholders "Corporate Purpose"' (2020) *Bocconi Legal Studies Research Paper*
Winter J, 'Addressing the Crisis of the Modern Corporation: The Duty of Societal Responsibility of the Board' (2022)
Winter J, 'The Dehumanisation of the Large Corporation' (2020) *SSRN Working Paper*
Zumbanssen P, 'Global Value Chain Legislation, Modern Slavery, Climate Change and Finance: Lessons from the European Corporate Sustainability Due Diligence Directive' (2024) *McGill SGI Research Paper in Business, Finance, Law and Society*

Index

www.ingramcontent.com/pod-product-compliance
Ingram Content Group UK Ltd.
Pitfield, Milton Keynes, MK11 3LW, UK
UKHW020820290926
15470UKWH00003B/1273